Professions and Professional Ideologies in America

*Published under the auspices of the
Shelby Cullom Davis Center
for Historical Studies, Princeton University*

Professions and Professional Ideologies in America

Edited by
Gerald L. Geison

The University of North Carolina Press
Chapel Hill and London

© 1983 The University of North Carolina Press

All rights reserved

Manufactured in the United States of America

Library of Congress Cataloging in Publication Data

Main entry under title:

Professions and professional ideologies in America.

   Bibliography: p.
   Includes index.
   1. Professions—United States—Social aspects—
Addresses, essays, lectures. 2. Ideology—Addresses,
essays, lectures. 3. Lectures and lecturing—United
States—History—19th century—Addresses, essays,
lectures. 4. Presbyterian Church—United States—Clergy
—History—18th century—Addresses, essays, lectures.
5. Judges—United States—History—Addresses, essays,
lectures. 6. Lawyers—United States—History—Addresses,
essays, lectures. I. Geison, Gerald L., 1943–
HT687.P759 1983   305.5′53′0973   83-5853
ISBN 0-8078-1568-3

For Lawrence Stone,
who shepherded me through it

Contents

	Preface	ix
1.	Introduction *Gerald L. Geison*	3
2.	The Profession That Vanished: Public Lecturing in Mid-Nineteenth-Century America *Donald M. Scott*	12
3.	"Stewards of the Mysteries of God": Clerical Authority and the Great Awakening in the Middle Colonies *Patricia U. Bonomi*	29
4.	"What We Shall Meet Afterwards in Heaven": Judgeship as a Symbol for Modern American Lawyers *Stephen Botein*	49
5.	Legal Thought and Legal Practice in the Age of American Enterprise, 1870–1920 *Robert W. Gordon*	70
	Notes	111
	Index	141
	Notes on Contributors	149

Preface

This collection of essays is a product of the research seminar of the Shelby Cullom Davis Center for Historical Studies at Princeton University. During the academic years 1978–79 and 1979–80, the Davis Center seminar focused on the history of the professions. Over that period, more than a hundred scholars participated in the seminar, including visiting fellows of the Davis Center, faculty at Princeton or other nearby institutions, invited speakers, and graduate students. More than forty speakers presented papers for discussion and criticism, including the five contributors to this volume. Three of the contributors (Professors Bonomi, Botein, and Scott) were visiting fellows at the Davis Center for a full academic year. Professor Gordon's essay is a revised version of the paper he presented as an invited speaker to the seminar. I participated in the seminar as a member of the faculty of the history department at Princeton.

On behalf of the other contributors, I thank the dozens of seminar participants who responded with useful criticisms and suggestions to earlier versions of the essays now gathered together here. The finished product has benefited immensely from the collective discussions of the Davis Center seminar. Special thanks are due to Professor Anthony J. LaVopa for his penetrating analysis of a larger collection of essays from which these four have been selected for publication in this format. By dedicating this book to Lawrence Stone, I seek to acknowledge his close and supportive participation in every phase of the enterprise, including the selection of speakers and essays, the editing of chapters, and the process of securing a publisher. My introduction has also been improved by his valuable suggestions. The Davis Center, which he directs, not only served as the forum in which these essays took shape but also provided financial support to the visiting fellows and other speakers, to me in the form of released time from teaching during one semester to edit this volume, and to the publisher in the form of a subsidy to cover a portion of the production costs. As anyone who has been to the Davis Center knows, its success owes much to Mrs. Joan Daviduk, its efficient and personable secretary. Finally, my thanks also go to Faye Angelozzi, who expertly typed (and retyped) portions of the volume and provided both clerical and human support throughout its production.

G. L. G.
Princeton, New Jersey
21 September 1982

Professions and
Professional Ideologies
in America

ic # 1 Introduction
Gerald L. Geison

In 1968, in a synoptic essay on "professions" for the *Encyclopedia of the Social Sciences*, the influential American sociologist Talcott Parsons left his readers in no doubt about the importance of his subject. The "professional complex," he wrote,

> has already become the most important single component in the structure of modern societies. It has displaced first the 'state,' in the relatively early modern sense of that term, and, more recently, the 'capitalistic' organization of the economy. The massive emergence of the professional complex, not the special status of capitalistic or socialistic modes of organization, is the crucial structural development in twentieth-century society.[1]

For Parsons, moreover, professions and professionals seemed to defy the usual conflict-laden categories of social analysis. Professionals were neither capitalists nor workers, neither peasants nor proprietors, nor were they even (except occasionally) government bureaucrats. The advance guard of the professional movement was to be found instead among academics. In Parsons's view, the professions and the research university were tightly linked, and their arm-in-arm march toward ever-increasing rationalization and efficiency was the most striking feature of modern life.[2]

Parsons's vision of the professions was widely shared at the time by other American academics. For most of this "American century," in fact, most Americans have looked upon the professions as a centrally important, increasingly effective, and basically apolitical component in modern society. Precisely because the professions have been so widely perceived as occupations of special value and importance, the scholarly literature about them has often reflected a concern with "gate-keeping." There have been repeated attempts to specify a set of distinctively professional attributes and to assess the extent to which this or that occupational group approached or diverged from the ideal type. At least since 1915, when Abraham Flexner produced his famous essay "Is Social Work a Profession?"[3] considerable energy has been invested in efforts to legislate the meaning and boundaries of the term itself. This long-standing tradition took on a special vitality and urgency as the "credentialed society" became ever more visible in the wake of World War II.[4]

During the 1950s and 1960s, American scholars reached a striking degree of consensus about the distinctive features of professions and professionals. As codified by Parsons in his essay of 1968, the characteristic features of a profession are (1) formal technical training, including especially an intellectual component, in an institutional setting that certifies quality and competence; (2) demonstrable skills in the pragmatic application of this formal training; and (3) institutional mechanisms to ensure that this competence and skill will be used in a socially responsible way.[5] These or very similar criteria stood at the core of a fairly coherent and widely accepted model of the professions. If sociologists were the chief architects of this model, historians proved more than ready to follow their lead. The history of the professions—insofar as it attracted interest at all—usually took the form of narrative accounts of the process by which this or that occupational group gradually acquired the full set of attributes that gave it legitimate claim to the status of a profession. The acceptance of a discipline or an activity within the university curriculum was often seen as the crucial stage in this process.[6] For the most part, professionalization was portrayed as a beneficial and virtually inevitable part of an increasingly complex and interdependent world.[7]

During the past decade or so, this way of looking at the professions has been subjected to increasingly critical scrutiny—sometimes, indeed, to vitriolic attack. Benign and "attributional" models of the professions have lost some of their appeal, among both academics and the wider public. Examples of demonstrable corruption or ineptitude on the part of some certified professionals have become more widely publicized. There has been a growing outcry against the alleged "tyranny of the experts."[8] The link between universities and "true" professions has become increasingly less clear as the university curriculum (especially in its "pluralistic" American form) has come to embrace virtually every form of vocational training. In the sociological literature, more nearly natural classifications of occupational groups are now being sought through ethnographic investigations of the richly ambiguous ways in which words like "profession" and "professional" are used by real people and real collectivities in real life.[9] And closer attention to the actual behavior and structure of professional groups has revealed the extent to which superficial similarities and harmonies can conceal important differences and conflicts underneath. What once looked like relatively passive, static, and homogeneous "communities of the competent" are increasingly perceived as segmented, hierarchical populations in flux and struggle.

Recent work in the history and historical sociology of the professions both reflects and reinforces this change of view. It is now less common to begin with the assumption that past professionals acted in a socially responsible way. It is now less common to assume in advance that past professional groups actually possessed the cognitive superiority and instrumental efficacy they claimed for themselves. And it is now less common to presume that there is some inevitable and automatically beneficial connection between professionalization and "progress." Increasing attention is being paid instead to some of the less edifying features of professional behavior—to the efforts of professional groups to enlarge their power, income, and status through monopolistic practices; to the sometimes bitter struggles between competing professions or between upper and lower branches of the same profession; and to the role that professions can play in legitimizing social stratification, economic disparities, and mechanisms of social control.[10]

Much has been gained from this shift of perspective and widening of concerns. Yet the resulting literature is sometimes strident or conspiratorial in tone and too sweepingly critical of Parsons and Parsonians. Despite its limitations, the Parsonian conception of the professions does have value and utility in certain contexts, especially when its categories are deployed as heuristic devices rather than as central elements in a rigid and universal model of the professions.[11] In fact, the "anti-Parsonian" literature itself often deploys Parsonian categories, if only to deny that professions and professionals actually conform to the model.[12] Similarly, in the course of rejecting Parsonian teleology, the critics often merely substitute one of their own. If the history of the professions was once dominated by a concern with the process by which occupational groups achieved the attributes of a "true" profession, much of the recent literature also assumes that the professions were headed somewhere from the outset. Particularly striking is the tendency to assume that the professions, which in their primitive or "traditional" form merely dispensed personal services to elite patrons, were destined to be swept upward on the escalator of "modernization" or industrial and corporate capitalism toward the current situation in which the "ideal-typical" professional is an employed servant of the state or a corporation.[13]

The most obvious objection to models that link professionalization with capitalism is that they leave us so deeply in the dark about the nature of the process in socialist or communist societies—one of the woefully neglected topics in the literature on the professions. But there are also reasons to doubt the universal applicability of such models in the case of capitalist societies themselves. Even Magali Larson—whose systematic, sophisticated, and often illuminating analysis emphasizes the general connection between professionalization and capitalism—nonetheless admits the need to exclude the clergy and the military from her account because these two traditional professions "do not transact their services on the market."[14] She further concedes that the distribution of personal services by self-employed lawyers and physicians, even in the United States today, involves "traditional" markets and "unproductive labor" having relatively little connection with the capitalist mode of production. Nor does she insist on the universal applicability of her model in the case of other occupational groups. She explicitly acknowledges that her focus on recent Anglo-American developments is a "restrictive" one and that her analysis of professionalization can "in no way be generalized."[15]

There is, in fact, good reason to suspect that all of the existing models of professions and professionalization are inadequate to some degree and in some respects. Whether they conceive of professionalization as the emergence of benign, apolitical, "non-economic," and homogeneous "communities of the competent," or whether they see it as a conspiratorial, stratifying, and exploitative process in tune with the needs of capitalism, the existing models are simply unable to account for the richly diverse forms and distribution of professional groups as we meet them in actual historical experience.

That conclusion is apparent, if by no means always explicit, in the four essays gathered together in this volume. This shared skepticism toward existing models is particularly noteworthy in a collection of essays on American professions. Historians who specialize in other countries, especially in pre-industrial Europe, have already complained that both "Parsonian" and "capitalist" models of the professions are artifacts of the attention thus far lavished on late-nineteenth- and twentieth-century Anglo-American developments.[16] By suggesting that both models are inadequate even in the American context, this collection of essays makes it clear just how much work needs to be done before a reasonably satisfying general theory of professions and professionalization can be constructed.

Given the direction of recent scholarship in the field, it will come as no surprise that the contributors to this volume find little appeal in the benign Parsonian conception of professions. What is perhaps more surprising is their reluctance to embrace the alternative "capitalist" model, especially those versions of it that embody George Bernard Shaw's famous definition of the professions as "a conspiracy against laymen." Without denying that professional groups try to constitute and control (that is, to monopolize) the market for their specialized services, these essays go beyond much of the recent literature by acknowledging that the public (or the laity) also plays a crucial role in the success of professional market strategies. The contributors recognize the limits of independent professional power and perceive the need to take account of the *demand* for professional services as well as the willingness of the public (or at least their elected representatives) to grant special status and privileges to specific occupational groups. Indeed, the contributors might even concede the quasi-Parsonian point that "something in the nature of things" helps to account for some part of professional power.[17]

But these four essays also share a still more specific and original theme. More or less explicitly, all four essays focus on professional "ideology" and "rhetoric" in the American context. What is particularly striking is the unity of their approach to this common theme. While they by no means adopt the ideologies purveyed by their historical actors, the contributors manage to avoid the current fashion for dismissing professional claims as mere self-serving verbiage—as deliberately deceitful smoke screens behind which professional groups can comfortably pursue their monopolistic goals. In these essays, unlike so much of the recent literature, there is a recognition that professionals have usually constructed their ideologies unself-consciously and sincerely, that whatever deception may be embodied in professional ideology and rhetoric is partly a matter of self-deception as well. Even in the case of the medical profession, which has been the focus of so much critical scholarship of late, there is evidence to suggest that many American physicians have genuinely believed in the extreme laissez-faire ideology that organized medicine has so long exploited in its efforts to avoid government "interference." Without accepting that ideology—indeed, it would be easy to mount a case that American physicians have been protected rather than threatened by their government—it is important to appreciate how fully the ideology has pervaded the profession.[18] In the four essays below, we are invited to consider that point in the case of other professions in the American context. More than that, we are asked to take seriously the actual *content* of professional ideologies. In doing so, we will be able to see the extent to which such ideologies reflect larger themes in American culture. And we will also be able to see that the history of the professions, like so much else in the historical experience of elites, makes vastly better sense when we try to forge strong and meaningful links between social and intellectual (or cultural) history.

In the opening essay, Donald M. Scott provides the only example known to me of a historical study of professional "failure." His analysis of a "profession that vanished"—public lecturing in mid-nineteenth-century America—stands alone in a body of literature replete with stories of successful "professional projects."[19] Of the essays in this volume, Scott's is also the most explicit in its treatment of existing models or conceptions of professions. He uses his study of public lecturing to argue that the meaning of "profession" is a sociocultural construct whose contours are constantly shifting in response to changing perceptions of the nature and role of particular occupational groups. According to Scott, public lecturing was fashioned into a career in the 1830s and 1840s by restless middle-class hustlers or even genteel young men who wanted to make their way in the world through possession and dissemination of knowledge but who found the conventional learned professions too crowded or too restrictive in the social role such occupations allowed them to play. Their improvised careers were made possible by an expanding demand for "useful knowledge" on the part of a public willing and able to pay for it. Between the late 1840s and 1870s, says Scott, public lecturing was transformed from a career into a profession when a fully developed public lecture system conferred authority and legitimacy on a group of itinerant speakers whose perceived role resembled that played by the clergy in eighteenth-century America. Although the activity of public lecturing has survived ever since, Scott argues that it ceased to be seen as a separate profession in any meaningful sense after about 1870. As the modern research university emerged and spread throughout the United States, the cognitive map was restructured in such a way that fields of knowledge became increasingly institutionalized into separate academic disciplines. Simultaneously, broadly literate cultural spokesmanship—the social role filled by the public lecturers—was largely replaced by academic scholarship, and the broad public audience for intellectual products gave way before specialized "communities of the competent."

Patricia U. Bonomi's essay explores the effects of the Great Awakening of the late 1730s and early 1740s on the professional image and standing of the Presbyterian clergy in the middle American colonies. She shows that internecine squabbles between "Old Sides" and "New Sides" (or revivalist) ministers demystified the Presbyterian clergy in the eyes of their congregations and more generally threatened clerical authority in Presbyterian communities. Lay men and women were emboldened to take independent positions in the face of pitched and public battles between Old Sides and New Sides ministers over such traditionally "professional" issues as clerical education, procedures for ordination, itinerant preaching, clerical discipline, and the proper division of authority among ministers, presbytery, and synod. Many worshippers were attracted by the evangelical fervor and semipopulist rhetoric of the New Sides ministers, who could then choose to break away from the institutional structures dominated by their Old Sides adversaries. Besides creating dissident presbyteries and synods, the New Sides ministers established innovative educational institutions and standards for ordination that allowed Presbyterian ministers to be trained outside the Old World universities or their New World counterparts, Harvard and Yale. There was, for a time, an open schism in the Presbyterian church. But ministers from both sides soon came to see that their continued public wrangling threatened to bring on a complete disintegration of clerical authority at a time when Presbyterians faced rising competition from more enthusiastically revivalist preachers and sects. Presbyterian ministers then sought to reclaim part of their authority and community standing by diverting some of their energy to secular functions, for example, making their churches centers of political action and military recruitment, especially on the frontier. At the same time, in the increasingly separate professional sphere, New Sides and Old Sides ministers moved gradually toward a reconciliation—finally achieved in 1758—in which the authority of church institutions and ministers was formally reaffirmed, even at the expense of losing many worshippers to more "democratic" or less structured denominations. By then, the once young and rebellious New Sides ministers had come to see the virtues of making common professional cause with their Old Sides brethren.

Stephen Botein's essay examines the exalted vision of judgeship that American lawyers have long held and purveyed as part of their construction of a professional ideology and rhetoric. Often using religious language and metaphor, the legal elite early portrayed judicial office as a fitting conclusion to a career of exceptional professional accomplishment and as a calling free from any debasing association with the world of daily affairs and entrepreneurial self-interest. This ideal—as the lawyers themselves recognized—was rarely approached in reality, for American judges usually won their office on the basis of social and political criteria rather than "professional" attainment. Yet the ideal of an unsullied and intellectually distinguished office at the top of the professional hierarchy served as a compelling and transforming symbol in the image the American legal elite could form of itself. It could also be a potent force in public relations. Twice in this century, the American Bar Association undertook major campaigns against efforts to "debase" the office of judgeship. In the 1910s, ABA spokesmen fulminated against the threat of the small but growing movement for "judicial recall," which would have made judges subject to periodic reexamination by the electorate. In 1937, when President Franklin Delano Roosevelt launched a notorious effort to "pack" the Supreme Court with his appointees, the ABA leadership was again outraged at such explicit political interference with the bench. Although rank-and-file lawyers were distinctly less unified than the ABA leadership on both issues, especially on Roosevelt's "court-packing," the ABA could claim to have defeated both of these threats to the professional integrity of judicial office. In an arguably irrational but surprisingly effective way, the transforming ideal of judgeship could even be extended to bestow a sense of dignity and professional tone on practitioners at the very lowest rungs of the legal ladder. If judgeship could be seen as a fitting and sublime capstone to a distinguished career, it was also a goal to which any American lawyer might aspire even in the midst of his usually mundane activities in the everyday world of American law.

In the closing essay, Robert W. Gordon offers an extended critique of prevailing approaches to American legal history and makes a preliminary case for an alternative model of his own. Above all, Gordon insists that historians must begin to pay proper attention to the relation between legal thought and legal practice. He joins other recent scholars by objecting to the body of literature that treats the history of legal doctrine as a species of pure intellectual history—as a strictly logical unfolding of disembodied ideas, elaborated in splendid isolation from the tumult of everyday affairs. But he also emphasizes the need to take the content of legal doctrine seriously, and most of his critical commentary is directed against the now fashionable tendency to dismiss legal thought as an inherently uninteresting "technological" response to new socioeconomic problems or as a trivially obvious expression of interest-group (or class) politics. Gordon concedes that such approaches do go part way toward explaining American legal history, but he stresses how incomplete they look when tested closely against particular cases or even long-term structural changes. His intellectual tour through three distinct ideologies of "legal science" in nineteenth-century America—the antebellum "Whig-Federalist" version, the Liberal version, and the Progressive version—suggests that these ideologies can be seen as the sometimes curious products of genuine efforts by elite lawyers to mediate between the realms of thought and action within "a traditional but continually self-renewing and self-transforming framework of justice" (p. 81). On this view, the elite lawyers were bound together less by shared economic interests and political beliefs than by their membership in a community of intellectual discourse and professional consciousness. Such a conception of legal "ideology" would, at the least, help us to comprehend the fact that American lawyers and judges have sometimes fashioned legal doctrines and instruments that turned out to be detrimental to their own immediate economic and political interests, or even those of their class and clients. In keeping with his central historiographic theme, Gordon ends by discussing two examples of the way in which Liberal legal doctrine was applied in practice—briefly in the case of the drafting of corporate charters and extensively in the case of the legal reorganization of troubled corporations, especially railroad companies. He argues that the Liberal version of rights definition, as elaborated through the ideological activities of practicing lawyers, sometimes worked against the needs of corporate capitalism and paved the way for the triumph of the Progressive version of legal science at the turn of the century. Conceding that we do not yet know whether or how far these two cases are typical, Gordon nonetheless presents them as examples of the potential fertility of applying his approach to other episodes in the history of American law.

This skeletal summary of the essays that follow cannot hope to do justice to their richness and interest. It seeks only to convey some sense of the freshness of their broadly similar approach toward a unified set of themes. Taken as a whole, the essays suggest that Parsons exaggerated the importance of the professions in modern society—or, more precisely, exaggerated the independence of the process of professionalization from larger social, economic, political, and cultural forces. The contributors to this volume would surely agree that professionalization is a dependent variable subject to these more powerful forces. They would probably also agree that the history of the professions is but one chapter in the history of social stratification in general and of elites in particular. But perhaps the history of elites and elite culture is ripe for renewed attention in the light of the recent efflorescence of "history from the bottom up." Important insights into popular beliefs (or whatever other impoverished translation one gives to *mentalités*) have resulted from this branch of the "new history." What this collection of essays suggests is that our understanding of professional elites will also benefit from systematic and empathetic efforts to penetrate the ways in which they, too, tried to make sense of the world around them.

2 The Profession That Vanished

Public Lecturing in Mid-Nineteenth-Century America

Donald M. Scott

As the editor of *Harper's Magazine* in February 1854 "looked out over the varied panorama of life and society in our country," he thought he discerned "a new profession growing up"—public or popular lecturing. Three years later *Putnam's Magazine*, like *Harper's* one of the arbiters of intellectual life in mid-nineteenth-century America, asserted that the lyceum was such a great success that it had founded a "new profession." And in 1859, when printing its annual list of major lecturers, the *New York Tribune* declared matter-of-factly that "the profession appears securely established."[1] From several vantage points such assertions seem well-founded. There was a fairly large and growing body of practitioners who had made lecturing before paying audiences a major if not the exclusive portion of their vocational activity and who thought of themselves, and were regarded by the public at large, as "professional" lecturers. Moreover, the public for this new profession numbered in the millions: by fairly conservative estimate, attendance at public lectures probably reached close to half a million people each week during the lecture season.[2] It was also a fairly lucrative profession, one that Park Benjamin, one-time lawyer, literary agent, editor, poet and journalist, adopted as his "sole profession" in 1849, partly because it could provide him "greater income than any other literary pursuit."[3] The leading figures of the profession, earning between $50 and $150 per lecture and lecturing between 50 and 120 times a season were indeed "well-paid for their labors." Bayard Taylor earned more than $6,000 in the 1854–55 season, nearly three times what was considered a very good salary for a clergyman. Lecturing also appeared to have become an important and honored profession that rivalled press and pulpit in its influence over the mind of the public.

Each of the leading lecturers addressed at least fifty thousand people during a season, and they were widely extolled as "an important and beneficent instrumentality for dispelling intellectual stagnation and training the American mind to habits of healthful activity, fearless investigation, and generous manly thought."[4] Nationally known and eagerly sought by lecture committees in towns and cities across the nation, the public lecturer by the 1850s had assumed "an honorable place among the intellectual sovereigns of the land."[5]

This essay examines the emergence and character of public lecturing as a "new profession." It is not intended, however, to herald a now-forgotten profession. The aim, instead, is to use the rise of professional lecturing to illuminate some of the issues surrounding the historical study of the professions and the concept of professionalization that has directed so much of that study.[6] Current perspectives have shaped the study of the professions more than most other areas of recent historical investigation. The models that have dominated scholarly thinking about the professions have been the modern academic professions—built around carefully bounded bodies of esoteric knowledge and controlled by clearly delimited and self-conscious "communities of the competent"—and the modern legal and medical professions, with the enormous collective power, prestige, and equally impressive wealth and status that are conferred on their members. What appears to have most impressed scholars about these professions has been their autonomy and power. Professionalization has accordingly been construed as the process by which a group secures an effective monopoly over a particular body of knowledge, arrogates to itself the authority to determine what constitutes knowledge in the field, and assumes effective control over who may enter and practice the profession. Most of the writing about professions in both the past and the present, moreover, has emphasized the development of the institutions and rituals by which professions define themselves and secure their autonomy as well as the politics of professionalization, the struggle for control over institutions and definitions by groups within or beyond the professional community as they try to maintain their essential monopoly or establish a new one.

This approach has been useful, especially for understanding the emergence and character of modern professions. In particular, it has directed attention to the relationship between professions and the way in which the cognitive universe is organized. It has revealed the extent to which the process of professionalization rationalizes intellectual life and gives practitioners at least some sense of control over their work and careers while also providing discernible paths to success and esteem. But this approach has not been very useful in helping us to understand professions that existed much before the last decades of the nineteenth century. Because it tends to reify mastery of a clearly delimited cognitive area and the existence of an autonomous community of the competent as the basic characteristics of a profession, it also tends to impose on the past a definition of profession that often bears little resemblance to many past professional groups.[7] Moreover, by projecting into the past our preoccupation with the autonomy and power of the modern professions, this approach tends to reduce professionalization to the more or less self-conscious quest for power, autonomy, and status. It thus overlooks both the wide variety of shapes that professions have assumed in the past and the broader social and cultural context within which professions existed as particular institutions in particular times and places.

In my view, it is more useful to approach "profession" as a changing social and cultural construct, encompassing different meanings of the idea of profession and different institutional arrangements at different times.[8] Professionalization can be usefully construed, moreover, not only as something people do to gain power and status but as a process that implicates the broader society. Profession, in this sense, is not only an identity that might be claimed or sought but also a cultural designation that is conferred. Whatever the legitimacy of a professional claim or the motives behind it, both the claim itself and the public acceptance of it—the bestowal of professional identity and standing—stem from the configuration of meanings that at any given time are associated with the idea of a profession. In this sense, professionalization can be construed not simply as an institutional but a cultural process as well: an activity, body of knowledge, or occupation can be seen as becoming a profession not only when it assumes a discernible institutional shape but also when it is granted public recognition and acceptance as a profession. It is within this framework that this essay examines the professionalization of public lecturing in mid-nineteenth-century America.

Before lecturing became a profession it became an occupation. People came to lecturing by several paths. Some turned to it because they were unable to establish themselves in the kind of intellectual or professional life to which they had originally aspired. Between 1820 and 1850 there was an enormous expansion in the number of people attempting a career in the traditional learned professions. Hordes of young men were abandoning the towns and the farmsteads that could no longer absorb them, and they were turning to education to increase their life choices. Scrounging up from a wide variety of sources the funds needed to attend the newly established provincial colleges and following various regimens of autodidacticism, they pursued knowledge and education with almost desperate intensity—not as a badge of gentility but as the equivalent of a patrimony: a precious stake by which they might escape the bleak prospects that family farm and home community held out to them and rise to the professional classes.[9]

The professional world often turned out to be a good deal harder to crack than their first dreams of success had led them to believe. Unlike the situation in the eighteenth century, *access* to the professions was not all that difficult: formal restrictions limiting entry to them were weak. (It was not until near the end of the nineteenth century that firmer mechanisms for controlling access to medicine, law, and the clergy were reinstituted.) The greatest difficulty many young men faced was not in becoming a lawyer, a doctor, or a clergyman but rather surviving and succeeding as one. There was a problem of overcrowding and competition: in many places aspiring young professionals had to vie for support among populations that were willing or able to support only a limited number of them.[10] The more serious problem, however, was that of finding a point of entry into a community that would enable them to secure a position or clientele sufficient to establish and maintain a career. Although few young men probably entered a town as total strangers, following at least some chain of personal ties and references, many nonetheless found it difficult to discern and gain access to the informal networks that could lead to success. Though the bustling, booming towns—the Worcesters, the Springfields, the Albanys, the Newarks—often appeared to them to be full of promise, ready to be conquered by anyone with the energy and will to take advantage of the opportunities they seemingly provided, the openness often proved illusory, and the young men encountered unforeseen obstacles as they discovered that the best positions usually went to those with ties and connections inaccessible to them.[11]

Finding themselves on the periphery of the traditional professional world and unable to secure a satisfactory place in it, such young men had to make their way by improvisation. When they encountered obstacles, they often had to jettison their plans, move on to another place, and grasp at unforeseen opportunities, as they tried to "get a hold" on life, to use the Lucian Boynton phrase. Boynton, in his own efforts, went from the clergy, to teaching, to law as he moved from Amoskeag, New Hampshire, to Newark, Delaware, then to three successive places in Virginia, back north to Worcester, and to Uxbridge, Massachusetts, before ending up—fourteen years after he had begun—in law in Springfield, Illinois.¹²

These young men, moreover, had few resources to fall back upon when they found their expectations dashed. They did, however, have the willingness to turn whatever knowledge they possessed or could garner into a vocational resource. Learning was about the only thing they had that could be turned into a vocation, and many of them amassed parcels of knowledge and doctrine and went about purveying these to any audience that would pay to hear them. Thus such people as Sylvester Graham, the Fowler brothers, and John Lord, for example, improvised careers as itinerant lecturers—people who would enter a town unsolicited and announce in lavish broadsides, filled with extravagant claims and endorsements, their intention to lecture on some grand historical or biblical theme, some surefire guide to health and happiness, or the mysteries of the natural, unseen, or spirit world. Dependent for their livelihood on their "take at the door," the itinerants often gave a free initial lecture and then gave as many more as would bring a sufficient take (at 10 to 12½ cents apiece) to make the effort worthwhile.¹³

Poor but aspiring young men who had to fall back on their ability to turn their knowledge to immediate vocational account were not, of course, the only people who became lecturers in the 1830s and 1840s. Oliver Wendell Holmes, Wendell Phillips, Ralph Waldo Emerson, Park Benjamin, and George William Curtis, for example—all of whom ranked among the prominent stars of the lecture system in the 1840s and 1850s—scarcely fit this characterization. In fact, they came from the genteel and professional elites that had traditionally provided public and intellectual leadership. For reasons having to do with social class, as well as personal taste and inclination, some young people of genteel origin were drawn to a life of culture and learning. But unlike their peers from "the middle classes downward to the cottages of the poor," they had little problem of access to a successful career in the learned professions. Their problem was in finding a satisfactory vocational outlet for their intellectual proclivities. These scions of the learned classes were motivated partly by a drive for self-culture—a drive that led them to resist "smothering their souls" in the world of commerce and power or in the narrowness and tedium of ordinary occupations. Some, like Park Benjamin (law) or Ralph Waldo Emerson (the clergy), entered the traditional learned professions but soon rejected them as intellectually confining or spiritually and emotionally unsatisfying. Others, including Thomas Wentworth Higginson and George William Curtis, engaged for a time in the purely personal pursuit of self-culture, but such a course quickly came to seem self-indulgent and morally unsustainable. At the same time, however, it no longer seemed viable to look to older models of genteel intellectuality in which culture was the pastime of a leisured class or in which men of affairs and social standing like Jefferson, Adams, Franklin, and Rush had engaged in highly disciplined study and reflection.[14]

In a certain sense these young people of genteel origins were what a later day would refer to as "intellectuals," people who possessed a serious vocational commitment to reflection but whose intellectual energies were not shaped by dedication to specific professions, positions, or disciplines. Like their less genteel peers, they too had a problem of getting a hold on a career. What they lacked was structure, and they, too, can be found improvising their intellectual careers, founding various short-lived journals and magazines, attaching themselves for a time to various kinds of literary institutions, moving in and out of various movements, trying out different genres in search of intellectual garb that might suit them. In the course of this search for an intellectual career that would enable them to follow their own dictates rather than channel their reflection through the routines and formulas of the conventional learned professions, many of these incipient intellectuals embraced public lecturing. It provided them with an intellectual forum that was especially openended, with a clear and immediate sense of a public to respond to their intellectual productions, and, ultimately, with a needed sense that they were performing an important public role, that their efforts were neither narcissistic nor trivial.[15]

There was a third path to public lecturing as a serious vocational activity. Many of those who remained stationed in the traditional professions and institutions of public intellectual leadership turned much of their energies to the lecture platform as they tried to find a broader social role than their particular offices provided. College professors and presidents began to use public lecturing as a way of expanding their intellectual roles and asserting a form of public leadership that extended beyond their formal responsibilities as college teachers. Though Edward Hitchcock and Benjamin Silliman, for example, remained in their professorships at Amherst and Yale respectively, they were assiduous in their efforts to convey science to as broad a public as possible. The importance they attached to their public lecturing, in fact, appears to have exceeded that which they gave to their classroom activities and almost to have matched their sense of commitment to their scientific peers. As men of science, in short, they saw themselves not simply as pedagogues or specialists inhabiting a carefully circumscribed disciplinary community but as "public men."[16] Similarly, as Wilson Smith has shown, college presidents in these years assumed a clear identity as moral philosophers and, almost without fail, they used the popular lecture as a major forum to address the public on questions of social ethics and morality.[17] Finally, statesmen and clergymen, the traditional guardians of moral and social order, had found their guardianship diminished by their partisan and denominational duties and allegiance. By the 1840s the pastoral clergy no longer occupied a position of general intellectual and public leadership. A pastor, simply as a pastor, no longer addressed a general public and even his own parishioners increasingly looked to him to attend to their devotional needs rather than define their public responsibilities. Consequently, the clergy turned increasingly to the popular lecture, both to expand the range of their intellectual activities (they lectured on subjects and in modes that were often far removed from their pulpit discourses) and to enhance their public influence. Indeed, almost half of the lecturers on the local and national circuits were clergymen.[18] As Frank Sanborn, casting about for a career in 1854, put it: "The clergyman quits his pulpit for the lectures . . . or assumes a double office. All the week days of the winter months he is a minister-at-large, and rushes from lecture room with the zeal of an apostate. What ideas he has he puts in his lectures rather than his sermons, being fully persuaded that his highest duty is towards his *audience*, not his *congregation*. Thus has lecturing become a profession."[19]

Lecturing emerged in this fashion as a career partly because of the particular conditions affecting those who, in the 1830s and 1840s, for one reason or another, had chosen to construct their vocations from the possession and dispersal of knowledge rather than from agriculture, commerce, or the mastery of a craft. Public lecturing was not an occupation they had aspired to and prepared for from the beginning. Instead, it was an activity they embraced along the way and turned into essential careers as they sought to make their way beyond original circumstances, whether to forge a new but unspecified kind of intellectual career or to alter the intellectual scope of the particular positions they held.

For lecturing to emerge as a career, however, it needed more than an intellectual cadre willing to lecture: it needed a public who valued the lecturers' intellectual product enough to attend and pay for lectures. What ultimately provided a paying public for lectures was the almost insatiable craving of vast numbers of people for what was called "useful knowledge," a category that included an almost limitless array of ideas, facts, and interpretations.[20] The vast population of middling Americans were a people on the make who looked to useful knowledge as the essential tool for getting a hold on life, bending conditions to one's will and aspirations, and thereby rising above their circumstances Lecturing was one of a broad array of new agencies they turned to in their unending quest for useful knowledge. Equally important, however, were the mechanisms for organizing this vast public into the specific audiences needed to sustain a career. The itinerants used techniques similar to those peddlers had always used: they essentially hawked their intellectual wares. By the 1840s, however, the majority of lecturers followed circuits organized around the various voluntary associations that had proliferated so rapidly in these years. Some worked the evangelical circuits—education, mission, bible, and tract societies—while others plied the reform networks, the health, temperance, abolition, and women's rights societies, all of which were organized around local affiliates of regional or national associations.

What really launched and sustained public lecturing as a career, however, was the emergence in the late 1840s of what came to be referred to as the popular or public lecture system, a national institution centering around a group of nationally or regionally prominent lecturers and reaching into more than three thousand communities. First, the avid reporting of lectures surrounded them with an aura that stamped them as important events and identified and spread the reputation of a corps of regional and national lecturers.[21] Second, the system was built around a coherently arranged lecture season. Running from late November to early April, the season consisted of a "course" of ten to fifteen lectures, each given by a different lecturer and covering a broad range of almost wholly unrelated subjects. For example, the typical course for the 1851–52 season in Belfast, Maine, consisted of lectures on astronomy, biology, and physiology (a single lecture), conversation, the cultivation of memory, popular delusions concerning the Middle Ages, the equality of the human condition, Iceland, the true mission of women, the domestic life of the Turks, the problem of the age, and the origins of letters.[22] In addition, all the lectures in the course were ordinarily delivered at the same hour on a weekday evening, on the same day, and at the same place. Finally, the season was arranged well in advance.

Lecturing in the public lecture system was solely by invitation. In the spring and summer preceding each season, the secretaries of the sponsoring societies, "sparing no pain to give the public a course of lectures from the first men in the country," would send out invitations to all the lecturers from whom they hoped to construct their course.[23] At the same time, many of the lecturers would send out circulars indicating what particular lectures they had available for the season.

Typical was Elias Nason's circular for the 1856 season, which declared that "the undersigned is now ready to enter into arrangements with committees of lyceums and other literary institutions for the delivery of his *New Lecture*, prepared expressly for the coming season: 'The Poetry of the Ocean.'" The circular went on to add that "he is also ready to lecture on the following topics: The Battle of Waterloo, The Crimean War, Robespierre and the French Revolution of 1789, The Music of Nature, The Mechanism of the Human Hand."[24] Often the secretaries of a particular locale—say, northern Illinois—would coordinate their efforts so that Starr King, for example, could lecture at Rockport, Dixon, and Freeport on consecutive nights of the same week. Similarly, after accepting an invitation from one town, lecturers would frequently write the lyceums in neighboring towns indicating that they were going to be in the area and would be available to lecture on certain dates. Sometimes lecturers who were fully booked and had to turn down invitations would recommend other lecturers in their place. Through this process, by late October at the latest, towns would have their courses fully set and the lecturers would have a full season of engagements.[25] Thus by the early 1850s, lecturing was a finely structured business, with modes of communication and smoothly working procedures for securing engagements which turned lecturing into a career that was predictably remunerative, personally and intellectually satisfying, and well-esteemed.

What was it that made this new career a profession? Partly it was a matter of structure. Although lecturing as a source of livelihood antedated the emergence of the public lecture by several decades, it was not until the lecture system was firmly established that people began referring widely to lecturing as a profession in the fullest sense. Essentially, the system institutionalized a particular kind of lecture as a genuine and legitimate public lecture. Sometimes the term "public lecture" was used to refer to any lecture directed to a broad, undifferentiated public. By the late 1840s, however, the term as applied to the performances under the auspices of the public lecture system carried a rather different set of connotations. The public lecture (as opposed to one given by an itinerant who lectured "on his own hook") was a carefully bounded public act. The societies that organized the courses functioned as quasi-civil institutions, acting, in a sense, for the public and in its name. (When lecture committees were thought to have broken this trust by acting exclusively or unfairly, an aggrieved group often organized a counter course usually dubbed "the people's" course). The genuine public lecture, moreover, was considered a disinterested act (whatever benefits of "F.A.M.E.—$50. and my expenses" it brought the lecturer).[26] It was consciously directed to the good of the audience and society and designed to "instruct and inspire" its hearers, to "elevate and enlarge the understanding and give broader, more comprehensive views" of the self, the nation, the world, and the cosmos. Partisan or sectarian discourse was carefully excluded, the lectures were held in at least neutral if not clearly designated public space, and they were expected to embrace all members of the community, whatever their occupation, social standing, or political and religious affiliation. Restricting the platform to those who were invited by duly constituted lecture committees was thought to protect it against invasion by humbugs and charlatans and to distinguish the public lecture from the itinerant system.[27] It was the popular lecture in this well-defined and bounded form that the cultural arbiters at *Harper's*, *Putnam's*, and *The New York Tribune* had in mind when they heralded lecturing as "a new profession."

What elevated this institutionalization of the public lecture into a process of professionalization? Lecturing did not become a profession by the process ordinarily associated with the professionalization of groups whose work consists of the creation and dissemination of knowledge. Though lecturers were certainly among those who asserted that lecturing was a new profession, it did not become one because of the efforts of practitioners to stake out their own cognitive territory or to organize themselves around institutions that fostered professional consciousness and autonomy. Essentially, public lecturing became a profession by attribution or declaration. It was a dramatically new institution, and as commentators and practitioners alike sought to identify and place it, they applied a grammar of professionalism to it, a grammar that described the kind of work lecturers did, situated that work within a cluster of social meanings and ethical prescriptions that reflected the cultural role public lecturers performed, and bestowed upon them a station of honor that reflected the value attached to that role.

On one level, "profession" was used synonymously with occupation or vocation to signify that lecturers earned much of their livelihood from lecturing and considered it their essential work. But at the same time, the word in this usage also contained social and moral connotations: the assertion and acceptance of a professional claim was built around shared expectations concerning both the character of the lecturers' commitment to their work and the quality of their performance. Professional lecturers were not triflers, but people whose performance was thought to embody preparation, skill, effort, seriousness of purpose, and honesty of intention. The fact of payment—the exchange of money (by the 1850s the essential token of value in American culture) for the privilege of hearing a lecture—was the ritual ratification of the belief that the public lecture was an occasion of importance served by professionals who could be expected to give an audience its money's worth. This distinction between the professional and amateur or "dabbler" was clearly reflected in patterns of attendance: when a society, because of last-minute cancellations or some other reason, filled one of its slots with a local figure who was not thought of as a professional lecturer, attendance fell off markedly, even though the subject might be identical to one given by a professional. As one commentator put it, "People will not go to a lecture if they think that the lecturer has 'given' his service. The public think that if not worth pay, it is not worth hearing."[28] It is this dimension of the lecturer's fee as the embodiment of worth that Park Benjamin appears to have had in mind when, in the circular he sent out announcing his adoption of lecturing as his profession, he made it clear that he would henceforth "devote his whole time and attention" to it. In this sense, his circular, with connotations similar to the notion of a profession of faith, was a public declaration of commitment and vocational identity, a formal statement that he had made lecturing his profession.[29]

The term profession applied mainly to certain types of vocations, those that involved the dissemination of knowledge or the performance of a service rather than the production and sale of a more tangible commodity. This distinction, however, was not solely taxonomic, but one that placed the true profession in a domain clearly separated from the burgeoning world of commerce, business, and profit. Although the desire for money, honor, and status might lead one to enter a profession, professional conduct itself was thought to be grounded in the faithful production or application of truth rather than the pursuit of profit. Indeed, many of the most important boundaries surrounding the professions, whatever other functions they may have performed, were those that were thought to protect the public from the charlatan who pretended to possess knowledge but who used deceit and falsehood to "humbug" people out of their money. The conventions surrounding the remuneration of professional work reflected this sense of the need to immunize the professions against the corruptions of the marketplace. Professionals were paid by stated salary (in the case of the clergymen) or by fees (or honoraria), regulated in part, at least, by custom rather than by a negotiable price that shifted according to the marketplace. When, in fact, clergymen appeared to be excessively calculating or grasping in negotiations over salary, they were often condemned as men of mammon rather than men of God; when lawyers seemed to stir up trouble and bring suits just to garner fees, they were condemned as shysters and pettifoggers. Both acts clearly seemed to cross the moral boundary that separated the true or faithful practitioner from the mere profit seeker.[30] When, in 1856, Henry Ward Beecher, the most prominent and widely sought-after public lecturer of the day, hired an agent, who promptly negotiated a fee at double the prevailing rate, Beecher was met with such an immediate and vehement condemnation (including a virtual boycott of his lectures) for having turned the platform into a business that he was forced to back down, to issue an explanation and an apology.[31]

The conviction, drawn largely from the models of law and divinity, that the professions inhabited a moral domain beyond the marketplace ultimately reflected the personal and public importance attached to the knowledge that the professions dispensed. Individual practitioners, to be sure, were important for the services and ministrations they provided for their specific audiences and clients. The value attached to their services did not lie, however, only in the success of their particular efforts but also in their role as mediators between the problems of everyday life and the broader set of ideas from which people derived their sense of the operation and order of things. Lawyers did not always secure their clients' claims, but they did provide them with a sense of access to and connection with the system of justice; a minister's prayers could not always stave off disaster or death, but his ministrations did explain such things in terms of the ideas and rituals by which his parishioners connected themselves with a Divine Order.[32] In addition, law and divinity were bodies of knowledge that possessed a clear public dimension and significance, one that gave the legal and clerical professions a collective role as guardians of the common weal. They had as a special office the preservation of the knowledge by which the American nation maintained itself as a Christian nation and a nation of laws.[33]

It was the interpretive and civic dimensions of the public lecture system that elevated public lecturing to the status of "a new profession" in the fullest sense and gave the lecturers their "honorable place among the intellectual sovereigns of the age." Neil Harris has written of how the 1880s and 1890s experienced an "explosion of knowledge" that affected every aspect of life and society,[34] but the expansion of knowledge and information in the 1830s and 1840s appears to have been almost as dramatic. More and new kinds of knowledge were promulgated by a vast array of cultural spokesmen who addressed a new and expanding democratic public in a variety of new forms. The newspapers of the day were compendia of data and information of all sorts. In addition to the news of local, national, and sometimes international events, they often contained compilations of statistics and commercial data, tidbits of historical and scientific fact, and accounts of travelers and missionaries among exotic peoples in distant lands. Their pages of advertisements were full of information about new products, new health cures, and additional sources of knowledge and information; and each issue had a large number of short items, undigested notations of miscellaneous, curious, and bizarre facts. There was also a vast proliferation of new genres—journals devoted to specialized topics or conducted by particular groups, magazines and miscellanies, tracts, treatises, addresses, pamphlets by the hundreds of thousands, and manuals of advice on almost every aspect of life. Almost as confusing as the sheer amount and variety of fact and opinion was the babble of voices competing for the attention of the public and seeking to instruct it. In addition to traditional opinion-makers—ministers, office-holders, gentlemen of letters and learning, college presidents and professors—there was a vast array of reformers, lecturers, self-proclaimed savants, and pundits of all sorts "crying," as one commentator put it, "lo here and lo there."[35]

It was within this context that the public lecture system came to the fore as a major new institution for "dispelling intellectual stagnation and training the American mind to habits of healthful activity, greater investigation, and generous, manly thought." It encompassed the almost limitless and expanding universe of useful knowledge. Over a few seasons, a lyceum's offerings would span an almost encyclopedic range of topics. A typical course provided a lecture or two on scientific topics, several travel lectures, some disquisition on a crucial American institution, an assessment of some troubling new phenomenon in American life (like "the woman question"), a literary and a historical lecture, the exploration of a grand theme such as the "law of progress," and several discourses on such crucial matters of manners and morals as marriage and money. The system also accommodated rapidly to events as well as to startling new knowledge. After the Hungarian Revolution, for example, there was a great demand for the lectures of Charles Loring Brace, who had just traveled in Hungary and had been captured for a time by the revolutionaries. He went about lecturing on "Hungary: Its Fitness for Democracy."[36] When E. K. Kane returned from an arctic expedition that had been avidly followed in the daily and weekly press, he was immediately flooded with "more than 100 invitations to lecture in various parts of the country."[37]

In addition to this intellectual scope, the lecture system operated under what in another context I have referred to as "an interpretive imperative."[38] Judging from what was most popular—i.e., the lectures that people were most willing to pay to hear—audiences expected lectures to place their particular kind of knowledge or topic in a broad, interpretive context. The good lecture had to be thoroughly grounded in something concrete; a lecture that strung together generalities was condemned as superficial. It was the connection of the specific topic or theme with some more comprehensive view that rendered thought and knowledge ultimately useful, at once "practical" and "ennobling," to use terms frequently employed in praise of lectures.[39] A scientific lecture, for example, whatever the particular field (geology and astronomy were the most popular), had science itself and the natural order as its implicit subjects. The effective lecture was thoroughly grounded in concrete facts and usually was accompanied by dramatic experiments or pictorial representations. By such display, as well as by the overall orchestration from the very particular and least grand specimen to the increasingly complex and encompassing ones, the scientific lecturer created a sense of what George Daniels has called the wonders of science, both as an intellectual enterprise or adventure and as a reflection of "the power, wisdom, and skill of the creator, God."[40]

Travel lectures had much the same character. Just as the scientific lecturer came before the audience as an explorer seeking out the mysteries of nature and the universe, the travel lecturer appeared before the audience as an explorer of human nature and the world. The travel lecture was thus less a travelogue than a kind of comparative ethnography. First-hand experience and observation provided the lecturer with what was thought to be unique and original knowledge. But the lecturer's essential purpose was to foster deeper understanding of human nature and mankind and, either explicitly or implicitly, to deepen the audience's awareness of American character and custom.[41] The large category of lectures that sought to explicate life in contemporary America followed a comparable rhetorical strategy. They focused on something familiar and of obvious concern—an institution like matrimony, a quality like beauty or character, a theme like success or progress. Then, drawing upon a broad array of concrete references and allusions taken from literature and history, the experiences of everyday life, and some of the most startling facts of the day, they connected their particular subject to commonly held moral precepts.[42] As Josiah Holland put it:

> American life is crowded with facts, to which the newspaper gives daily record and diffusion. . . . Men wish for nothing

more than to know how to classify their facts, what to do with them, how to govern them, and how far to be governed by them. The man who takes the facts with which the popular life has come into contact and association, and draws from them their nutritive and motive power, and points out their relation to individual and universal good, and organizes around them the popular life, and does all this with masterly skill, is the man whose houses are never large enough to contain those who throng to hear him. This is the popular lecturer, *par excellence*.[43]

Finally, the lecture system was thought to bind far-flung and disparate Americans into a common culture, transcending the divisions that fragmented American society. The miscellaneous audiences, drawn together in public space to attend an event that was held under neither sectarian nor partisan dominion, was thought to be an embodiment of the entire democratic community. As one commentator put it, "the lecture room [was] neutral ground upon which all parties and conditions ... meet."[44] The system also transcended intellectual fragmentation: men of letters, science, and literature; reformers and conservatives; lawyers; physicians; professors; poets; editors; and statesmen—all made their way onto the platform, but they came to fashion what one writer called "a common ground."[45] As Thomas Wentworth Higginson, one of the leading extollers of the system put it, the popular lecturer, "moving to and fro [provided] a living shuttle, to weave together this new web of national civilization."[46]

The public lecture system thus appeared to encompass the whole, expansive world of knowledge, organize it, and thereby "elevate and enlarge the understanding" and give its vast public "broader and more comprehensive views." It did this not by providing new cognitive structures for organizing knowledge but by bringing the full range of spokesmen who were thought to possess useful knowledge into a forum organized and accepted as a fully legitimate agency for creating the "intelligent progress" that was thought to guide American democracy. Thus did public lecturing take on the shape of a "new profession," new because the institution was new, a profession because the role it performed was much like that performed by the quintessential learned profession of the eighteenth century, the clergy.

Public lecturing's standing as a new profession was short-lived. Emerging rapidly in the late 1840s, it flourished for a little more than two decades in the fullest mid-nineteenth-century sense of the term, then the "profession" of public lecturing virtually disappeared. Public lecturing itself, however, continued. The lecturer remained a familiar figure on the cultural landscape well into the twentieth century. By 1870, moreover, the lecture system had become even more efficiently organized than it had been in the 1850s—as central booking agencies like Redpath Agency took over management of the system, signing up lecturers and arranging their engagements in towns all over the country.[47] It was thus not paid lecturing itself that disappeared in the 1870s. Instead, what had dissolved by the 1870s was the idea that lecturing constituted a profession beyond the vocational sense in which the term had been used. The growing emphasis upon lecturing as entertainment rather than instruction and inspiration may have had something to do with this. But the loss of lecturing's standing as a full profession appears to have had less to do with changes in the popular lecture itself than with changes in the idea of a profession that had once allowed itself to be perceived as a profession.

By the 1870s a very different kind of professionalism was coming to dominate formal intellectual life in America, one built not around new ways of institutionalizing the cultural and interpretive roles traditionally performed by the learned professions, but rather around new ways of organizing their cognitive base.[48] This professionalization of knowledge transformed not only the order of knowledge but also the idea of a profession. At the core of this development was the increasing division of the cognitive universe into discrete and fairly well-bounded disciplines and the subsequent institutionalization of these disciplines into relatively autonomous professional communities that were able to assert their authority as the ultimate arbiters of what constituted real knowledge in their respective disciplines. This process, moreover, institutionalized a differently structured and oriented kind of intellectual career. The essential "work" of one who "professed" a discipline was the production of scholarship rather than cultural spokesmanship. It was the challenge and discipline of inquiry and investigation, rather than their standing as "public men," that gave these new professionals their sense of satisfaction. Finally, of course, the emergence of the modern research university established careers that were organized around and gave prestige and rewards to a life of scholarship, thus providing the broader institutional context that underlay the emergence in the 1880s and 1890s of the modern academic professions. Unlike public lecturing, which had been a new profession built on an older model, these were new kinds of professions—constituting, in fact, a new kind of social institution that was located in a very different social and cultural space from that occupied by professions on the older model. The primary orientation of the academic profession was not to the public-at-large; indeed, it institutionalized a sense of an unbridgeable cognitive gap between professionals and nonprofessionals (a gap of a sort that had not existed between the traditional learned professions and the public). Professional academics addressed themselves instead to the self-isolated and relatively autonomous "community of the competent." Their primary role, moreover, was not the public and interpretive one of the sort that public lecturers had performed but the pursuit of truth and science free from the interference of those outside the professional community.

By the last decades of the nineteenth century, this new kind of professional structure had come to dominate the idea of a profession as it was applied to the creation of knowledge. The newly established and institutionalized academics were rapidly becoming the new "intellectual sovereigns of the age." As in most revolutions, they achieved this position by overthrowing the old. As the well-bounded disciplinary communities became the essential model that defined the idea of a profession, public lecturing became unrecognizable as a genuine intellectual profession. Public lecturing vanished as a profession less because the activity itself had disappeared than because the cultural lens that had led to its perception as a "new profession" in the 1850s had been shattered.

3 "Stewards of the Mysteries of God"
Clerical Authority and the Great Awakening in the Middle Colonies

Patricia U. Bonomi

The Great Awakening in the mid-eighteenth-century American colonies has been studied from many angles, but only recently has its effect on the professional development of the colonial clergy attracted interest.[1] To be sure, the influence of the Awakening was felt at every level of provincial life. Yet only the ministers experienced it as a crisis that immediately affected their careers and the institutions that nurtured them. One could argue, of course, that the ministers themselves provoked the crisis. That is, the revivalists' bold assaults on the body of the church—on its governing structures, professional standards, and the authority of its elites—as well as their insistence on discussing these matters publicly, turned a debate between ministers into a broad popular controversy. Since the revivalists began as a minority in every church, they sought to advance their religious ideology by forming alliances with the people. And because the Great Awakening occurred at a time of shifting values, it broadened into a popular movement that gave expression to a range of social and political as well as religious discontents. Still it started out in every case as a contest between clerical factions. Thus only those churches with a "professional" clergy and organized governing structure were split apart by the revival;[2] the newer German churches and the pietistic sects, having little structure to overturn, remained largely outside the conflict.

These events have usually been viewed from the perspective of New England Congregationalism. In this essay I wish to direct attention to less familiar territory—to the middle colonies and the Presbyterian clergy. As the great influx of Ulster Irish after 1725 led to a rapid expansion of the Presbyterian church, all of the strains and readjustments experienced by other colonial denominations over a longer time span were compressed, in the Presbyterian case, into a fifty-year period. Thus the Presbyterian example may serve as a kind of paradigm for the pattern of professional development experienced by all ministerial groups from their initial formation through the Great Awakening and its aftermath.

Presbyterians looked to the future with reasonably high hopes by the third decade of the eighteenth century. To all appearances they possessed a more stable and orderly church structure than any of their middle-colony competitors. Unlike the Anglicans, they required no bishop to perform the essential rites of ordination and confirmation; nor did they suffer quite the same shortage of ministers as the German churches. The supply of Presbyterian clergy, if never adequate, had at least been sufficient to support the formation of a rudimentary governing structure. Three presbyteries and the Synod of Philadelphia were in place before the first wave of immigration from Ulster reached the Delaware basin in the 1720s, enabling the twenty-five to thirty ministers active in the middle colonies to guide growth and protect professional standards in the period of expansion after 1725. Congregations were under the care of elders and, when available, ministers. Supervising presbyteries in each region maintained oversight of local congregations and protected professional standards by ordaining and disciplining the clergy. At the top was the synod, which provided a setting in which disputes over church doctrine and governing authority could be resolved *in camera*.[3]

Despite this orderly beginning, it was the Presbyterian church that exploded in fratricidal strife and schism after 1739, while the immigrant German churches, for example, proceeded peacefully to create governing structures that enhanced their stability and discipline. The controls imposed by the Presbyterian hierarchy were hardly all that they appeared to be. Beneath orderly processes were tensions that had been expanding steadily before finally bursting forth in 1739. Any reading of eighteenth-century Presbyterian records discloses at least three kinds of strains beneath the surface: between parishioners, between people and minister, and within the professional clergy itself.

The Presbyterian church was the focal point and mediator of Scotch-Irish community life from the late 1720s on, when thousands of Ulster Scots began entering the colonies annually. As the westward-migrating settlers moved beyond the reach of government and law, the Presbyterian church was the only institution that kept pace with settlement. By stretching resources to the limit, the synod, and especially the presbyteries, kept in touch with their scattered brethren through itinerant preachers and presbyterial visitations. Ministers, invariably the best-educated persons on the early frontier, were looked to for leadership in both religious and community affairs, and they often took up multiple roles as doctors, teachers, and even lawyers. So closely did the Scotch-Irish identify with the Kirk that it was often said they "could not live without it."[4]

But if the church was a vital center, it was also an agency of control. Presbyterian ministers—whom some regarded as a "stiff-necked . . . [and] pedantick crew"[5]—expected to continue surveillance of their parishioners' spiritual growth and moral safety in America as they had done in the old country, and at first, by and large, they succeeded. Congregations gathered spontaneously in Scotch-Irish settlements, much as they did in immigrant German communities. A major difference between the two societies was that from an early stage the Scotch-Irish Presbyterians submitted themselves to clerical authority, whereas laymen and ministers in the German church shared power more equally. As soon as a Presbyterian congregation was formed, commissioners were chosen to appear before the local presbytery to request recognition and the supply of a minister. Often the presbytery could provide only a probationer or itinerant preacher for the Sabbath, and many settlements were fortunate to hear a sermon one or two Sundays a month. The congregations nonetheless proceeded to organize themselves, often under the supervision of a moderator sent out by the presbytery. They elected elders, deacons to care for the poor and sick, and trustees to oversee the collection of tithes for the minister's salary. The governing session, comprised of elders and the minister, was responsible for promoting doctrinal purity and maintaining moral oversight of the congregation. The session heard charges and ruled on a variety of matters, including disputes between parishioners over land or debt, domestic difficulties, and church doctrine, but its main responsibility was to enforce moral discipline. Sessions' rulings could be appealed to the supervising presbytery, comprised of all ministers and elders in the region.[6] The presbytery minutes consequently have much to tell us about the quality of clerical authority. But they also disclose the growing undercurrent of resistance it aroused among the freer spirits in the Scotch-Irish settlements.[7]

Reading over the minutes of the westernmost presbytery of Donegal, with their unceasing concern for communal harmony and moral order, one is reminded of early New England Puritan communities, where the religious culture also was a source of both cohesion and strain. Donegal

Presbytery met seventeen times between October 1732 and November 1735 at nine different locations, an itinerary that enabled it to assert direct authority over widely dispersed congregations. During these "visitations," members of the presbytery dealt with administrative problems, questioned parishioners and ministers on points of religion, and presided over trials—for such they were—in cases of moral discipline. In the early years appeals were handled with dispatch, as when one parishioner requested reconsideration of the session's refusal to baptize his child who had been born "before the time in reference to his marriage." After investigating the marriage and finding it sound, the presbytery granted his request.[8] Cases of fornication and adultery were so common in one church that the elders requested guidance from the presbytery about granting membership to persons "guilty of uncleanness." The presbytery admonished all sessions "not to be hasty or precipitant in admitting of persons guilty of fornication" but to wait until evidence was obtained in private discussion "of their true & sincere sense of sorrow for their sin," after which a "publick profession" was required. The same rule applied in cases of adultery, whether "single or double" (by one or both parties); one couple was forced to appear on the Sabbath "in publick . . . Confession . . . twice from the woman & three times from the man (it being Adultery in him)." Other cases involved disputes over "false swearing," drunkenness, an alleged breach of contract regarding a five pound loan, an argument between two neighbors about timber rights, and the barring of parishioners from church privileges for failure to pay their share of the minister's salary.[9]

The case of Elizabeth Ross, heard by the presbytery on 16 October 1734, illustrates both the judicial and the consensual character of these proceedings. Mrs. Ross had been accused by Thomas Wilkie, a fellow parishioner, of appearing drunk in public, and the local session, after hearing witnesses and taking depositions, had found Wilkie's charge to be false. The accused's husband, John Ross, then demanded that Wilkie "publickly own that he wronged Elizabeth Ross," pending which Ross refused to accept the session's authority and appealed the case to the presbytery. This appeal over his head offended Ross's minister, who made a public display of his anger. At the presbytery hearing, two witnesses testified that they had not seen "any symptoms of drunkeness" in Mrs. Ross. The decision handed down by the presbytery is a masterpiece of nicely balanced justice. John Ross was declared "very culpable" for abusing the witnesses against his wife and was admonished for refusing to accept the judgment of the session. The presbytery also concluded that Thomas Wilkie did not have "Just ground" to charge Mrs. Ross with drunkenness, but because Wilkie did not lie intentionally, he was declared not guilty of perjury. Further, the minister was admonished for wrangling publicly with John Ross "inasmuch as his Character & Station require that he should be Examplary in meekness & patience." The final scene before the presbytery was heavy with the symbolism of consensus. The clerk records that the decision was greeted with "great Joy and Satisfaction," after which "all Parties did in a vary Christian manner Submit to and acquiesce in the above determination . . . by Joining of hands & agreeable words declaring their mutual reconciliation to Each other."[10]

The conciliatory efficacy of such proceedings, and the clergy's warrant to preside over them, persisted as long as the church fathers spoke with one voice. The clergy's power to withhold church privileges—membership, baptism, and communion—to say nothing of the influence they exerted for community approval or nonapproval, gave ministers a strong hold over their parishioners. But should unity within the clergy loosen, other tensions below the surface of provincial society might be difficult to contain.

The first portent of trouble for Donegal Presbytery came as early as 1735. The Nottingham church in Lancaster County had become divided over points of doctrine—though it may be doubted whether "doctrine" can begin to cover the case—and the minister, William Orr (a rather volatile sort), had aroused a lively opposition from a portion of his congregation. One of them, a Mrs. Robinson, went so far as to accuse him of "unchast behaviour with Mary Barns." When the furor of denials and counterdenials so widened the breach in the congregation that Orr asked for a separation from the Nottingham church, the entire affair was referred to the presbytery. In a long and vividly detailed hearing, Orr's witnesses testified that Mrs. Robinson was a notorious woman whose word was not to be trusted. One of them declared that she had threatened to "be Even" with Mary Barnes for not assisting in "the breaking of wool" at Mrs. Robinson's house. Another said that Mrs. Robinson's shipmates on the voyage from Ireland had suspected her of witchcraft and had wanted to make her recite the Lord's Prayer as a test. She was further accused of drunkenness, of "Cursing & swearing profanely," and of having a stormy domestic life.

Although Mrs. Robinson was to some a person of bad repute, she was clearly useful to the disaffected faction of the Nottingham church. Orr, protesting that the opposition party "first attacked My principles & now has Entered upon my Character," found himself repelling charges of drunkenness, of neglecting family worship, and of misconduct with "Married women & young women too." Most of the witnesses seem to have vouched for Orr's sobriety and morals; thus after arbitration by "two indifferent persons" appointed by the presbytery, the charges against him were finally withdrawn. Nevertheless tension failed to subside, and shortly thereafter Orr once again asked for, and this time obtained, his release. When the presbytery was slow to grant him a certificate of good standing (perhaps in the hope of persuading him to stay, though one wonders), Orr refused to preach any longer at Nottingham. Denouncing the presbytery as "a company of damn'd Hypocrites," he departed the district in the spring of 1736 without a certificate, for which he was subsequently censured.[11]

Here was a new and ominous note. The presbytery had now moved from arbitrating the petty disputes of disgruntled parishioners to engaging in semipublic debate with a fellow minister. By the late 1730s, moreover, the procedures developed by the synod and presbyteries to regulate clerical conduct and standards were under steady assault from an evangelical faction in the church. When several members of that faction formed the New Brunswick Presbytery in 1738 to facilitate the ordination of evangelical preachers,[12] the stage was set for a showdown that would shatter ministerial unity, elevate discontent within congregations, and usher in the Great Awakening.

The Great Awakening split the Presbyterian church apart, and from the break rose long-suppressed clouds of acrimony and vituperation that would change the face of authority in Pennsylvania and elsewhere. As the passions of the Awakening reached their height in the early 1740s, evangelical New Side Presbyterians turned on rationalist Old Sides with a ferocity that is peculiar to the zealot, charging them with the most extravagant doctrinal and moral enormities. The internecine spectacle that ensued, the loss of proportion and professional decorum, hastened the demystification of the clergy, weakened the authority of the church, and forced each Presbyterian minister to reevaluate his position in provincial society. Issues of professionalism were at the heart of the schism in every phase of the controversy.

The division that surfaced in 1740-41 had been developing for more than a decade. Presbyterian ministers had no sooner organized their central association, the Synod of Philadelphia, in 1715 than the first lines of stress appeared, though it was not until a cohesive evangelical faction emerged in the 1730s that an open split was threatened. Most members of the synod hoped to model American Presbyterianism along orderly lines, and in 1729 an act requiring all ministers and ministerial candidates to subscribe publicly to the Westminster Confession had been approved.[13] In 1738 the synod had further ruled that no minister would be licensed unless he could display a degree from a British or European university, or from one of the New England colleges (Harvard or Yale). New candidates were to submit to an examination by a commission of the synod on the soundness of their theological training and spiritual condition. The emergent evangelical faction rightly saw these restrictions as an effort to control their own activities. They had reluctantly accepted subscription to the Westminster Confession, but synodical screening of new candidates struck them as an intolerable invasion of the local presbyteries' right of ordination.[14]

The insurgents were led by the Scotsman William Tennent, Sr., and his sons, William, Jr., Charles, and Gilbert. William, Sr., had been educated at the University of Edinburgh, receiving a bachelor's degree in 1693 and an M.A. in 1695. Tennent may have been exposed to European pietism at Edinburgh, where "new life was stirring" in the last quarter of the seventeenth century.[15] Though ordained a priest of the Anglican church in 1706, Tennent did not gain a parish of his own, and in 1718 he departed the Old World for the New. When he applied for a license from the Synod of Philadelphia in 1718, Tennent was asked his reasons for leaving the Church of England. He declared that he had come to view government by bishops as antiscriptural, that he opposed ecclesiastical courts and plural benefices, that the church was leaning toward Arminianism, and that he disapproved of their ceremonial way of worship. All this seemed sound enough to the Presbyterians, and Tennent was licensed forthwith.[16] Having a strong interest in scholarship and pedagogy,[17] Tennent built a one-room schoolhouse in about 1730 in Neshaminy, Bucks County—the Log College, as it was later derisively called—where he set about training young men for the ministry. Exactly when Tennent began to pull away from the regular synod leadership is unclear, but by 1736 his church at Neshaminy was split down the middle and the antievangelical members were attempting to expel him as minister.[18]

In 1739 the synod was confronted with a question of professional standards that brought the two factions closer to a complete break. When the previous year's synod had erected commissions to examine the training of all ministerial candidates not holding degrees from approved universities, Gilbert Tennent had charged that the qualification was designed "to prevent his father's school from training gracious men for the Ministry." Overriding the synod's rule in 1739, the radical New Brunswick Presbytery licensed one John Rowland without reference to any committee, though Rowland had received "a private education"— the synod's euphemism for the Log College. Sharply criticizing the presbytery for its disorderly and divisive action, the synod refused to approve Rowland unless he agreed to submit himself for examination, which he refused to do.[19]

Since education was central to the dispute, it is unfortunate that no Log College records have survived to describe the training given the remarkable group of men that came under the tutelage of William Tennent, Sr. We do know that they emerged to become leaders of the revivalist movement and would in turn prepare other religious and educational leaders of the middle and southern colonies. What evidence does exist casts doubt on the synod's charge that Tennent and his followers were "destroyers of good learning" who persisted in foisting unlettered Log College students upon an undiscriminating public. As Gilbert Tennent insisted, the insurgents "desired and designed a well-qualified Ministry as much as our Brethren." To be sure, their theological emphasis was at variance with that of the rationalist clergy, and there may have been parts of the traditional curriculum they did not value as highly, as was true with the innovative dissenting academies in Britain at the time. But as competition between the two factions intensified, restrained criticism gave way to censoriousness. Thus when the synod charged that Gilbert Tennent had called "Physicks, Ethicks, Metophysicks and Pneumaticks [the rubric under which Aristotelian philosophy was taught in medieval universities] meer Criticks, and consequently useless," its members could not resist adding that he did so "because his Father cannot or doth not teach them."[20]

Yet there is much that attests to both the senior Tennent's learning and his pedagogical talents. Many who knew him agreed that he was a polished scholar of the classics, spoke Latin and English with equal fluency, and was a master of the Greek language. He also "had some acquaintance with the ... Sciences."[21] A hint of the training Tennent offered comes from the licensing examination given his youngest son, Charles, in 1736 by the Philadelphia Presbytery, among whose members were several who would later emerge as chief critics of the Tennents. Young Charles was tested on his "ability in prayer" and "in the Languages," in the delivery of a sermon and exegesis, and on his answers to "various suitable questions on the arts and sciences, especially Theology and out of Scripture." The record also shows that he was examined on the state of his soul. Charles Tennent was apparently approved without question.[22]

The strongest evidence of the quality of a Log College education comes, however, from the subsequent careers and accomplishments of its eighteen to twenty-one "alumni."[23] Their deep commitment to formal education is demonstrated by the number of academies they themselves founded, including Samuel Blair's "classical school" at Faggs Manor in Pennsylvania, Samuel Finley's academy at Nottingham, and several others.[24] Two early presidents of the College of New Jersey (Princeton) were Samuel Finley and Samuel Davies (the latter having been educated by Blair at Faggs Manor); three Log College men were founding trustees of the college and five others served as trustees in the early years.[25] The published sermons and essays of Samuel Finley, Samuel Blair, and Gilbert Tennent not only throb with evangelical passion but also display wide learning. In the opinion of a leading Presbyterian historian the intellectual accomplishments of the Log College revivalists far outshone those of the opposers, among whom only the scholarly Francis Alison produced significant writings.[26] As George Whitefield observed when he visited Neshaminy in 1739 and saw the rough structure of logs that housed the school: "All that we can say of most universities is, that they are glorious without."[27]

The distinction that the Log College men would achieve was still unknown in 1739, however, when the New Brunswick Presbytery defied the synod by licensing John Rowland. It was at this juncture, moreover, that the twenty-six-year-old English evangelist, George Whitefield, made his sensational appearance. Whitefield's visits to New Jersey and Pennsylvania in the winter of 1739–40 provided tremendous support for the Presbyterian insurgents, as thousands of provincials flocked to hear him and realized, perhaps for the first time, something of what the American evangelists had been up to. The public support that now flowed to the Presbyterian New Side exhilarated its members, inciting them to ever bolder assaults on the synod. The revivalists had to this point preached only in their own churches or in temporarily vacant pulpits, but that winter they began to invade the territory of the regular clergy. This raised the issue of itinerant preaching, perhaps the thorniest of the entire conflict, for it brought the parties face to face on the question of who was better qualified to interpret the word of God. It was in this setting that Gilbert Tennent was moved on 8 March 1740 to deliver his celebrated sermon, "The Danger of an Unconverted Ministry," to a Nottingham congregation that was then engaged in choosing a new minister. It was an audacious, not to say reckless, attack on the rationalist clergy, and Tennent would later qualify some of his strongest language. But the sermon reveals in its starkest light the gulf that separated the two factions by 1740. It also demonstrates the revivalists' sublime disregard for the traditional limits on public discussion of what amounted to professional questions.

Tennent began by drawing an analogy between the rationalist opposition in the Philadelphia Synod which was in the process of rejecting experiential religion, and the legalistic Pharisees of old who had rejected the radical teachings of Jesus. The Pharisees, he declared, were bloated with intellectual conceit, "Letter-learned" but blind to the truths of the Saviour. They "loved the uppermost Seats in the Synagogues, and to be called Rabbi, Rabbi." They were masterly and positive in their sayings, "as if forsooth Knowledge must die with them." Worst of all, they "had their Eyes, with Judas, fixed upon the Bag. Why, they came into the Priest's Office for a Piece of Bread; they took it up as a Trade. . . . O Shame!"[28] For all these worldly conceits Jesus had denounced them as hypocrites and a "Generation of Vipers." Tennent went on to pronounce a similar judgment on the Pharisees of his own time, "unconverted [and] wicked Men . . . who as nearly resemble . . . the old Pharisees . . . as one Crow's Egg does another." Men had to be called to the ministry by a "New Birth. . . . How else can they avoid being greedy of filthy Lucre?" Unconverted ministers might be "better polished with Wit and Rhetorick," but "their Discourses are cold and sapless, and as it were freeze between their lips."[29]

Tennent's solution to the problem of unconverted ministers, in addition to prayer for their "dear fainting Souls," was "to encourage private Schools, or Seminaries of Learning, which are under the Care of skilful and experienced Christians." As for itinerant preachers, Tennent assured his Nottingham congregation that it was no sin but a right well within their "Christian Liberty" to desert their parish minister for a converted preacher. "Birds of the Air fly to warmer Climates" to shun the cold and get better food; should humankind do less? In the only light moment of the sermon, Tennent exclaimed: "*Faith* is said to come by *Hearing.* . . . But the Apostle doesn't add, *Your Parish-Minister.*" The itinerants may have been a divisive influence, upsetting presbyterial order and "Breaking. . . Congregations to Pieces," but "Blessed Paul was accounted a common Disturber of the Peace. . . . And yet he left not off Preaching for all that." Thus Tennent concluded: "Let those who live under the Ministry of dead Men . . . repair to the Living, where they may be edified."[30]

Tennent set forth in this influential and widely disseminated sermon[31] the three principal issues over which Presbyterians would divide: the conversion experience, education of the clergy, and itinerant preaching. While his tone may have owed something to Whitefield's recent influence—humility was never a strong point with the evangelists—it also reflected the growing self-confidence of the revivalist party, as a wave of public support lifted them to heights of popularity. During the synod of 1740 the rationalist clergy, in a demonstration of their reasonableness, agreed to certain compromises on the issues of itinerancy and licensing,[32] but when the revivalists continued to denounce them publicly as carnal and unconverted, their patience came to an end.

The break between Old Side and New Side Presbyterians came during the synod of 1741 when a protest signed by twelve ministers and eight elders charged the evangelical party with "barefaced arrogance" and "heterodox and anarchical" principles. These "unwearied, unscriptural, anti-presbyterial, uncharitable, divisive practices" made continued union between the two parties "monstrous." The protest closed with a demand that the revivalists be expelled from the synod. Samuel Finley and Gilbert Tennent promptly took the Old Sides to task for spreading "groundless and slanderous" reports and for putting "a religious Face upon their Envy."[33] In June 1741, the New Side clergy withdrew from the Philadelphia Synod to their presbyteries, where their work continued with great zeal and a success that would outshine that of their rivals. In 1745 the expelled party, joined by other friends of the revival from the middle colonies, formed the Synod of New York, which would sustain a lively existence until 1758 when the Presbyterian schism was finally repaired.

Disagreements over theological emphasis, professional standards, and centralized authority were the most immediate causes of the Presbyterian schism, but other differences between Old and New Sides had the effect of making the conflict sharper. Disparities in education, age (and therefore career expectations), and cultural bias are of special interest.

The twelve Old Sides who expelled the revivalist radicals in 1741 have sometimes been labeled the "Scotch-Irish" party, and for good reason.[34] Ten were born in Northern Ireland, one in Scotland, and the birthplace of the twelfth is unknown.[35] All were educated abroad, mainly in Scotland, especially at the University of Glasgow. Most came to the colonies between the ages of twenty-eight and thirty-two, after having completed their education.[36] The typical Old Side clergyman was about forty-two at the time of the schism. The New Side ministers who formed the Synod of New York in 1745 numbered twenty-two. Of the twenty-one whose places of birth can be ascertained, ten were born in New England or on the eastern end of Long Island, one in Newark, New Jersey, eight in Northern Ireland (including Gilbert, William, Jr., and Charles Tennent), one in Scotland, and one in England. Most of those born abroad emigrated to the colonies during their middle teens;

Charles Tennent was but seven, and the oldest was William Robinson, son of an English Quaker doctor, who emigrated at about twenty-eight after an ill-spent youth.[37] The educational profile of the New Side preachers is in striking contrast to that of the Old. Of the twenty-two, nine received degrees from Yale College, two were Harvard men, and ten were educated at the Log College. One had probably gone to a Scottish university. The typical New Side minister was around thirty-two at the time of the schism or a decade younger than his Old Side counterpart.[38]

Several tendencies suggest themselves. The Old Sides, being more mature than their adversaries, were also more settled in their professional careers; further, their Scottish education and early professional experiences in Ulster may have instilled a respect for discipline and ecclesiastical order that could not easily be cast aside.[39] They knew it was difficult to keep up standards in provincial societies, especially the heterodox middle colonies where competition in religion, as in everything else, was a constant challenge to good order. Still, it was irritating to be treated as intruders by the resident notables or by such as the Anglicans, who pretended to look down on the Presbyterians as "men of small talents and mean education."[40] There was security in knowing that the first generation of Presbyterian leaders had been educated and licensed in accordance with the highest Old World criteria, and the tradition must be continued, for succeeding generations would gain respect only if the ministry were settled on a firm professional base. Though Harvard and Yale were not Edinburgh or Glasgow, they did base their curricula largely on the British universities and to that extent could serve until the Presbyterian church was able to erect a college of its own.[41] And only if Presbyterian leaders controlled the education and admission of candidates to the ministry could they hold their heads high among rival religious groups. A professional ministry was thus crucial to the "Scotch-Irish" party's pride and sense of place.

The New Side party, on the other hand, cared less about professional niceties than about converting sinners. Its members were at the beginning of their careers, and most, being native-born or coming to the colonies in their youth, were not imbued with an Old World fondness for prerogative and order.[42] They never doubted that an educated clergy was essential, but the education had to be of the right sort. By the 1730s Harvard and Yale were being guided, in their view, by men of rationalist leanings who simply did not provide the type of training wanted by the revivalists.[43] Thus the New Sides chafed against the controls favored by their more conservative elders, controls that restricted their freedom of action, slowed their careers, and were in their opinion out of touch with New World ways.

The anti-institutionalism of the revivalists would cause some critics to portray them as social levelers, though there were no significant distinctions in social outlook or family background between Old and New Sides.[44] As with any insurgent group that relies in part on public support for its momentum, the New Sides tended to clothe their appeals in popular dress. At every opportunity they pictured the opposers as "the Noble & Mighty" elders of the church and identified themselves with "the Poor" and "common People"—images reinforced by Old Sides references to the evangelists' followers as an "ignorant" and "mobbish ... Rabble." Embracing their role as insurrectionists, the New Sides identified themselves with Paul and Elijah: "Both they and we are Turners of the World upside down, Subverters of Peace and Church-Government," but only to save the church from its enemies.[45]

The revivalists may not have been deliberate social levelers, but their words and actions had the effect of elevating individual values above collective ones. Everything they did, from disrupting orderly processes and encouraging greater lay participation in church government, to promoting mass assemblies and the close physical proximity that went with them, raised popular emotions. Most important, they insisted that there were choices and that the individual himself was free to make them. As Samuel Finley declared in 1741: "I look upon all Neutres, as Enemies, in Affairs of Religion. Away with your carnal Prudence! And either follow God or Baal. He that is not actually with us, is against us."[46]

The people, it might be suspected, had been waiting for this. The long years of imposed consensus and oversight by the Kirk had taken their toll, and undercurrents of resentment had strengthened as communities stabilized and Old World values receded. Still, the habit of deferring to the clergy was deeply seated in Scotch-Irish culture, making inertia an accomplice of church authority. By 1740, however, with part of the clergy themselves openly promoting rebellion, many Presbyterians, "in imitation of their example," seized the chance to throw off controls. The result was turbulence, "shattered and divided" congregations, and a rash of "slanderous reports ... against Ministers of the Gospel."[47] As aspersions against the ministerial character reached new peaks of ardor and entered the arena of public debate, it became increasingly clear just how effectively the schisms of the Awakening were breaking down the old structures of authority and order.

Examples of competition between clerical factions leading to popular tumults are too numerous to describe here, but the case of Middle Octerara Church in western Pennsylvania and its pastor, the Rev. Alexander Craighead, is typical. Craighead was tending toward evangelical attitudes by the later 1730s as was demonstrated by his refusal to baptize children of couples who had not experienced conversion. By the end of the decade his church had divided into pro- and anti-Craighead factions, and in December 1740 the controversy was referred to Donegal Presbytery, where a trial was held to determine whether Craighead was fit to continue at his post. Since the presbytery was dominated by Old Sides, the embattled minister denied that its carnal and graceless members had any authority over him. He then cut loose publicly, accusing them of "whoredom, drunkenness, Sabbath breaking, Lying etc." With such charges resonating through the parish, Craighead's supporters were emboldened to add their voices to the clamor, and the presbytery's proceedings were "interrupted by the people rising into a tumult, and railing at the Members in the most Scurrilous & opprobrious terms." The scandalized presbytery charged Craighead with slander and with offering "harrangues to amuse the populace." He had invited "the whole Congregation, which was very great, to the tent, where they were entertained with the reading of a paper he calls his defence," and in which he denounced the Old Sides "by name." All of this had heaped such "reproach & contempt on the Presbytery" that there was no choice but to suspend Craighead from his pastorate.[48] Clearly undeterred by the presbytery's action, laymen loyal to the New Sides appeared at the presbytery's spring meetings in 1741 to bring charges against four sitting members for drunkenness, blasphemy, and other wickedness. New and Old Sides meanwhile continued to belabor each other publicly as "dead Drones," "blackguard Ruffians," "Quacks or Mountebanks," liars, and heretics.[49]

In 1742 one woman accused her minister to his face of immoral conduct, explaining that she did so because of "the regard I bear to the profession & coat you wear."[50] Yet obviously that regard, so readily accorded in earlier days, had suffered a decline. The lengthening sequence of public wrangling between clergymen had exposed their frailties and dispelled some of the aura that traditionally surrounded their office; ministers openly scuffling with each other no longer looked so different from anyone else. This lowering of dignity, this demystification of the clergy, was a primary legacy of the Great Awakening. The ministers had been brought to this critical juncture, moreover, by a more complex process than the somewhat elusive intellectual transformation emphasized by historians of ideas. It included institutional disorders, professional rivalries, and social tensions both inside and outside the church.

The Great Awakening thus marked a turning point for the Presbyterian clergy by challenging its traditional position and authority in provincial life. Yet as ministers accommodated and adapted to the currents they themselves had helped to unloose, they found new ways to assert their influence. Although that story cannot be told fully here, a brief glimpse at the years after 1742 may suggest both the resilience of the clergy and the changing character of the American Presbyterian church.

Presbyterian clergymen responded to the challenges and shifting values of the early eighteenth century in at least two major ways. One was to identify their office more closely with the broader problems of the communities they served, a secularization of function that significantly expanded the minister's social role. Another was to unify and revitalize ecclesiastical structures and practices so as to enhance the clergy's self-image and sharpen the boundaries of their professional territory.[51]

The tendency toward secularization was quite striking, as New and Old Sides alike participated directly in two very unecclesiastical activities—military life and provincial politics. Presbyterian frontier settlements, exposed to French and Indian raids and underrepresented in the Pennsylvania assembly, desperately needed articulate spokesmen in the 1750s and 1760s. Though some Presbyterian ministers might have recoiled from such worldly doings, the response of most of them was one of passionate involvement.[52] They bombarded public officials with letters about frontier grievances, circulated petitions at services, and made their churches into centers for military recruitment. In an arrangement that may be unique in modern church history, frontier militia units were in a number of cases under the direct and active command of Presbyterian preachers—a mingling of roles that may be read in one official's reference to a certain John Steel, clergyman and captain of militia, as "The Reverend Capt. Steel."[53]

Presbyterian preachers entered even more directly into Pennsylvania politics after 1763, when a furious anti-Presbyterianism gripped the colony following murderous raids by some hot-headed westerners (most of them Presbyterians) on the Conestoga Indians in Lancaster County and the "March of the Paxton Boys" on Philadelphia in early 1764. As laymen and ministers were roundly denounced in the public press, a denominational partisanship flared that galvanized Presbyterians throughout the colony. From 1764 on, Presbyterian ministers, released from any lingering inhibitions they may have had about political activism, proceeded to convert their pulpits into "drums for politics." Through pastoral letters, congregational "committees of correspondence," the manipulation of denominational sensibilities in local elections, ticket balancing, and general conventions, Presbyterians learned "to act as a body... to defend our civil or religious liberties."[54] So thoroughly were Presbyterians politicized in this period that their churches and ministers would continue to serve as focal points for insurgent propaganda and activity in the 1770s as the revolutionary crisis approached.

At the more personal level of the ministers' professional concerns, the schism within Presbyterianism itself had to be closed if the church was to compete in the post-Awakening era of denominational pluralism. New and Old Sides debated their differences after 1742 and went on contending for dominance, but finally coalesced in an ostensibly reunited church in 1758.[55] The main impetus for reconciliation came from the evangelical party, possibly because the New Sides had rapidly outdistanced the Old in popular support and expected to set the direction of a reunited church. The Synod of New York, founded by twenty-two ministers in 1745 as a counterweight to the Old Side Synod of Philadelphia, had doubled in size by 1750 and risen to seventy-three members by 1758. In comparison, the Synod of Philadelphia reached a peak of twenty-six members in 1742, dropped to eighteen in 1754, and then stabilized at around twenty to twenty-three members by 1758.[56] But if the New Side clergy led in numbers, they also would draw back more sharply from the extreme positions taken in 1740 and 1741. Once their evangelical fever broke in 1742, the revivalists' vision cleared, and their overtures for reconciliation became so persistent that only the intransigence of the starchy Old Sides kept the parties apart until 1758. Not that the revivalists turned their backs on experimental religion, for the issues of conversion and internal piety continued to divide Presbyterians into the 1750s and beyond, but after 1742 the debate was largely contained within synods and presbyteries. The noisy censuring of fellow preachers and the public disputes of the revival had unloosed popular tumults and congregational schisms that had run swiftly out of control. The evangelical leaders thus experienced another sort of awakening when they saw how vulnerable their New World churches were to such wayward currents.

Gilbert Tennent had perhaps the most publicized second thoughts after two particular events alerted him to the dangers posed by public disorder. One was the bizarre behavior of his fellow Presbyterian the Reverend James Davenport in Connecticut during the latter part of 1741. Davenport was not content merely to denounce clergymen as unconverted; he had been instrumental in the division of a number of Connecticut congregations. Caught up in an extreme mental excitement, Davenport acquired wide notoriety as a fanatic when he led crowds singing through the streets, preached in a wild manner, and claimed that God had told him the end of the world was at hand. Called to explain these antics before the bar of the Connecticut assembly, Davenport's response was to mimic the posture of the crucified Christ.[57] When Gilbert Tennent got word of these "extraordinary Things," he recognized their "awful Tendency to rend and tear the Church." Coincident with Davenport's excesses, moreover, Tennent became sharply aware of the threat posed to his New Side parishioners by the proselytizing Moravians. A meeting with Count Zinzendorf, the Moravian leader, convinced him that the sect represented an emotional and undisciplined universalism that threatened to seduce the unwary, to "divide the People of God, and set them a jangling." All of this, as Tennent candidly confessed in a letter that soon found its way into the public press, caused him immense spiritual desolation and gave him "a greater Discovery of myself, then I think I ever had before." Acknowledging his own mismanagement and warmth of temper, Tennent now had "a clear view of the Danger of every Thing which tends to ENTHUSIASM and DIVISION in the visible Church." Most important, he saw that compared with the "enthusiastical Moravians" all Presbyterian clergymen "are in the main of sound Principles of Religion." "My Soul is sick" of divisions, he concluded; "I would to God, the Breach were healed."[58]

The growing concern of the New Sides about the Moravians—and about the Baptists too—encouraged several moderate clergymen to initiate steps toward a reunion in 1743.[59] The fifteen-year-long record of that effort shows that reconciliation was not significantly impeded by differences of theology. The real difficulty arose from the same set of problems that had inserted the wedge in the first place: professional issues such as ministerial education and licensing, the division of authority between synod and presbytery, itinerant preaching, and clerical discipline. A number of these were resolved by time. The Old Sides had initially demanded the equivalent of an apology from the schismatics, but by 1758 a majority of the New Side Synod of New York had taken no part in the events of seventeen years before, and the matter was allowed to drop. The issue of ministerial training was much eased by the 1746 founding of the College of New Jersey, though the Old Sides made further attempts to start their own seminary.[60] On the question of itinerancy, however, the New Sides remained obdurate, resisting "coercive measures to oblige people to be under the ministry of those whom they do not choose." The Old Sides, on the other hand, pressed for greater centralization of power in the synod; they also spurned the evangelicals' demand for a "joint testimony" affirming that the Great Awakening had been a work of God. These points, debated each year by the respective synods, were finally compromised in 1757. Ministers could preach in neighboring presbyteries when invited to do so; presbyterial authority to ordain and license was confirmed; and a carefully worded statement proclaimed that "religious appearances" that led the converted to "glorify God and to do good to their fellow men," but avoided the extremes of enthusiasm and delusion, indeed showed the hand of God.[61]

Finally, we might ask how laymen fared under the settlement of 1758 and whether they exercised any direct influence over it. Considering the New Side populist rhetoric and the prominent part taken by ordinary parishioners in the church separations of the early 1740s, we should expect lay authority to be increased after the Great Awakening. True, the Old Sides' casual approach to the appointment of elders and deacons was corrected, probably because the New Sides had encouraged all congregations to select lay officers. The New York Synod also made a concerted effort to increase lay involvement in, or at least attendance upon, presbytery meetings. By the later colonial years, most congregations were supplied with elders, and the ministers' power over such appointments was declining.[62] But if lay power was slightly enlarged at the local level, both New and Old Sides relegated the laity to a distinctly subordinate role at the higher, more professional, levels of church government. Presbytery and synod committees were composed largely of ministers. Moreover, the work of those bodies was dominated by such professional concerns as the training and ordination of ministers, parish assignments, and the payment of clerical salaries. Some elders attended every meeting, to be sure, but their presence is known only because their names appear in the initial roll call. The rapid rotation of elders also limited their power (few served longer than one year, especially in the synod), while the ministers' involvement was continuous until transfer to another district or death.

Parishioners did become visible when cases were heard on appeal from the local sessions, though for the most part such matters were settled at the presbyterial level. An exception was the New York Synod's involvement over several years in a simmering dispute between two factions in the New York City church. The synod's final ruling on the matter in 1756 is revealing of how the New Side attitude toward the laity had evolved since the Awakening. Defiant parties within congregations may have been tolerated—or even encouraged—in 1740, but with professional self-consciousness on the rise by 1756 neither New nor Old Sides had much patience with parishioners who were "not walking orderly." Thus when one of the New York City factions presented a list of grievances against the synod's handling of their dispute, the ministers found it to contain "insulting and even threatening expressions." Such conduct toward "a judicature of Jesus Christ is insufferably arrogant, presumptuous, and of evil tendency," they charged, for Scripture directed them "to suffer no man to despise us acting properly in our own office."[63]

The professional assertiveness shown by the clergy in this episode would grow as the Presbyterian church moved through the years of reconstruction toward maturity. A few ministers caught up in the passions of the Awakening may have briefly glimpsed an American church in which pastor and flock stood on more equal ground, but the excesses of the untutored and their tendency to confuse piety with enthusiasm soon convinced the clergy that popularity could not be pursued at the expense of order.

It was equally apparent that frail sinners would discern the True Church only if they were led to it by trained guides. "An ignorant Minister of God is a great Absurdity, a plain Contradicion," declared the New Side leader Samuel Finley in 1749. In an obvious thrust at lay exhorters (always disapproved by both Presbyterian factions), Finley observed that it was not enough for a preacher to have "good natural Parts . . . these must be cultivated by Learning" so that he could "resolve perplexing Cases of Conscience; explain Difficult Points of Doctrine; defend all necessary Truth against Subtle Opponents; and make intricate Subjects easy to vulgar Apprehensions."[64]

The consequences of this reaffirmation of professional standards were profound. By maintaining a certain distance between pastor and people, the church was conserving some of the mystery in the ministerial calling, even as the minister's external office was being widened in a secular direction.

At the same time, the insistence on a fully trained, professional clergy would confine the Presbyterian church to a less competitive position in the years ahead. Already Baptist and Methodist lay exhorters, with their plain speaking and proletarian ways, were leading an expansion that would cause their denominations by 1805 to soar beyond all others in America.[65] At least one Presbyterian minister was having second thoughts in 1775 about the course his church had chosen. From "Albany to Georgia we want 300 preachers," wrote the Reverend Jacob Green in alarm. Yet by requiring their candidates to complete college and a year or more of divinity training before ordination, the Presbyterian church "first make men gentlemen and then make them preachers," and so "our candidates have no idea of being gospel ministers without living politely."[66] Only by sending young men of parts and prudence to live and preach on the frontier before completing their education could the Presbyterian church hope to compete with the lay preachers.

Green's was, indeed, a voice in the wilderness. The emergent professional self-image of the clergy required that no further compromises be made which would vitiate their authority, and New Sides—now older and more settled—and Old Sides alike understood this. Stability had been achieved at some cost, and the time had come to draw a line. Thus Samuel Finley spoke for the present and future Presbyterian church when he declared that a minister must be "stored with Knowledge," for he was "a Steward of the Mysteries of God." Learning, above all else, would secure him from contempt and cause his congregation "to Honour, and *Esteem him very highly*, not merely as a Gentleman, but chiefly *for his Work's sake*, as a Minister."[67]

4 "What We Shall Meet Afterwards in Heaven"

Judgeship as a Symbol for
Modern American Lawyers

Stephen Botein

Historians seeking to understand the "professionalization" of American law have tended to minimize the significance of the judiciary.[1] There is an abundance of scholarship concerned with the historical development of courts in the United States, but most has focused on judicial statements of legal doctrine.[2] Compared with law professors, for example, judges do not loom large as participants in the process by which lawyers articulated ideology to establish their professional authority in modern American society.

This is a pattern of inattention that reflects received professional wisdom. As of the middle of the twentieth century, when the American Bar Association sponsored a massive Survey of the Legal Profession, few observers doubted that the professoriate of the modern law school had been at least moderately successful in enhancing opportunities for American lawyers to persuade the general public of their claim to "esoteric knowledge."[3] Numbering approximately one thousand at the time, law teachers were believed to fulfill important responsibilities as custodians of professional culture, whatever its recognizable shortcomings.[4] Judges, of whom there were then more than seven thousand in the country, appeared to have contributed less conspicuously to the agenda of professionalism. Most were selected by localistic popular procedures seemingly at odds with the ABA's second canon of ethics, which required lawyers to "prevent political considerations from outweighing judicial fitness" in evaluating personnel for the bench. Only the most accomplished members of the profession were supposed to become judges. "The aspiration of lawyers for judicial office," stipulated the second canon, "should be governed by an impartial estimate of their ability to add honor to the office and not by a desire for the distinction which the position may bring to themselves." Within the decentralized American system of electoral politics, no one could imagine that reality approached this ideal. Even at the federal level, where all judges were appointed, the organized bar had only begun to develop mechanisms for asserting professional influence.[5]

Yet the ABA's first canon of ethics insisted that it was the "duty of the lawyer to maintain towards the Courts a respectful attitude, not for the sake of the temporary incumbent of the judicial office, but for the maintenance of its supreme importance."[6] This curious formula illustrates a recurrent and often quixotic theme of discourse in the history of the American legal profession. What follows is intended as an exploratory essay on the meaning and uses of such discourse. As early as the middle of the eighteenth century, and through the next two hundred years, elite lawyers confronted a bench that mostly failed to meet their professional norms. Nevertheless, the bar in America needed exemplary judges to sustain its professional ideology and was prepared to invent them if necessary. Judgeship, representing an ideal of "primary orientation to the community interest," was an essential ingredient in the symbolic language of the American legal profession.[7] Prominent lawyers first defined and extolled judicial office in such a way as to promote a general image of themselves as a kind of "traditional" intelligentsia, ostensibly as "autonomous" as the clergy.[8] Then, at two key moments in the modern era, they made a cause of rallying to the defense of that office. Thus, while dissatisfied with the politics of judicial selection in America, the organized bar of the twentieth century was able to affirm the solidarity of a profession devoted not to private ambitions but to "ecumenic" values. Probably in their own minds and certainly for the benefit of the laity, professional ideologues used judgeship to deny internal divisions and to take maximum public advantage of their special relationship to the American "state."[9]

In 1862 a prominent Presbyterian minister in Philadelphia named Henry A. Boardman delivered a thanksgiving address to local lawyers on "the JUDICIAL SYSTEM of the United States, and the characters and services of the leading men by whom it has been administered." The occupation of the speaker was unusual but not inappropriate for a lengthy recital of motifs that the American bar had already come to associate with judgeship. The ideal judge was of course a member of the federal bench, preferably the Supreme Court, that "awful shrine" that had been formed as a "sanctuary" of liberty by the "doctrine of the Fathers." Guided by the "hand of a beneficent Providence," John Marshall had done his "great work" well. The "purest branch" of government, entrusted with the "sublime instrument" of a written constitution and dwelling in a "serene atmosphere" above the "turbulent region of party politics," the Supreme Court had to be protected from "desecration" by unhallowed men. "It will not do to recruit this Bench from the second and third ranks of the Profession," Boardman emphasized. Although political affiliation would unavoidably figure in appointments, "every one understands the distinction between a lawyer who makes his profession a hewer of wood to his politics, and a lawyer who makes his politics wait on his profession."[10]

Summarized here was the basic meaning of judgeship as it had evolved since colonial times—and as it would unfold in the discourse of lawyers for the next century. The model originated in English experience, although it had acquired an overlay of metaphor reflecting distinctively American circumstances. As any young colonist studying law in London would have been certain to appreciate, English judges were drawn exclusively from the upper echelon of the legal profession. With the help of favorable political connections, a well-esteemed barrister could hope to cap his career with service on a bench of the royal courts; from that summit of professional status, located within the national government, he might be all the more openly contemptuous of inferior practitioners, whether solicitors or the "almost necessarily disreputable" order of attorneys, none of whom could aspire to the eminence of such office. By the middle of the nineteenth century, strengthened by more attractive salary provisions, the position of the English judiciary as a professional elite was secure.[11]

From the perspective of a professionalizing American lawyer, there was much to recommend so hierarchical a system, but it was not precisely replicable outside England. By the 1750s, ambitious young gentlemen entering law in the colonies could display more impressive professional credentials than their judiciary. Despite Whitehall's best efforts to suppress "Domestick Justice" in America, there remained many judges at the county level who were admired more for common sense than for "knowledge of words and language." At the provincial level, where judges were meant to serve "upon the pleasure of the Crown," appointments were apt to be enmeshed in the clannish factionalism of Anglo-American politics. The most offensive of such appointments occurred in 1760, when Thomas Hutchinson became chief justice of Massachusetts; the emerging bar of Boston and vicinity was infuriated by his lack of legal training and his previous record of only minor judicial service.[12]

During the long formative period of legal development that preceded the Civil War, the characteristic features of the American judiciary took permanent structural form within a multilayered constitutional system. The federal courts of the new republic were buffeted about in the bitter controversies that soon enveloped the national scene. Although insulated by the appointment process from the immediate pressures of electoral competition, judges sat on these courts less by virtue of professional reputation than by means of adroit maneuvering through the byways of personal and party politics.[13] At the state level, elite lawyers and their allies made early gains at centralizing authority within court systems and imposing minimal standards of legal competence for the bench, but by the mid-1830s there was a "secret tendency to diminish the judicial power," as Tocqueville reported. Within the next couple of decades, many states adopted constitutional amendments requiring that judges be elected and forced at intervals to stand for reelection.[14] This was not a method of judicial selection that automatically prevented lawyers of high professional standing or ability from reaching the bench; strong judges here and there produced volumes of creative case law.[15] Especially within a legal system that had abandoned the formal ranked divisions of English practice, however, no elective bench could be certified with confidence as the preserve of leadership at the bar. The egalitarian challenge to social as well as professional hierarchy had been apparent in Philadelphia from 1825, when the legal patriciate there worried that a new president-judge of the Court of Common Pleas was a "man whose birth and position were not up to the old-time judicial standards."[16]

In the face of such troubling realities, leading members of the profession began to elaborate the metaphorical conventions that would surround judicial office in the modern era. "At length we follow the successful lawyer," proclaimed Timothy Walker in his inaugural law lecture of 1837 at Cincinnati College, "from the bar, to the bench. The counsellor has at last become the judge. The topmost rung of the ladder is now reached." Here was the classic English conception of status, coming from a man who had studied at Harvard under Justice Joseph Story of the United States Supreme Court. Such an appreciation of judgeship, celebrating law as an occupation with its own internal order of honorific advancement, appealed particularly to professional ideologues at a time when countless American lawyers were winning election to high executive and legislative office. "I would hold up the legal profession, as an end in itself," Walker took care to explain, "not as a stepping stone to something higher. In fact there is nothing higher. He who stands at the head of this profession, is on a level with the most elevated in the land."[17]

The symbolism of judgeship was more broadly useful, too. However fervently it might be argued that lawyers should labor "not for those alone who can afford the *honorarium*, but the widow, the fatherless, and the oppressed,"[18] there was a skeptical Anglo-American tradition suggesting that they did nothing of the kind. Unlike barristers in England, leading practitioners in America could not deflect such criticism by disclaiming crass involvement in the everyday affairs of clients or by abusing solicitors and attorneys who were so involved.[19] Sensitive to charges that lawyers were mercenary casuists exploiting the productive people of the land, professional ideologues were quick to see the advantage of fashioning the bar in an image of the bench. Judges could be said to epitomize the public ethos expected of all who pursued legal careers.

By means of judgeship, professional ideology could be stretched to encompass mainstream American belief in the "rule of law." As nineteenth-century legal orators never tired of repeating, the glory of the American constitutional system was its reliance on written fundamental law as interpreted by the courts. Although in practice the doctrine of judicial review was seldom applied at either the federal or the state level before the Civil War, it had come to be "held as a professional dogma" long before—"rather as a matter of faith than of reason," according to a dissident jurist in Pennsylvania.[20] One reason for the rapid acceptance of this doctrine in some quarters may have been the part it played in professional discourse. Here was the ultimate and distinctive mission of American lawyers: they joined judges "as sentinels upon the outposts of the constitution," as Justice Story put it. "The discussion of constitutional questions throws a lustre round the Bar," he observed proudly, "and gives a dignity to its functions, which can rarely belong to the profession in any other country."[21]

Like the ideal judge, then, the ideal lawyer was a statesman opposed to both executive and legislative tyranny in the name of republican principles that were the legacy of the American Revolution. Those principles, which of course included the "rights of property," were "sacred."[22] Particularly for New Englanders, whose eighteenth-century forebears had frequently entered law after prolonged vocational crises in which they considered the clerical alternative, it was second nature to fill professional discourse with vaguely religious metaphor.[23] Such metaphor created a peculiarly fitting context for contemplation of the judiciary. Judges on circuit might resemble traveling lecturers, preaching moralistically on contemporary topics in their charges to grand juries.[24] Like clergymen of an earlier day, they questioned whether their salaries and tenure were sufficient to maintain the integrity of their office.[25] Their literary output was voluminous, as though divinity had made way for jurisprudence in the cultural life of the new nation.

Lemuel Shaw signed more than two thousand opinions in his thirty years as chief justice of Massachusetts's Supreme Judicial Court; his father, whose pastorate in Barnstable lasted almost fifty years, was said in an obituary to have written more sermons than any living minister in New England—"if not in the world."[26]

Conceived as a kind of latter-day ecclesiastical order, the judiciary had the appearance of austere disinterestedness. Although Chief Justice Shaw and others like him might be architects of a new legal framework for business in America, the symbol of judgeship in professional discourse implied an outlook free from entanglement in the world of entrepreneurial development.[27] That implication could then be extended to the profession as a whole. Advocates as well as judges were said by Story to be "ministers" standing "in the temple and in the presence of the law."[28]

According to a sermon that had been delivered in 1760 at the ordination of Lemuel Shaw's father, the true ministry of the gospel was of "vast Importance to a People," yet a true minister could not expect to be "applauded" by them or rewarded with "affluent Circumstances."[29] Such also was the situation of the nineteenth-century judge, at least for the credulous. In 1863, when Stephen J. Field was named to the United States Supreme Court, a former colleague of his on California's highest bench was moved to comment on the sacrifices demanded by judicial office. "Millions might have been amassed by venality," noted Joseph G. Baldwin in praising Field's years as California's chief justice. "He retires as poor as when he entered, owing nothing and owning little." There were those who suspected that both Field and Baldwin had made quite enough for themselves while on the bench, but these allegations were never proven and were properly ignored. Baldwin, better known for short stories than jurisprudence, understood a higher truth.[30]

Fancifully or not, elite lawyers of the antebellum period had to stake out a claim to social independence by invigorating the language of public spirit that was essential to their ideology of professionalism. Without a transforming vision of judgeship, given the judiciary available to them, they would have found it difficult if not impossible to advance what has been termed the "massive philosophical formulation" that accompanied and facilitated their "amazing rise ... to a position of political and intellectual domination."[31]

Following the Civil War, the reputation of the judiciary in America eroded. Led by Stephen Field, citing such noble principles as freedom of contract and due process, judges acted to protect business enterprise from rising popular antagonism. Well-paid lawyers manipulated the court system on behalf of an aggressive moneyed class. David Dudley Field, Stephen's brother, was said by Henry Adams to have a "silken halter" around the neck of one New York judge and a "hempen one" around another's.[32] Perhaps most deplorable, to keepers of the professional conscience, was the tendency of prominent judges to resign from the bench and resume private practice, most often to represent railroads.[33] By 1900, on the threshold of the Progressive era, the courts faced severe criticism not only from labor leaders, populists, and socialists, but also from some respectable members of the legal profession, which was at long last beginning to develop a formal apparatus for collective deliberation and policymaking.[34]

Amid widespread fears of "judicial oligarchy," various politicians at the state level tried to gather support for constitutional propositions that adapted a device originally designed for executive and legislative officers and subjected judges to recall by popular vote. The judicial recall movement agitated the newly organized American bar to a greater extent than any other public issue before the 1930s. It "overshadows the tariff," a lawyer told the Chicago Bar Association in 1912.[35] For the American Bar Association, in the second quarter century of its existence, the issue provided a welcome opportunity to undertake a national campaign of public education. In defense of judgeship, if not of judges, the ABA could try to establish its credentials as America's first and foremost voluntary organization in the field of law.[36] Traditional antebellum ideology would allow leaders of the bar to comprehend divergent experiences and purposes within a profession that was growing rapidly and becoming more heterogeneous.[37]

In 1908 Oregon became the first state to apply a recall amendment to the judiciary. Then, in 1911, judicial recall was instituted in California. In that same year, Arizona asked to be admitted to the union with a constitution that included the same basic provision, which President Taft believed would make a judge the "instrument and servant of a majority of the people and subject to their momentary will." In August, upon Taft's veto of the statehood bill that had finally passed Congress, Arizona was left with the option of withdrawing its recall provision as a prerequisite of entering the nation. As one popular periodical noted, the president's intervention had "precipitated this new issue into the national arena."[38]

Around the country, local and state bar associations heard speakers assail judicial recall and adopted resolutions condemning it. At the end of August, in an effort to lead and coordinate this activity, the American Bar Association approved a statement expressing alarm that judicial recall would be "destructive of our system of government" and urging "members of the bar in every state, through existing organizations or others to be formed, to cause to be presented to the people the reasons well understood by the legal profession why the recall should not be made applicable to judges." In addition, the ABA formed a special committee, including a lawyer from every state and territory, "to take such steps as it may deem best to expose the fallacy of judicial recall."[39]

The ABA's Committee to Oppose the Judicial Recall operated for a total of eight years. In all but the first, its chairman was Rome Green Brown of Minneapolis, a former president of the Minnesota State Bar Association; the other members of the committee were drawn from the leadership of the ABA and various state bar associations. Republicans and Democrats were equally represented.[40] For the first few years, this group conducted its business in an atmosphere of crisis. Initially, according to Brown, the case of Oregon had seemed little worse than a "local and temporary lapse from reason"; when California and Arizona followed the same path, "thinking people were awakened." In 1913 the situation looked rather bleak. Nevada and Colorado had adopted judicial recall toward the close of the previous year, and Arizona—once admitted to the union—had blithely restored judicial recall to its constitution. The legislatures of Kansas and Minnesota had approved recall bills, which awaited popular ratification in November 1914. A recall amendment had been averted in Arkansas only because the Supreme Court of that state had ruled that the procedure by which it had been adopted was irregular. The legislature of North Dakota had defeated a recall bill by a single vote. Agitation for judicial recall was said to be on the rise in Wisconsin, Ohio, Illinois, Nebraska, Oklahoma, even in Massachusetts, and there was sentiment stirring in Congress to try somehow to introduce the mechanism within the federal judicial system. The movement, reported Chairman Brown, seemed to be one "originating upon the Pacific Coast . . . and spreading east." Already, he warned, it had a foot across the Mississippi.[41]

By the next year, it was apparent that there had been what William Howard Taft, then president of the ABA, called a "distinct falling off in the support of these fundamentally unwise and dangerous proposals." This, explained Taft, was due to the "great work" of Rome Brown's committee. "I assert with confidence," Chairman Brown told the ABA, "that the advocacy of judicial recall is on the wane," although still liable to "appear at the time and in the locality where you least expect it."[42] By 1915 Brown's committee could report that the situation was no longer of serious concern. It was true that Kansas had finally approved judicial recall, but Brown's home state of Minnesota had not. Elsewhere, recall agitation was at a minimum, and efforts were underway to repeal the new amendments in Nevada and Colorado. Judicial recall was "apparently dead," declared Brown, although of course it still needed vigilant watching.[43]

Such was the success of Brown's campaign that one official historian of the ABA, as late as 1932, considered it the "most significant and daring" ever sponsored by the organization.[44] ABA leaders were evidently convinced that they had accomplished something of importance by means of their crusade against judicial recall. Viewed from a distance, the entire episode had an air of unreality and even comedy about it, but the ABA's first strenuous exercise in imagemaking was sustained by symbolism that mattered greatly to professional ideologues.

Judicial recall was, in practice, far less startling and drastic a constitutional remedy than ABA leaders imagined. By 1914, regardless of recall provisions, only seven American states did not elect their judges; life tenure was enjoyed by the judiciary in only four states. As advocates of judicial recall hastened to point out, their proposals did not fundamentally alter the basis of judicial service in most states since a judge who had to run for reelection was already exposed to a kind of recall procedure. Moreover, early experience with the system indicated that it was normally cumbersome enough to shield judges from short-term pressures.[45] No such sobering thoughts kept statesmen of the bar from fulminating against the "vicious" innovation in apocalyptic tones. "It is not progress," Elihu Root announced; "it is not reform; it is degeneracy." The republic was in peril. "Why not abolish courts?" asked one professional editorialist. "It is but a step further."[46]

If leaders of the organized bar habitually magnified the evils of judicial recall, as measured against the political facts of life that they had long learned to live with, they also greatly exaggerated the scope of their struggle to defeat the movement. When the issue surfaced, the ABA was an organization of fewer than five thousand lawyers, about 4 percent of the national total, and its annual budget was approximately $30,000. Appropriations for the Judicial Recall Committee during its lifetime added up to less than $5,000. Through all the sound and fury of the controversy, it was the proudest achievement of the committee to distribute about 750,000 copies of about 30 different pamphlets to libraries, schools, and other civic institutions.[47] In any case, the judicial recall movement never generated much popular enthusiasm beyond some half a dozen states; most avowedly progressive politicians with national visibility were at pains to dissociate themselves from the issue.[48]

Of the few resources that the ABA could marshal in its battle to save the American judiciary, Rome Brown himself was the most formidable. The Committee to Oppose the Judicial Recall was largely a one-man show, as colorful an example of political theater as the organized bar was capable of producing. Much of the ABA's anti-recall literature was mailed out directly from Brown's office in Minneapolis, where he represented such clients as Cream of Wheat, the Great Northern Railway, and the power company network of one William J. Murphy. According to one Minnesotan, Brown was generally recognized as the "most extreme, stand-pat . . . corporation product."[49] As counsel to the Murphy interests, he had made a name as a decidedly partial authority on water rights. In 1914, too, he made an appearance before the United States Supreme Court to argue against the constitutionality of "socialistic" minimum wage legislation, which he regarded as a "forced contribution to the purely individual needs of the worker." Walter Lippmann, a tongue-in-cheek student of the Minneapolis lawyer's writings, described him as a "kind of specialist in the business of finding fault with the minimum wage." There was no ignoring Brown, said Lippmann, for he was the "heavy artillery on the other side." Despite a crowded political agenda, Brown found the time to travel thirty thousand miles and deliver some twenty-five addresses denouncing judicial recall.[50]

Brown was quite certain that the new proposals "sprang from socialism," and only an independent judiciary could maintain constitutional guarantees "that private property shall not be taken for public use without compensation." Recall was the stratagem of a few "dynamiters" who styled themselves progressive but secretly aimed at "confiscation." Their methods were insidious. "This nation is now afflicted with a widely spreading plague of misinformation," Brown told the Oklahoma State Bar Association in December 1913, "of a poisoning of the public mind against the very safeguards of our free institutions. A deadly infection works upon the misguided prejudices and discontents of the elements of unrest. This infection is fertilized and spread by certain classes of citizens who have become purveyors of error and all of whom are shouting for the judicial recall." His ABA committee was engaged in a "course of hygiene, to educate citizens . . . to a healthful, wholesome intellectual attitude."[51]

With so much at stake, Brown was sometimes sufficiently aroused to ignore the protocol of his profession—oddly enough, even to violate the ABA's first canon of ethics, requiring respect for the judiciary. Among the many enemies that Brown identified throughout the land, no one angered him more than Chief Justice Walter Clark of the North Carolina Supreme Court. Here was a judge so heedless of his position as to have befriended such notorious "radicals" as Bryan, Gompers, and La Follette and to have publicly criticized the whole American court system for succumbing to the "influence of the great vested interests."[52] Invited to address the North Carolina State Bar Association in 1914, Brown saw his chance to confront the renegade jurist unflinchingly. With the chief justice present in the audience, Brown spoke sharply of "one of these conspicuous, if not shining, exceptions to the generally sane attitude . . . which has been held by the American bench and bar." Predictably, most lawyers in North Carolina responded to this performance with outbursts of professional and regional pride. Clark himself was enraged by the "spectacle of an imported Yankee" coming down to abuse a "Southern soldier." On the day following his speech, Brown apparently concluded that it would be prudent for him to see the chief justice and apologize for his "rough northern way."[53]

It was an antic reactionary, then, who staged the first great demonstration of the organized American bar on behalf of judgeship. The wonder is, given such leadership, that the recall issue served the ABA so well. The fact that it did is indicated by the results of a membership drive that doubled the size of the organization between 1912 and 1916. William Howard Taft would later say that Rome Brown's energies and abilities had earned him the "merited gratitude of . . . his fellow members of the legal profession."[54] Certainly he had been willing to make the personal commitment of time and money without which a fledgling voluntary society could not hope to persuade anyone that it was accomplishing anything. Although judgeship may have meant little more to Brown than protection of corporate capital in the private rather than the community interest, his tireless promotion of the cause was essential to an organization that was seeking acknowledgment of its authority to proclaim professional orthodoxy to a national audience.[55]

In spite of Brown's grand promise to conduct a "general propaganda of education" that would reach the "every-day citizen," the work of his committee tended to concentrate on the memberships of state bar associations. Hence the ABA was appealing mainly to groups already on record, after Taft's Arizona veto, as being opposed to judicial recall. It "avails little to discuss these questions merely before lawyers," Chairman Brown conceded, but he did little else.[56] That, however, was perhaps the most valuable accomplishment of the anti-recall campaign—to give the appearance of agreement within the organized bar on a major public issue. From the "whole membership of a learned profession entitled to authoritative expression of opinion on this question," reported Brown in 1912, "have come deliberate protests against this greatest of modern fallacies." Although young Felix Frankfurter might confide to his diary that the "sacrosanct notion" of the judiciary had to be "hit" whenever possible, public avowals of such thinking were uncommon and regarded as professionally undecorous. Only an intrepid soul would break with his brethren to espouse recall, or even to suggest that the issue called for "investigation, not vituperation."[57] As one ABA speaker would observe after the furor had died down, the heretics seemed to be a few disaffected lawyers bent on "making their appeal to the American electorate." It was outrageous that such unscrupulous men could force leaders of the bar to "discuss the question upon reason rather than authority." Few or not, such dissidents were limited in their opportunity to find a rank-and-file following within a profession that counted no more than 30 percent of its practitioners in any bar organization whatsoever.[58] Meanwhile, at the upper levels of the organized bar, there was a loose consensus against recall.

Other ABA leaders joined Brown in the crusade for judicial independence, but his mandate to fight "radicals" was less broad than he wished. At the annual meeting of 1919, with the issue of recall quite stale, Brown attempted to prolong the life of his committee as a means of heading off further "anti-constitutional and socialistic" measures that might pave the way in America for a "Bolshevism as bad as that in Russia." One lawyer rose to object. "I do not think there are any of us who are socialists or revolutionists," he said. "But I do not think we should find if we all got together that we always agreed exactly as to what is a revolutionary measure and what is not." He advised that the ABA refuse to give carte blanche to Brown's committee to war on "anything and everything that in their opinion may be revolutionary." Others concurred, and the Committee to Oppose the Judicial Recall finally expired.[59]

Although Brown and probably a majority of his committee belonged to that conspicuous class of lawyers who not only participated actively in the management of the corporate firms they represented but more generally functioned as public spokesmen for business interests, many leaders of the bar located themselves closer to the center of the national political spectrum.[60] However cautious, these were self-styled reformers who shared Woodrow Wilson's concern that American lawyers had been "sucked into the maelstrom of the new business system of the country" to become "mere expert counsellors" of private enterprise. In particular, remarked ABA President Stephen Gregory in 1912, those practicing "at the lower end of Manhattan Island" were apt to be identified with "large interests" that confined their freedom to assume public responsibilities.[61] It was a persistent refrain of many ABA speakers during the progressive era that "serving the client is not always a lawyer's highest duty." Otherwise, how could the traditional morality of the profession be upheld? Lawyers "are as intelligent, generous, patriotic, self-sacrificing and sympathetic a class as there is in society," William Howard Taft contended plaintively. "We are not opposed to progress, real progress."[62] The requirements of professional ideology were such that leaders of the bar needed a cause to which they could speak as both lawyers and citizens. Judgeship, defined more liberally than Rome Brown would have liked, was advantageous to this cause.

Even if it were true that all the "lawyers and lobbyists of the trusts, railroads, and public-service corporations" were allied with Brown, as a well-known "people's lawyer" charged, [63] prominent ABA opponents of judicial recall included two men of markedly reformist sympathies. One was Edgar Farrar of New Orleans, ABA president in 1911, who played a key role in establishing the Committee to Oppose the Judicial Recall. Like many lawyers of the time, Farrar managed to chart an uneasy career combining private practice on behalf of large corporate clients with public criticism of monopolistic capital. In his widely reprinted presidential address of 1911, Farrar was vehement in warning his brethren against not only the "virus" of judicial recall but also a "corporation debauch" that endangered the future of the country.[64] In 1913, the ABA's president was Frank B. Kellogg, a proponent of the "New Nationalism," whom Theodore Roosevelt had once called the "best trust-buster of them all." To Rome Brown, Roosevelt was "an ex-president preaching Socialism," and Kellogg was not much better. From 1911 to 1912, however, Kellogg had served as the first chairman of the Committee to Oppose the Judicial Recall; for a year, he and not Brown was the ABA's spokesman for the constitutional order.[65]

Unlike Brown, many ABA leaders opposed recall specifically because they considered themselves reformers. Taft and Kellogg, for example, claimed to be convinced that procedural deficiencies in the administration of American justice were at the root of popular discontent with the courts. "I have been preaching reform in our judicial procedure for years," Taft wrote in 1913. Once implemented, "it will do the poor man more good ten times than the shining nostrums held out to him as a ground for electing their inventors." A year earlier, Kellogg had told the Ohio State Bar Association that "expense and delays in trials" were responsible for the very agitation to recall judges.[66] Such academic lawyers as Harvard's Roscoe Pound were inclined to agree, while stressing as well that judges had to modernize their understanding of substantive law.[67]

Perversely, from the perspective of professional leaders who were championing reform as an alternative to fundamental social change, the logic of judicial recall seemed to point in quite the wrong direction. Procedural reform depended upon "professional experts of the highest proficiency," as Taft referred to them, and orthodox sentiment within the organized bar left no room for doubt that there would be a "higher average of experts for the Bench" if they were selected by the appointive system of life tenure used in the federal courts. Presumably, appointed judges would be recruited more often from the ranks of professional leadership than from political wards. Judicial recall was therefore a "case of atavism," in Taft's phrase, enlarging instead of reducing the element of electoral politics in judicial selection.[68] The threat of recall would also hinder judges from fulfilling the proper administrative role that professional reformers envisioned for them. As one authority on procedure told the ABA, "progressive democratization of the courts" was a backward step that made it more difficult for judges to command deference and thus exercise larger discretion to disregard technicalities in the interest of efficient courtroom management. The first task of procedural reform should be "to retrace our steps, and vest not less, but more independence in our judges."[69] Academic lawyers concerned with substance as well as procedure were of the same mind. Although displeased by many court decisions, they believed that "hard and fast" legislation would prevent judicial "engineers" from adapting the law to suit the variety of circumstances in a complex industrial society.[70]

From differing points of view, then, professional opinion converged around the issue of judicial recall to give an impression of near unanimity that was useful to a national organization purporting to represent the common public creed of lawyers. A "stand-pat" figure like the energetic Rome Brown could be helpful to the ABA, but at the true ideological middle there was a program of professional reform that focused on the twin topics of judicial selection and administrative efficiency. If such a program was narrowly conceived and quite recognizably compatible with the "selfish interest" of business lawyers,[71] it also resonated with the traditional discourse of the bar and was in keeping with the constitutional tradition of the country. ABA leaders of all persuasions were far better attuned to the classical themes of both professional and political culture in America than were the defenders of judicial recall. "Adoption of the recall," explained one of the latter, "is nothing more than the application of good business principles to government affairs." After all, every "wise employer" reserves the right to fire an employee "whenever the service rendered is unsatisfactory," and there "hangs no halo of sanctity around the head of the judiciary."[72] Apparently, many people felt otherwise.

"To a lawyer," observed one speaker at the 1912 ABA meeting, "a judge is the symbol of a system—the exponent of an abstract idea—whom by education, training and every tradition of his profession he is bound to reverence." Long ago, added this acolyte of the bench, "all judges were bishops, abbots and other church dignitaries, just as all lawyers were once upon a time men in holy order." And so they remained, "in a true poetic sense."[73] Not only did independent judges seem necessary to ensure orderly progress for the country, by maintaining "constitutional safeguards" that protected the "cottage or the liberty of the humblest citizen"; they also epitomized the personal aspirations of many practicing lawyers. Like independent judges, it was often said within the profession, lawyers should adopt a neutral public posture. In the Progressive era, unlike antebellum times, the urgent challenge was less to keep executive and legislative power in check than to restrain the "predatory classes . . . both the rich and the poor."[74] In fighting for an independent bench, then, lawyers were perhaps also asserting indirectly their own ideal of an independent bar. If, moreover, this was a standard that sometimes eluded them, because of the pressures of private practice, at least they might have the satisfaction of preserving it intact at a higher professional level.

Within this context, devotion to judgeship during the first decades of the twentieth century became almost cultist in intensity. Appropriately, it was not Rome Green Brown but William Howard Taft who led the organized bar in celebrating the glories of judicial office, even while regretting the quality of many occupants. "Judge Taft," as the bar thought of him, was a "man dear to the heart of all American lawyers," and this warm feeling was generously reciprocated. At the ABA's 1911 meeting in Baltimore, amid a discussion of judicial recall, Taft suddenly arrived to interrupt the proceedings. He had been vacationing nearby, but, he explained, "I could not resist the temptation to come and be one of you for a while." It was a mere two weeks after the Arizona veto. "There are a lot of things between us which go without saying," Taft happily told the convention. "We start with our reasoning pretty far along because we have reasoned together up to conclusions upon which we all agree."[75] Little wonder, then, that the president's message on Arizona appealed so powerfully to the organized profession. He was hailed continually for his "brave and wise words," for his "sturdy, judicial and fearless attitude" toward the statehood bill.[76]

Nothing engaged Taft more during his presidency than judicial appointments, and it was his good fortune to fill six vacancies on the Supreme Court alone. In part because he attributed his popularity with the organized bar to expectations that he would be "conscientious in the selection of judges," he examined each candidate with the fastidiousness of a connoisseur. The same instinct for the reformist center that underlay his nomination of Charles Evans Hughes would later cause him publicly to question whether Louis Brandeis was "fit" for service on so august a tribunal. The chief justiceship was the most rewarding phase of his own long career. "I love judges and I love courts," Taft is reported once to have said. "They are my ideals on earth of what we shall meet afterwards in Heaven under a just God."[77] Cloaked in a mantle of nonpartisanship and professionalism, judges offered assurance that the nation could survive the "present agitation." Standing at the head of the bar, they attested to the disinterested, public-spirited functions of lawyers. In such an atmosphere of self-affirmation, the issue of judicial recall allowed the ABA to elevate its image as the national organization of professional lawyers, committed to basic principles of American belief.

Just a little more than a quarter of a century after Taft's veto of the Arizona statehood bill, another president—also a lawyer, but no admirer of the legal profession—moved dramatically not to safeguard but to undermine the independence of the judiciary. On 5 February 1937, Franklin D. Roosevelt startled the country with a set of proposals that he and Attorney General Homer Cummings had devised to add as many as six new justices to the United States Supreme Court. The story of this ill-fated stratagem—packaged within a comprehensive plan to increase the efficiency of the federal court system, but transparently intended to make the Supreme Court more conciliatory toward the New Deal—is familiar enough and needs no reciting here.[78] As a chapter in the history of American judgeship, however, the court-packing episode is revealing. Compared with its campaign against judicial recall, the response of the American Bar Association to the crisis of 1937 was indicative of changes taking place not only in a single organization but within the public culture of professional lawyers.

According to the ABA, the bar was "more aroused over the Supreme Court proposal, and the threat to an independent judiciary, than . . . on any previous occasion since the Civil War." Once again, professional oratory dating from the formative antebellum period seemed relevant, perhaps all the more so because this time the assault came from a popular executive in the Jacksonian mold. "I think we are in great danger at the moment," declared ABA President Frederick H. Stinchfield, who was, like Rome Brown, a Minneapolis lawyer. The Supreme Court "must not be destroyed," he warned, "and the Constitution must stay." Americans had become an "exceedingly nervous, even impressionable people"; judicial restraint of majoritarian impulses was essential to the survival of free government.[79]

This was predictable, as was the ABA's claim that it had never fulfilled a more useful public function than in its efforts to persuade Congress to reject FDR's scheme. "It . . . seems reasonable to conclude that the people have largely entrusted the business of government to lawyers," observed ABA spokesmen. The people "know what lawyers in the past have done in making and preserving the United States." Since it was their business "to deal with the courts," lawyers were peculiarly well qualified to pronounce FDR's plan unconstitutional "in a moral and spiritual sense." The usual special committee was appointed and the usual appeals were made to expand membership.[80]

Yet the ABA was not the same organization that had rallied to the defense of the bench in the Progressive era. It had grown in size to almost thirty thousand lawyers, nearly 18 percent of the national total; its annual budget exceeded $200,000. In addition, it had been reorganized just the year before on a so-called federal model, in partial imitation of the American congressional system. Instead of making decisions by a quorum of its membership at annual meetings, the new ABA was governed principally by a House of Delegates that included lawyers selected by ABA members in each state and territory, along with representatives from state and some local bar associations, and officials of such national groups as the American Judicature Society and the American Law Institute. The object of this revision was to "correlate the activities of the Bar organizations of the respective states on a representative basis in the interest of the legal profession and of the public throughout the United States."[81] Auspiciously, since the central issue could be defined in terms of judgeship, court-packing was the first major test of the federated ABA.

The most striking organizational feature of ABA activity in 1937 was a more heightened degree of political sophistication than had been demonstrated in its operations in the controversy over judicial recall. It was still true that campaign techniques were amateurish for lack of a paid staff assigned to public education. For the most part, the ABA's struggle against FDR was carried on in Washington by volunteers from the Junior Bar Conference, members of the association under the age of thirty-six, who—according to the ABA *Journal*—"swung into action" as soon as Congress began to debate court-packing.[82] Whatever the limitations of this group, however, the ABA recognized that a certain subtlety of approach was required, lest its work backfire. Word was passed that "stand-pat" corporation lawyers like John W. Davis would best remain "conspicuously absent" from the public eye. The chairman of the special committee named to present ABA views to Congress was Sylvester C. Smith, Jr., a New Deal Democrat from a small city in New Jersey, a man who could identify himself as one of many "plain country lawyers representing the man on the street, the people back home." The secretary of the Junior Bar Conference, Paul F. Hannah, insisted that he regarded FDR as "one of the greatest of Presidents," under whose leadership the country had achieved significant "social and economic progress."[83]

In further contrast to its handling of judicial recall, the ABA went out of its way to acknowledge divergent opinion within the profession. In accordance with a general policy that both sides should be heard, the ABA *Journal* offered readers two "able and authoritative presentations" of FDR's case. Both authors were academic lawyers. One, Thurman Arnold, mischievously asked that the "practical men" in the ABA be "realists" with regard to the Supreme Court, rather than leave FDR's proposals "smothered in symbolism and garnished with poetry."[84]

With a wit that probably eluded most ABA members, Arnold was gesturing here toward new circumstances that affected the professional response to court-packing. It was not simply that in 1937—unlike 1911—the ABA was challenging a powerful national politician, nor that the organization had motives to alter its image as a quasi-affiliate of the right-wing American Liberty League.[85] In addition, the new ABA of 1937 could no longer expect ready assent to the proposition that it spoke for a profession unified by devotion to the symbol of independent judgeship. Traditions were still potent and the issue was doubtless as convenient as any that might have surfaced—but not quite as convenient as it had been twenty-five years earlier.

By 1937, almost two-thirds of the lawyers in America belonged to some bar group or another; specialized organizations were proliferating.[86] One, the National Lawyers Guild, had just been formed as an alternative to the ABA, to "function as an effective social force . . . to the end that human rights shall be regarded as more sacred than property rights." The guild endorsed court-packing and assailed the "intemperate" leadership of the ABA for encouraging "a somewhat hysterical, a certainly emotional, a completely irresponsible attack on the President of the United States for his earnest efforts on behalf of the underprivileged of the country."[87] Many lawyers active in government as well as the academy were at least inclined to sympathize with FDR's reasons for trying to enlarge the Supreme Court and were unimpressed by harangues on the sanctity of the judiciary. An "Isaiah" like Brandeis they might revere, but it was not so with every judge. As "realists," after all, they had far less confidence than Chief Justice Hughes in the "capacity for independence, impartiality and balanced judgment" of nine or, for that matter, fifteen presidential appointees, old or otherwise. Although Hughes himself might look and talk "like God," as one

New Dealer would later say, some of his colleagues on the Supreme Court appeared actively malign.[88] To the extent that the faith of the Progressives in legal expertise endured, it had come to be nourished as much by the professoriate as by the judiciary. A few years earlier, Harvard's Felix Frankfurter had chosen to decline the United States solicitor generalship and stay for the time being in Cambridge, despite FDR's tempting assurances that the appointment would smooth the way for eventual nomination to the Supreme Court.[89]

In part because the structure of the American legal profession had become more complex in the decades following World War I, it was difficult to keep up an appearance of consensus through discourse at the level of leadership, even when judgeship was at risk. Dissidents within the ABA's House of Delegates could muster only 7 votes for court-packing, against 130 for professional orthodoxy, but academic and government lawyers had many more opportunities to espouse contrary views than had been available in previous times. Shrewdly, facing the prospect of fragmented elite opinion, the ABA determined to position itself in the public view as a "truly democratic national organization" that consulted with the mass of practitioners. "Leaders of small and unrepresentative organizations of lawyers may *presume* to speak" on general public issues, it was said, but the ABA was able to do much more. First, before taking an official stance on court-packing, it conducted a referendum of its membership; it then attempted to poll the entire American profession.[90]

As an exercise in public relations, this maneuver proved successful enough. Only about 14 percent of ABA members were reported to favor FDR's Supreme Court proposal; of nonmembers, about 23 percent. While conceding some minor variances in their returns, ABA leaders triumphantly announced that the results were "significantly similar" in "virtually all parts" of the country, "among non-members as well as among members." Court-packing was not a political question as far as lawyers were concerned. "This should end the assertion or assumption," it was proclaimed, "that members of the Association think and act differently from lawyers who are not members."[91]

Up to a point, it did, but some ABA leaders were uneasily aware that the figures were not as overwhelming as they seemed at first glance. After all, 37 percent of ABA members and 63 percent of nonmembers had failed to submit ballots, and even officials of the organization admitted that among those nonrespondents were lawyers who looked on the ABA with "indifference or hostility" or who doubted whether the voting would be "really secret."[92] Such a group might well be attracted to court-packing. In any case, 23 percent of the nonmembers was not exactly negligible professional support for FDR's move, since rudimentary polls had indicated initial approval of no more than 45 percent of the general public and later of as little as 31 percent.[93] In fact, the voting of nonmembers was more sensitive to politics than ABA leaders were willing to appreciate. Of nonmembers from the ten states that had been least supportive of FDR in the 1936 election, only about 11 percent favored court-packing; from the ten states that had been most supportive, about 33 percent. One ABA leader hinted darkly that "lawyers of foreign birth or origin" were a source of such unprofessional opinion, but the rate of approval for court-packing in returns from southern as well as northern industrial states suggested a broadly partisan pattern of response.[94] In view of the probability that the ABA's poll overrepresented Republican lawyers, there was nothing in the evidence thus assembled to demonstrate conclusively that American lawyers thought much differently about court-packing than other citizens.

So the crisis of 1937 ended on a somewhat uncertain note. The ABA had come a long way since the days of Rome Brown and his Committee to Oppose the Judicial Recall, but the future of the organization as the national guardian of traditional public values cherished by all professional lawyers was in doubt. It was problematic whether an enlarged ABA could continue to maintain the illusion of consensus on major political issues involving the legal profession.[95] The usefulness of judgeship, as a symbol for elite American lawyers, could no longer be taken for granted.

Perhaps the most brazen personal example of high-level professional heresy to undermine the cult of judgeship after 1937 was that of William O. Douglas. When he joined the Supreme Court in 1939, the youngest man to be appointed after Joseph Story, Douglas was prepared to wear his judicial robes casually. According to his autobiography, he had never dreamed of attaining the position and had no deep sense of fulfillment when he did. It was in a sense an "empty achievement" for him, a job that he found neither fully satisfying nor fully time-consuming. Early in his judicial career, he determined to enjoy first-class citizenship by participating in a wide range of public projects. "A man or a woman who becomes a Justice," he later said, "should try to stay alive." Frankly interested in exploring political routes to the presidency, which luck almost bestowed on him, he never bothered to display the kind of delicate sensibility that in 1916 had led Charles Evans Hughes to fret over the morality of leaving the Court to run against Woodrow Wilson.[96]

In his heyday, Douglas was a hero of what might be termed a professional counterculture. As of mid-century, it had a following that appeared likely to increase over time. In the court of public opinion, however, judgeship was perhaps a more vital symbol than in legal circles. By the measurement of one survey conducted in 1947, Americans rated a seat on the United States Supreme Court as the most prestigious job in the country. Possibly the lay public was prepared to embrace the discourse of elite modern lawyers even as dissent became more noticeable within the profession. The same survey of popular attitudes in 1947 indicated that people forty years old and over were far more respectful of county-level judges than they were of lawyers in general, whereas younger people were inclined to reverse that ranking and to display increasing respect for lawyers by comparison with other professions.[97] If indeed Americans gradually came to appreciate the symbolism of judgeship, while growing less deferential to their rank-and-file judiciary, the organized bar was surely the stronger for it. Along with the public image of the modern law school, the public image of ideal judicial character in America may have contributed to a favorable climate in which the professionalizing claims of the ABA and other bar associations would seem more credible.

5 Legal Thought and Legal Practice in the Age of American Enterprise

1870–1920

Robert W. Gordon

This essay surveys some of the problems and possibilities of trying to relate the more abstract thought produced by legal elites of the late nineteenth and early twentieth centuries to their practices—to their ordinary ways of acting and making a living in society.[1] This is a task that most legal history quite sensibly does not attempt, preferring to detach legal ideas from their social setting and to treat their development as an autonomous process with a logic, coherence, and dynamic of its own. Historians who *do* undertake to relate legal thought to practice usually do so in one or both of two ways: (1) They treat law—its institutions, doctrines, processes, norms—as a kind of problem-solving technology, developed as a functional response to certain social needs. From this perspective, corporate law is seen as a response to the need to mobilize capital in larger amounts than family-based partnerships permit; doctrines that increase the negotiability of commercial paper or recognize the binding effect of new forms of secured financing are seen as responses to the need for greater predictability in marketplace dealing; and legislation or adjudication that substitutes uniform for local regulation is supposed to respond to the need to reduce uncertainty about the flow of interstate capital.[2] In this mode of legal history, the "social needs" themselves are usually rather vaguely conceived as unproblematic social universals (stability, the organization of claims to scarce resources) or as inherent elements in some process of large-scale historical change (Western capitalism, economic development, the extension of the market, secularization). (2) Otherwise historians who try to relate legal thought to practice tend to treat law simply as the product of interest-group politics, the outcome of struggle fought to victory or compromise among various social factions.[3]

When applied to the legal history of the late nineteenth century, these approaches—"instrumental" approaches, let us agree to call them—have combined to produce an image of the law of that time that is probably still dominant, though in recent years it has begun to fade. This is the image of legal "formalism" or "mechanical jurisprudence." On this view, there supposedly arose a body of legal ideas that was either so abstract or trivial as to have been hopelessly inadequate to control the social consequences of large-scale industrial enterprise or that functioned simply as a smoke screen for factional, class, or occupational interest. Legal doctrine is thus variously portrayed as the outcome of compromise deals between farmers, shippers, carriers, and labor; as a laissez-faire ideology for corporations to use against regulation; or as a status ideology for lawyers anxious to set themselves off from laymen and lower-order professionals.

In what follows I will set forth examples of instrumental approaches to some specific aspects of American law, suggest what may be said for and against such approaches, and put forward an alternative, "ideological" approach. To anticipate a bit, one of the problems with instrumental approaches in general is that they fail to take seriously the doctrinal content of law on its own terms. Unfortunately, to get serious treatment that recognizes the integrity and coherence of bodies of legal doctrine, one must have recourse to the internal dogmatic writings of the profession. These are often completely idealist, treating legal ideas as evolving spontaneously out of other legal ideas, a species of philosophic reflection completely unconnected to the affairs of lawyers and their clients.[4] In other words, our histories have tended to see legal ideas either as the client (or social planner) sees them, as strategic instruments amid an arsenal of others to achieve specific ends for a group or client, or else as the jurist sees them, in relation to other legal ideas of the past or present. The realms of thought and practice thus often appear to us as totally discontinuous, different worlds governed by different rules—legal thought as pure intellection, untouched by politics; legal practice as a pragmatic craft activity, unaffected by ideas.

The first working premise of this study is that the way to try to bridge this gulf between legal theory and legal practice is to look at what lawyers actually do. It is, after all, supposedly the lawyer's task to mediate between these realms, to accommodate the desires of clients to the framework of legal ideas. The second working premise is that what lawyers do should be examined as, among other things, the production of ideology. This second premise is equivalent to a recognition that both jurists (judges, doctrinal writers, any lawyers making a general statement about law of any kind) and legal practitioners (representing a particular client's interest) are engaged in the task of trying to explain and rationalize what they see happening in the world in terms of some general normative conceptions. It recognizes that every legal practice—from drafting a complaint for simple debt to writing a constitution—makes a contribution to building a general ideological scheme or political language out of such explaining and rationalizing conceptions. (The qualifying phrase "among other things" is an acknowledgment that every legal act has a specific local purpose and consequence quite apart from its role in the construction of an ideological framework. To file a complaint for simple debt might also be a means of carrying on a family feud, to write a constitution might also be a means of buying off a liberal opposition movement.)

Using these two working premises as underpinning, this essay will argue that the leading academic and practicing lawyers in late nineteenth- and early twentieth-century America can be seen as members of a community of intellectual discourse who developed a common ideological consciousness that cut across divisions in practice specialty and political orientation. To put it another way, I am trying to illustrate the claim that the same basic ways of thinking about law can be detected in all activities of this elite—in their abstract academic writing, in their law reform and public service work, and in their day-to-day practice. It is a corollary of this claim that important transformations in legal ideology were paralleled in all other spheres as well.[5] If valid, this conception of lawyers' work as ideology should explain the connections between what they thought and did more persuasively than the currently fashionable instrumental approaches or than the idealist and hyper-realist views that simply deny such connections.[6]

The limits of instrumental approaches are nicely illustrated by a familiar example from my period. It has been widely noticed that the modern law school and the corporate law firm grew up together and achieved a symbiotic relationship to one another. By the 1900s, the leading schools produced lawyers for the leading firms; the firms in turn made the schools prosperous by donations. This would be a simple story if the schools had undertaken to train lawyers in the technical skills of corporate practice. But in fact they did not though their founders had originally aspired to do so. Thus C. C. Langdell and C. W. Eliot of Harvard and Theodore Dwight of Columbia, the heroes of the revival of legal education, argued for the *practical* superiority of their teaching to apprenticeship training because of its basis in scientific principles: "When a young man [said Eliot in 1871] has thoroughly mastered at a good school the principles and methods of the law, when he has become familiar with law books and has learned how to investigate and prepare a case, how to find precedents and how to use them,—he is ready to be of some service in a lawyer's office."[7]

Early demand for the products of this "scientific" training was, however, limited. Langdell, Eliot, and Dwight traced this lack of demand to the bar's failure to make a properly sharp distinction between the work of an attorney, which consisted chiefly of filling out forms in routine client service, and that of a counselor, which involved pleading cases in court. Once a need for counselors was admitted, the need for law schools was plain. They could do something to train advocates which law offices could not do, namely, give them extensive clinical training in arguing cases.[8] Moreover, as Langdell put it, the "art of the attorney, being in its nature local, should be acquired in the place where it is to be practiced; while the science of the advocate, being confined within no narrower limits than the system of English and American law, may best be acquired, other things being equal, in the place where that system of thought is studied and taught most exclusively as a science, i.e. exclusively of everything local, temporary, or arbitrary."[9] Thus, for Langdell and other would-be reformers of American law schools, the project was to create through formal legal training both the caste that would maintain the future demand for itself—that is, an upper body of the bar modeled deliberately on English example and devoted above all to appellate advocacy—as well as the transatlantic jurisprudence on which this body would rely.

This project was not as fantastic as it looks in retrospect. As will become clear, it was a long-standing project of the American legal elite, and its jurisprudential ambitions, at least, were partially fulfilled. But the conditions for its success as an instrumental method never materialized, for its presumed virtues were being touted during exactly that period in which the business of the upper bracket of the bar was undergoing a shift in emphasis from advocacy to office practice.[10] This newly valued work was firmly tied to local law, especially to state statutory corporation law, administrative rules of regulatory commissions, and municipal ordinances and by-laws. It consisted mostly of drafting instruments such as charters, leases, mortgages, bond indentures, and reorganization plans to comply with such laws, or else of passing on their validity. In these cases, lawyers were most likely to use litigation as a tactic for harassment or delay, the aim being to avoid any resolution on the merits of the case. Toward that end, the unscientific, haphazard, and heterogeneous nature of unreformed state law and procedure was a positive advantage.[11] The lawsuits seeking substantive legal outcomes were usually of two highly specialized sorts. One was litigation over receiverships and reorganizations (of which more later); the other, constitutional litigation, which at the United States Supreme Court level was virtually monopolized by a handful of advocates (in New York, at one point, Choate, J. C. Carter, Dillon, and Guthrie) who were usually retained specially to handle it. The routine business of a Wall Street office by 1900, according to the most exhaustive firm history we possess, demanded skills quite different from those of the counselor. As W. D. Guthrie complained in 1897: "Most of our work is in the management of large corporate enterprise which requires capacity for detail and also great accuracy and much business judgment. We find little difficulty in obtaining assistance in litigated work, but we have found it almost impossible to secure men who can attend to the details of these corporate matters capably and accurately."[12] To judge from the bulk of problems that came to that office from the late 1880s onward, the substantive knowledge its young associates would have to pick up first would concern corporate finance and public utility rate regulation.

The new law schools could not afford to ignore entirely these discrepancies between the legal curriculum and legal practice. In the 1870s Langdell of Harvard offered a course in the New York Code of Procedure and in 1893 brought in a Boston lawyer to teach "Peculiarities of Massachusetts Practice."[13] At Columbia, at the time when the law school's graduates could be admitted to practice in New York without taking a bar examination, Dwight was careful to sprinkle his lectures on general, national common-law principles with references to specific points on New York state law.[14] Harvard taught bits and pieces of general corporate law through its courses on the law of persons (Gray) and on partnerships and corporations (Ames's third-year elective). Harvard also hired Jeremiah Smith to teach corporations (again as a third-year elective) full time in 1889 and added elective courses on insurance law and carriers in the 1890s and on public service companies after 1900.[15]

But no school with pretensions altered its basic approach in the face of the changing character of law practice. Common-law subjects remained at the heart of the curriculum. Even Smith's corporations course—though decidedly more au courant than most Harvard Law School courses in its concentration on recent American rather than early nineteenth-century English case law—did not concern itself with a single corporation law of any state nor any company's charter except as these might appear piecemeal in a case.[16] If someone suggested teaching a business subject, such as principles of insurance or corporate finance, he was referred to the newly developing schools of business. If someone wanted to teach a course involving issues of public policy, such as trade regulation, taxation, industrial organization, or labor, he was directed to the departments of history and government or economics. The Harvard Law School faculty's opposition to teaching anything but "pure law in our department" seemed to be obsessive. The faculty resisted all of Eliot's attempts to turn the Law School into a general graduate school to train men for public service through such subjects as Roman law, comparative legislation, science of government, international law, or colonial administration, saying that these belonged in a separate school of political science.[17]

At Columbia, where the political science faculty had separated from the Law School in part because of Dwight's animosity, a rapprochement was ultimately attained by hiring Wall Street lawyers to teach political science and allowing law students to cross-register in the department. Some 320 law students, two-thirds of the student body, did so in 1902–3, which shows the strength of the demand.[18] Yet Dean Keener, the Harvard man who was hired to modernize the Columbia Law School in 1891, remained adamantly opposed to appointing a professor of public law in the school;[19] and Joseph Beale, his one-time Harvard colleague, thought that even Columbia's limited indulgence towards political science instruction helped account for that law school's "striking failure" to "take the position to which her location, her wealth, and the ability of her faculty seem to entitle her." [20]

In a well-known exchange with President Harper of the University of Chicago, Dean Ames of Harvard refused to let Beale go there to head the Law School unless Chicago committed itself to teaching only "pure law," contrary to the plans of its leading professor, Ernst Freund, to include courses on administrative law, comparative jurisprudence, "relation of state to industry," and "railroad transportation."[21]

On this record it is tempting to call the law faculties donnish ostriches, totally out of touch with their times. There remains, however, the problem of accounting for their success. Eliot thought the Law School his most brilliant creation[22]—it was also one of the richest— and by 1910 its model of legal education had completely swept the field of its rivals.[23] Most important, the Harvard Law School had sold its system to the new law firms. Starting with Walter Carter's firm in New York, the new law firms initiated what came to be called the "Cravath system" of hiring high-ranking young law school graduates with no prior experience in practice as salaried associates.[24] The law schools were obviously doing *something* right.

A tempting mode of explanation would begin by filtering out the substantive content of the curriculum—private-law science—as secondary. In this mode, it could be asserted, with some justice, that the firms did not really want new associates with a technical training because the firm could better provide the training on the job. Since types of clients and business changed so rapidly, no faculty not actively engaged in practice could hope to keep up. The young law school graduates had at least been drilled in an exacting if not precisely relevant discipline, perhaps all the more useful for its irrelevance because it deprived them of preconceived ideas. A man who had adapted himself to one demanding system, and had worked hard enough to do well in it, could presumably adapt to another of analogous kind.

In an especially ingenious exploration in this mode, Anthony Chase proposes that the case method, the sequenced curriculum, and regular examinations were at the heart of the law school project. The central goal, argues Chase, was the inculcation of an essentially *clinical* method that Eliot had promoted in the Medical School as well as in the Law School and that socialized students into a work discipline and semantic code appropriate to the newly emerging intensive forms of professional practice.[25] There is clearly something to this argument, since the endless wrangles over legal education within the profession between 1890 and 1920 all took the "Harvard system" to stand primarily for the "case method," and Chase makes a persuasive case that the reforms in lègal education paralleled those in other fields. Yet even he remains vague on the central point—the nature of the relation between the case-study method of legal training and the realities of law practice.

Another kind of instrumental explanation argues that it was the law graduates' social class rather than their actual training that made them desirable to the firms. Indeed Jerold Auerbach's main point is that the interests of the bar leaders and law professors converged only in the effort to stratify the bar and exclude immigrants by raising standards. Until the bar recognized the appeal of post-graduate legal education as a simple means of siphoning off "the best men"—those who could afford it—practitioners and professors fought each other, the bar finding the dons impractical and too liberal, the dons finding the bar parochial and reactionary.[26] Evidence of this exclusionary alliance undoubtedly exists, but for my purposes is not entirely persuasive. I think the thesis overstates the degree of early enmity between the bar and the law schools, and it tends to the reductionist in its explanation of the subsequent amity between them. Before 1900 the law faculties could not have survived, much less prospered, without a constituency among scholarly practitioners who shared their intellectual aspirations and frequently their mildly reformist politics as well.[27] Moreover, as Auerbach himself shows elsewhere in his book, the Wall Street firms never had to use an immigrant lawyer's lack of education as a reason to deny him a job, and they turned away plenty of Jewish law review editors.[28]

In a recent dissertation Andrew Barlow has proposed another version of the class alliance thesis. He argues that capitalists in the 1870s and 1880s wanted to achieve national coordination of enterprise to avoid the destructive effects of competition and the instability of alliances with machine-based politicians, but the existing elites were local, family-based small groups ("class fractions") with insufficient capacity or capital to coordinate their activities on a national scale. In the face of this difficulty, Eliot and Langdell created in the Harvard Law School an institution that could be promoted as the training ground for a national elite capable of "providing the decentralized capitalist class with a national administrative framework" and of "rationaliz[ing] the competition which was devastating the capitalist economy."[29]

This thesis, though suggestive, rests in part on a misconception of the Harvard Law School curriculum—its graduates were actually equipped only to advise and argue in private-law controversies—and overlooks the faculty's determined resistance to its becoming a school for government and business leaders. The Law School faculty, until Felix Frankfurter joined it, never shared Eliot's ambition to create an American counterpart to the European university-trained elite of civil servants. Of course law schools did eventually supply many government and business leaders, as some lawyers moved from corporate practice onto the boards of corporations and from there into management and as others moved into public office (usually appointive) or onto regulatory commissions.[30]

What of those who stayed in practice? Barlow's thesis has a famous ancestor in James Bryce's *American Commonwealth* (1888). Bryce, too, maintained that corporate lawyers were a key element in the patrician elite that he and his American informants, including Eliot and his Law School's faculty, called the "best men"—the college-bred group that supposedly controlled many sectors of American economic and social life and could have dominated still others if it chose.[31] Yet neither Bryce nor Barlow describes in any detail *how* lawyers played this dominating or coordinating role, or exactly what that role involved. At the core, assertions about the instrumental importance of lawyers in American society often turn out to be frustratingly imprecise,[32] as one would expect if this essay is correct in arguing that the primary social role of lawyers is the production of ideology. In fact, existing research does not allow us to evaluate very reliably the legal elite's claims to influence, but it may be helpful to make a brief effort at sorting out and assessing the various claims.

(1) The social homogeneity of the leading corporate lawyers, at least

in the Northeast, is undeniable. Exclusively white and overwhelmingly Protestant, they were native born, college educated, and (after 1880) law-school trained, usually at Harvard or Columbia. More often than not, they were the sons of local gentry—doctors, lawyers, clergymen, business leaders—from small towns in New England and upstate New York.[33] As the law schools expanded, the pool of such men available for recruitment by Wall Street and State Street very likely increased as well. But if a common social background made the bar an exclusive club, it could not, at least by itself, have created a national alliance of economic and political *managers*. After all, exclusiveness can be a way of depriving one's group of power as well as a means of achieving it. What besides their native gentry stock might have made them influential?

(2) The Barlow thesis suggests a strategic role for lawyers in the direction of economic enterprise. This suggestion is by no means entirely wrong but should be treated with reserve. There is little support for it, either in the older school of entrepreneurial history, which assigned the major role in the coordination and rationalization of late nineteenth-century American capitalism to the investment bankers led by J. P. Morgan,[34] or in the newer work of Alfred D. Chandler, Jr., and his associates, which gives the credit to engineers and managers who reorganized the structure of enterprise from inside.[35] A search of business histories for the period (which may, of course, understate the influence of lawyers because they are not looking for it) suggests that in all three of the major phases of post-Civil War organization of enterprise—competition, combination by alliance, and consolidation by integration—the contribution of counsel was chiefly tactical. For the most part, corporate lawyers did little more than select and in some instances devise the most legally defensible and advantageous forms through which decisions already made could be executed.[36] In the first phase, this meant carrying on economic warfare through strike litigation and through efforts to secure legislative favors. In the combination-by-alliance phase, the chief task of corporate lawyers was to negotiate alliances and reduce them to contractual agreement. In the consolidation-by-integration phase, corporate lawyers mainly crafted new legal structures for consolidated enterprise.

I will later argue that this process of rationalization through legal form was of fundamental importance *as ideological activity*. But on the narrower question of what matters of corporate policy brought lawyers' voices into the boardroom, the evidence suggests that they were secondary. Lawyers did not choose whom to squeeze out or buy out, or whom to bring into the pool, cartel, or holding company. Nor did they contribute much beyond technical advice to decisions involving investments, expansion to new product lines, pricing policy, management structure, operations, marketing, or even labor policy, except under unusual circumstances.

Sometimes, of course, what were ordinarily secondary issues became primary and tactics dictated strategy.[37] In some situations, none of them surprising, the lawyer did become a critical figure in decision-making: (a) when the company was engaged in litigation critical to its existence, as when it faced an antitrust or patent-infringement suit, or when it sought to control its labor problems through injunctions; (b) when it was in process of formation; (c) when it was on the verge of receivership, with the need to reorganize and attract fresh capital; (d) when some important new legislative or administrative scheme to regulate it was in prospect; and (e) when it required a special franchise—public land, traction route, utilities service monopoly—from some governmental authority. Further exploration of the last four of these situations might bolster the Barlow thesis, for in all of them lawyers acted as brokers and intermediaries between management and strangers to it: investment bankers, underwriters, syndicates of foreign bondholders, government officials. Metropolitan lawyers were, of course, insiders in the financial centers, whereas managers had often spent their whole adult lives in their businesses.[38] It was doubtless helpful to Standard Oil of California that its general counsel knew President Taft personally at a time when the federal government was withdrawing public oil lands from sale.[39] Some corporate jobs *required* lawyers who were known to and trusted by financiers. One could not seriously think of marketing one's bonds among Boston investors without an opinion on their validity from respected Boston bond counsel. And to be trusted in such circles presumably meant that one had to be a gentleman.[40]

Yet one must not overextend the point. If a client needed a concession from the Iowa legislature, it did not help that its lawyer had gone to Harvard. Furthermore, by the late 1890s the market for industrial securities had been broadened by promoters well beyond the conservative financial groups that provided the capital for the early phase of the merger movement. In this stockholders' market, the lawyer's personal endorsement was no longer so useful.[41]

(3) Another way of trying to establish the instrumental importance of lawyers in the direction of large enterprise would be to focus on their product rather than on their personal roles, on the legal forms they devised rather than on their presence in the boardroom. Willard Hurst has provided a model for those historians who have stressed the contri-

bution of legal-technological innovation: new forms of security financing (the trust receipt, the equipment trust certificate, the "open end" mortgage that secures an indefinite amount of issuable bonds); new forms of corporate securities (preferred stock, no-par stock, convertible debentures), which offered diverse risks and opportunities and thus attracted many different kinds of investors; and new forms of corporate organization (the trust, the pool, the joint-traffic association, the holding company, the patent agreement), which were designed to consolidate enterprise and control competition within the statutory limits erected by suspicion of monopolies.[42]

Examples of American legal-technological ingenuity in the late nineteenth and early twentieth centuries could easily be multiplied, for we are fortunate to have an unusually rich and detailed literature on the subject. But it has yet to be established that this technical contribution was of primary causal significance in determining strategies and structures of enterprise. Here again, all one can say is that the principal business historians of the subject have explicitly declined to assign it such a role. Here and there one will find a concession to the significance of legal form: corporate counsel's interpretations of the Sherman Act, for example, seem to have influenced the general trend after 1890 away from horizontal mergers in cartels and holding companies and toward integration in single operating companies.[43] Such legal factors, according to Professor Chandler, only "reinforce[d] technological and market imperatives."[44]

Of course the whole issue of the contribution of legal technology to entrepreneurship is an enormously complicated one, which (because economic historians are rarely interested in it) has yet to be adequately explored and cannot be casually disposed of in a few paragraphs. But whenever one hears an argument for the importance of the part played by the corporate lawyer and of particular forms of law in the construction of modern capitalism, one has to remember that large-scale capitalism has developed in a huge variety of social environments in which the peculiar tasks of the American corporate bar and the particular legal forms it developed have often been wholly absent.

(4) The case for some version of Barlow's "best men" thesis improves only slightly when one moves from assessing lawyers' influence on enterprise to their influence on politics. During our period, the corporate elite of the bar, unlike leading lawyers before the Civil War, rarely went into national politics. To be sure, elite corporate lawyers may be found in large numbers, usually in dominating roles, in the urban reform movements of the late nineteenth century, whether Mugwump, regular, or Progressive.[45] But did they, in this capacity, consti-

tute a national managerial class? Not according to David Hammack's thorough recent survey of the vast literature on the influence of patrician elites in city politics. Hammack concludes that, in New York City in this period, the power of the patrician elite over urban decisionmaking was sometimes considerable but always sporadic, and in any case this power had to be shared with several competing elites. In particular, he argues that the experts, including the lawyers, who did most of the actual work of political organization and decisionmaking, would not have been allowed such a role had they lost the support or confidence of their "wealthy clients, employers, and sponsors"—namely, the industrial and mercantile elite.[46] Here too one finds lawyers now and again given the main stage but mostly playing subordinate parts.

(5) A more promising place to look for evidence that lawyers played a major role in national enterprise during this period would be in the institutions of the modern regulatory state, especially its administrative commissions. This is obviously extremely important, and I plan to discuss it extensively in the larger study of which this essay is a part. For the moment, I can only say that the exact extent of lawyers' influence in the construction and operation of the modern regulatory state remains to be explored and is perhaps all too easy to exaggerate.

In summary, no compelling evidence exists for any of the efforts thus far made to assign lawyers a major instrumental role in the Age of American Enterprise. Yet contemporaries seemed to think that lawyers were influential in their own right, not simply as the henchmen of their business or banker clients. Moreover, corporate lawyers were frequently treated with a public deference (or fearfulness) beyond that usually accorded to expediters, clerks, and go-betweens. Could it be that the key to their influence lies precisely where the instrumental approaches decline to search for it—in the substance of the ideas they propagated, including the ideas in which their law schools trained them? Perhaps, after all, their main importance, both in their work for clients and in reform politics and public service, derived from their position as curators of and contributors to what many people in the society supposed to be vital forms and categories of public discourse. To express this hypothesis in another way, the main task of the legal elite may have been to show that the activities and goals of their clients and reform constituencies fit into a traditional but continually self-renewing and self-transforming framework of justice. Or as Lord Bryce put it, trying to explain why he thought lawyers as a class might be just as powerful as capitalists: "Their function is to educate opinion from the technical side, and to put things in a telling way before the people."[47]

When the elite lawyers themselves undertook (as they did eagerly and often) to account for the sources of their influence, they rarely failed at some point to mention their command over a traditional body of learning, "legal science." The idea of legal science is now completely out of fashion, and modern lawyers tend to treat their ancestors' scientific pretensions with derision, a response that is certainly tempting, given the self-indulgent hyperbole of professional speeches. There is even a notion wandering around in American legal historiography that legal science was just a weird fantasy of Langdell's which caught on because science was prestigious in the late nineteenth century and indispensable to any profession's claim to status in a period of "professionalization."

But this view is woefully misleading. Those who spoke of legal science in the late nineteenth century may well have been exploiting the rising prestige of natural science. But they were also echoing their own profession's ancient usage of the term, which comes from classical Roman law and signifies nothing more, or less, than the self-conscious attempt to make legal argument and decisionmaking into systematic activities that are regulated by a coherent theoretical structure (instead of a random jumble of disaggregated rules and forms), along with the body of law and legal commentary that results from such an attempt.

How the idea of legal science came into the discourse of American lawyers, and achieved in the process an accommodation with the notoriously unscientific English common law, would be a long and difficult story to tell. The main reference points in the English tradition were Bacon, Hale, Blackstone, and Mansfield, who were all to some extent interested in rationalizing the common law and giving it a more analytic structure, using Romanist and continental civilian schemes less as models than as analogues.[48] By the early nineteenth century, in any event, the idea that law could be practiced as a science had already become a cornerstone of the Federalist-Whig lawyers' *thèse nobiliaire*. Their claim, urged in practically all of their treatises, lectures, or other forms of public discourse from the Revolution forward, was that the law should constitute a mediating force in society between the wealthy and the masses, between the excesses of commercial acquisition and levelling democratic politics. Reduced to its barest essentials, the claim was this: people should be free to pursue their own ends, to enter society and interact with one another, but not to dominate or kill others. The *legal* contribution to liberal thought about this ancient problem lies in the realm of personal and property rights, which define how far one may go in exercising one's liberty and where one must stop to avoid infringing upon that of others. The state is instituted to define and enforce rights; its medium of rights-definition is law, which both facilitates liberty as freedom of action and protects liberty as security, including security against the state itself.

This much was orthodoxy. The argument among lawyers was about the proper method of defining rights. What follows is a highly compressed version of the early nineteenth-century American debate over this issue (really just a variant of the Bentham-Burke debate in England), shorn of all but its central points for the sake of brevity.[49]

Jeffersonian-Jacksonian law reformers and antilawyers took the position that the knowledge of rights was accessible to ordinary reason, which meant that (1) democratic legislatures, subject to the suprademocratic executive veto, were capable of defining them in such a form that the citizenry would be capable of understanding and acting upon them, or that (2) ordinary intuition could derive them from customary morality without the mediation of official definition. Unfortunately the common law, then the chief source of reference for definitions of private rights, was a mass of unintelligible feudal barbarities, most of which should be thrown away and the rest reduced to a clear and definite statutory code.

The Whig-Federalist response was its *thèse nobiliaire*: rights definition was a process of almost unbearable complexity since it was inherent in the concept of rights that they be certain, yet society was constantly changing. A code of laws would be too rigid to accommodate change; an unlimited power of legislative revision would subject rights to the fluctuating opinions of temporary majorities. Fortunately there was available to the extremely learned a science capable of developing a progressively more precise mode of rights definition. The primary but not exclusive data of this science were the common law and equity reports, a vast storehouse of collective experience wiser than any single man could be, containing past decisions of ordinary people about the customary and right ways to settle particular controversies as filtered through the perception and judgments of judges trained to tell good custom from bad. The first step in the *method* (following Bacon) was inductive: the lawyer was to gather all the judgments on similar and analogous facts and from them to generalize a principle. The legal scientist went further: he developed the principles into a system, classifying them and, ideally, relating them harmoniously to one another. The final step for the practitioner was to descend once more from the general to the particular and to apply the appropriate principle to the case at hand.

The Whig-Federalist thinkers did not presume that this historical-empirical method for deriving principles would always work, as precedent was indeed often rooted in the barbarity of feudalism or the idiosyncracies of irrational procedural forms. Moreover, new situations did sometimes arise for which no convincing common-law analogies could be found. The corrective for the occasional irrationality of custom was to submit its principles to a critical and creative control technique, a complex amalgam of (1) a special theory of history, (2) a comparative method, (3) and an appeal to certain extrahistorical criteria of reason. Lord Mansfield was acknowledged to be the all-time master of this method. (1) The special historical theory was that history had direction, especially in the American republic, away from hierarchy, superstition, technicality, and restraints on disposition of property and labor and towards political equality, rationality, free disposition, and liberality in rights definition. Modern legal science was itself part of this trend. History could thus be used critically as well as conservatively. (2) The comparative method consisted of looking to the practices of other civilized nations—especially, in matters of commercial law, to international commercial custom and European civilian writers on it. (3) The final component of the technique was natural reason, not just anyone's but a highly educated reason steeped in classical and historical studies, political theory, and the law of nations. There were also metarules about when to apply the technique liberally (when one was trying to facilitate commercial convenience) and when to hold strictly to precedent (when one was trying to protect vested rights).

While the Jefferson-Jackson scheme counted on the democratic legislature, this Whig-Federalist conception looked to the judiciary as the primary definer of rights, assisted by a chorus of practitioners trained in "legal science" and by a smaller band of treatise writers devoted to expounding it. In the rhetoric of this scheme, the term "trustee" was habitually used to describe the lawyer's role in society, a metaphor that put the lawyer in charge because of his superior learning but subordinated him to the service of his settlors and beneficiaries, the People. In fact the whole society was visualized as a network of interlaced fiduciary relationships preserving hierarchies within a republican framework. Thus corporate directors were portrayed as trustees for their stockholders and creditors, lawyers for their clients, judges for the constitution. And all were supervised by high court judges. Just as trustees for spendthrift children are supposed to care for both the parents' desires and (through changing and unpredictable circumstances) the children's own long-term interests, so the legal elite was to help the People guard their collective customary wisdom and realize their historical destiny as Americans, to preserve for them their own best selves by taking customs and norms from the People and elevating them above the People. The science that made lawyers worthy of this trust, if they invested the pains to master it, did so because its study and practice inculcated not only learning but also virtue, acquired by habit through the study and cultivation of the example of Republican Romans and through safeguarding the secrets and the money of clients.

These arguments about legitimacy and authority in defining rights were carried on at a level of rhetorical elevation so distant from the preoccupations of everyday practice (routine conveyancing and debt collection) that the reader often wants to dismiss the whole debate as side-show entertainment for a few legal intellectuals. The programs of making every lawyer a scientist and of reducing the whole law to a code seem completely visionary, but the fact is that the arguments were also concretized in political activity and resulted in some significant, if limited, victories for the partisans of legal science. They produced an upper-court judiciary and a group of treatise writers (sometimes, as with Story and Kent, the same men) who brilliantly exemplified the Whig ideal of the liberal judge, a man learned in the common-law tradition of principles that protected the rights of property but as free-handed as Mansfield to adapt them to the liberalizing tendencies of history and to the requirements of commercial policy. Through the general acceptance of the Federalist idea that even the constitution was only law and therefore subject to the judicial technique of rights definition, these partisans of legal science acquired more political authority for judges than anywhere in Europe. Even where they had to submit to election, the process was genteel and usually ended in their reelection. The occasional threat of reforms that might have seriously undercut the authority of the courts was politically neutralized.[50]

No less importantly, a popular version of this Whig view of law had gained widespread acceptance in the profession by 1800 through Blackstone's *Commentaries* (via the American editions that offset its Toryisms). This was the only modern treatise that attempted any systematic treatment of the common law as a whole until Kent's *Commentaries* (1826–30), which were themselves modeled on Blackstone's.[51]

Yet the hegemony of Whig legal science was strictly limited. By their own report, the elite lawyers never persuaded the journeymen of the bar to practice law scientifically. Most lawyers, trained in the desultory reading of nisi prius books (formbooks) and digests in unsupervised apprenticeships, could never see through the pleading forms to the structures of obligation beneath them. These lawyers wanted neither science *nor* codes.

> To such a one [said James Wilson in 1792], the least deviation from even the most unessential form, appears equally fatal with the greatest departure from the most important principles: for they agree in the only circumstances, by which he can distinguish either: they are not within the sphere of his practice. Tied to the centre of precedent, he treads, for life, the same dull, and small, and uniform circle around it, without daring to view or to enjoy a single object on either side.[52]

Moreover, the partisanship of advocacy (always a bit of an embarrassment to the antebellum Whig ideal) caused lawyers to hunt down just those cases that suited their interest:

> Because principles [said H. W. Warner in 1832], as distinguished from cases, are too few, and simple, and unbending, to meet all the wants of litigant parties—of whom one half at least are ever in the wrong, and the other half right only in part,—it is found convenient, and has grown into general usage among us, to serve clients with cases rather than with principles,—cases, I may say, instead and to neglect of principles. The course of science is from particulars to generals; while that of professional exertion, taking the opposite direction, terminates too often in those very particulars where science begins.[53]

Finally, the hegemony of Whig legal science was weakened as the bar increasingly refused to acknowledge that the elite should have social authority as trustees merely because of their command of "scientific method." The Jacksonian opinion was that anyone with natural genius who hustled could succeed at the bar, an entrepreneurial ideology that seemed to be confirmed in experience.[54] This is not just the familiar story of an aristocratic model of learning coming to grief in a democratic society. Here the model of learning, with its underlying theory of historically evolving liberalism and its freehanded rational technique for facilitating commerce, had helped to *make* the society.

In any case, when the college-bred sons of the professionals who were coming to dominate the bar helped to revive legal education in the 1840s, the proponents of legal science compromised with their Jacksonian opponents.[55] The sporadic attempts to impart legal science in its full Whig-Federalist regalia as a branch of general ethics and politics had failed pathetically. The symbols of this failure were Kent's lectures (1794–98) to successive audiences of seven students plus "thirty-six gentlemen," of two students plus his own clerk, and then none at all; and the collapse of David Hoffmann's projected "Course of Legal

Study" at Maryland.[56] It was Story himself, when he took over at Harvard in the 1840s, who reduced the content of legal science to private law though, as a good nationalist, he insisted that the legal curriculum should not be local but should concern itself with synthetic general common law and equity based on English, federal, and leading state decisions. Except for constitutional law, all else was excluded: politics, legislation, civil law, international law, and liberal learning. Law study was to be rigorous (not that it actually was so under Justice Story, who liked to tell rambling war stories) but not out of the reach of students of ordinary attainments (no college degree was required). Legal training was to be based on principles instead of pleading forms, but the principles were to be imparted by a scientific faculty, rather than by trying to make every lawyer a scientist. In effect, the faculty was to give lectures that codified and simplified the common-law subjects and made the textbooks easily intelligible.[57] Story's compromise was thus a vulgarized version of Whig legal science, shorn of its pretension to elegance, public statesmanship, and Ciceronian virtue and squeezed into the Jacksonian mold of standardized practical expertise. This compromise also became a foundation for successful American academic training in law and for a revised conception of the professional lawyer that would reach its fullest development after 1870.

Enough has been said to show that Langdell's generation did not invent the idea of an American legal science. In some fundamental ways the situation remained as it was before the Civil War. The problem to be solved was still the problem of rights definition; the solution was still the development of legal science to make rights more certain and the use of judges as the administrators of that science. The case method was originally seen simply as a more efficient pedagogical method for *imparting* legal science,[58] though it later came to be thought important in its own right and has survived to a time in which "legal science" sounds archaic or foreign. In its central features, the method of this science also remained the same, i.e., the extraction of general principles by means of historical study and the arrangement of them in rational relation to one another.

Occasionally, to be sure, one does find an effort in the late nineteenth century to compare legal science with modern rather than Baconian natural science, as, for example, Frederick Pollock's notion that the lawyer makes probabilistic predictions based on past statistical regularities of decisions on similar facts. But this sort of modish claim was rare until well into this century.[59] In fact, while the historiographic resources for practicing the old "scientific method" had greatly improved—the work of Ames, Thayer, and Holmes in legal history was miles above that of their predecessors—history continued to function as both the source and critic of dogmatic science. History remained a repository of deeply embedded traditional principles and a means of dismissing unwanted ones as anachronistic. It was still assumed to have direction, indeed a direction very much like that ascribed to it before the Civil War, except that now it was Maine, Freeman, and Stubbs who were invoked as authorities on the historical unchaining of individual liberty, on the evolution from status to contract. Comparative law was still used as a check on conclusions; if a principle was found, its counterpart could probably be found in other developed civilizations, at least in commercial matters. To be sure, the law of nations was dropped as a source, but otherwise, the science of *deriving* basic principles used much the same materials and seemed at first to proceed in much the same loose, ad hoc way as before the war, mixing appeals to tradition, critical history, eminent judicial authority, commercial convenience, and notions of fundamental morality.[60]

Yet, for all the continuities and similarities, there were significant differences as well. In late nineteenth-century legal science, the principles were to be integrated into a highly abstract comprehensive system whose distinctive characteristics differed very sharply in some ways from the antebellum scheme.[61] The differences are hard to express, but the most basic one seems to be this: the Whig-Federalist lawyers had claimed that their science gave them an authority of virtue and learning that entitled them to declare *how people should behave toward one another* in a wide range of social situations in which neither they themselves nor the legislature had prescribed express obligations. Their private law, to put this another way, was full of what we would call obligations implied by law, inhering in good custom, precedent, and general considerations of public policy concerning persons of different status in their relations with one another. In the minds of the Whig-Federalist lawyers, "principles" of science were entangled with "principles" of conduct.[62] The postwar legal elite, by contrast, disclaimed any special competence on the part of legal scholars or judges to prescribe behavior in particular situations. The function of legal science was rather to draw as clearly and sharply as possible the boundary lines beyond which the conduct of social actors would be sanctioned and behind which it would not. Legal science would thus create, as it were, combat zones of free conduct in which individuals might do as they willed without fear of legal reprisal, and it would specify the precise legal consequences of infringing on someone else's zone. The working principles of this system of thought, variously known as "formal," "mechanical," or "classical" law (but which I shall call Liberal, to emphasize its correspondences with liberal thought in England and Europe) are worth trying to summarize. In essence, the principles were embodied in three major and closely related aims:

1. One aim was to make all (adult male) persons juristically equal, having the same rights and obligations as all others. This meant among other things purging the law of special rights and obligations deriving from status (a social condition unalterable by will).

2. A second aim was to recast all legal obligations so that they derived from an exercise of will, either the will of private individuals or the will of the state. This meant purging the law of obligations deriving from notions of custom, morality, or public policy that could not plausibly be so recast. In practice it meant the rather heroic doctrinal task of trying to derive all private-law liability from contract or fault; and, within contract, from promise rather than unjust enrichment or reliance.

3. The final aim was to make the whole system formally realizable, that is, to standardize the definition of rights and duties. When this was accomplished, parties (with lawyers) would know in advance whether their actions did or did not fall within the combat zone of unrestricted exercise of will. At the same time, the judge would be able to enforce the rules without exercising any discretion of his own. He would act, or decline to act, only as the agent of someone else's will. When enforcing a legal contract, he carried out the will of the parties. When invalidating an illegal contract, he carried out the will of the state.

Legal science was to achieve this final aim through the following steps: (a) it was to establish as first principles, by means of the traditional historical-comparative-rational method described above, a few core propositions of obligation that were as inclusive as they could be of existing common-law doctrine but purged of pre-Liberal nonwill-based conceptions of duty; (b) legal science was then to show how all of the subrules of the law could be derived from the core principles by deduction, eliminating any subrules that could not be so deduced (the best-known of these projects being the subsuming of all tort liability under the fault principle); and, finally, (c) legal science was to "objectify" the definition of "liability behavior" by attention to external signs. Among other things, this last step meant that parties outwardly manifesting the signs of intent to contract—words constituting an offer, signs constituting an acceptance—were bound whatever their private reservations; that their agreement would be interpreted in its "reasonable" meaning rather than any private meaning that they may have attached to it; and that "negligence" must be determined by how a "reasonable man" would behave under the circumstances. In addition, it meant that the signs must be plain and binary, designating on/off categories for determining liability: one has made a contract or one has not, the state has "taken" property or it has not. Clearly, this mode of thinking is alien to our current legal notion that a multiplicity of factors must be elaborated and balanced before coming to a decision about liability.

In any case, the overarching unity of these three central aims of Liberal legal science was their conception of freedom as a set of barriers against coercive intrusion into zones of autonomous conduct. To borrow the words of Fredrich Hayek, who in our own time has expressed as eloquently as anyone the nineteenth-century Liberal ideal:

> The conception of freedom under the law . . . rests on the contention that when we obey laws, in the sense of general abstract rules laid down irrespective of their application to us, we are not subject to another man's will and are therefore free. It is because the lawgiver does not know the particular cases to which his rules will apply, and it is because the judge who applies them has no choice in drawing the conclusions that follow from the existing body of rules and the particular facts of the case, that it can be said that laws and not men rule. . . . This generally is probably the most important aspect of that attribute of law which we have called its "abstractness." As a true law should not name any persons, so it should especially not single out any specific persons or group of persons.[63]
>
> The significance for the individual of the knowledge that certain rules will be universally applied is that . . . the different objects and forms of action acquire for him new properties. He knows of man-made cause-and-effect relations which he can make use of for any purpose he wishes. . . . Like the laws of nature, the laws of the state provide fixed features in the environment in which he has to move; though they eliminate certain choices open to him they do not, as a rule, limit the choice to some specific action that somebody wants him to take.[64]

In this way, argues Hayek, freedom and jural equality, regardless of status, are made to depend on the abstract, formally realizable, nondiscretionary, and above all *general* nature of legal principles.

If Hayek's position is now unfashionable, it reflects what was once a collective consciousness, a way of organizing thinking about legal rights, that articulate members of the late nineteenth-century American legal elite constructed and held in common. Of course no new way of thinking can take over an entire legal system in the space of a generation. Liberalism never existed in completely pure form in any single mind but always in conjunction with both older and newer ways of thought. Yet its leading tenets, which began to appear as early as 1850, became most conspicuously abundant in Anglo-American academic circles during the 1870s and 1880s and in the writings of practitioners and judges during the 1880s and 1890s. As soon as it was elaborated, it started to decay under attack. Sometimes the same lawyers—most notably Holmes—served as both architect and destroyer of the system. When it reached its height as a political force, in the decisions of the United States Supreme Court majority between 1890 and 1920, the criticisms that were to destroy it had already been developed, within the legal elite as well as in political challenges from outside.

Although there is a surprising scholarly consensus on the content of this Liberal phase in American legal thought, there is a vast diversity of opinion on its social and intellectual sources. The question deserves extensive treatment elsewhere; for the moment, I can only record and briefly assess three standard ways of accounting for its emergence.

1. Some accounts seek the origins of this legal Liberalism in strictly American phenomena, such as antislavery natural-law jurisprudence[65] or the revulsion against the active state because of its supposed abuses during Reconstruction.[66] Such explanations seem unduly parochial, since legal thought went through comparable phases in England and Germany, neither of which suffered a Civil War.[67] Indeed, American Liberal science was itself a genuinely transatlantic project, carried on in its first, academic phase through the mutual influence and friendship of the Harvard lawyers and a group of legal scholars at the Oxford Law School (Anson, Bryce, Dicey, Holland, Markby, and Pollock), who were continuing a process of systematizing English law through the study of Roman law which Austin had begun in 1832.[68] In one aspect, to be sure, the American version of Liberal science was unique—it was obsessively judge-centered, as much in public law as in private-law writing, and this characteristic may very well have been due in part to the fact that the vacuum of central power left by the retreat from Reconstruction was occupied by the judiciary as the most legitimate and least corrupted organ of the state.[69]

2. Accounts confined to law and the legal profession also seem too narrow, given the obvious parallels between Liberal legal science and other branches of thought, especially political science and economics. Nonetheless, in looking for the intellectual sources of Liberal legal

science, one is paradoxically better off giving the legal literature priority over extralegal literatures (of, say, Social Darwinism or Scottish common-sense philosophy, to take two popular candidates), since lawyers seem to have absorbed the common fund of ideas of their time through the versions given them in judicial and juristic writing (just as lawyers now learn their economics from Calabresi, Posner, or Justice Traynor, rather than from economists).

3. Most important for my present purposes are the various explanations that seek to establish instrumental connections between Liberal legal ideology and large-scale economic organization. A general Weberian type of explanation is that formally rational legal systems serve the needs of the capitalist class for predictability in its transactions and help to legitimate its domination over others by masking the class system under a formal facade of equality of individuals as abstract rights-bearing units.[70] (This is the ideological counterpart of the instrumental class-alliance thesis referred to in my first pages above). Such explanations have some validity, but one must be careful not to overstate the point. It is undeniably true that the partisans of legal science claimed as one of its virtues its supposed capacity to give security to expectations (not only those of capitalists, however, but of everyone else as well). It is also true that an ideology of formal equality is always of more help to those on the top than to those on the bottom, at least unless and until those on the bottom convert it into one of substantive equality. Nor can there be any doubt that the wealthy and powerful in late nineteenth-century America deployed this legal ideology against social reform movements and labor.

For all of that, however, it must be recognized that Liberal legal science—through its formal, objective character, its deliberate unconcern with real intentions—was always frustrating expectations, as when, for example, strict construction of the common law of contract denied enforceability to such common business deals as the long-term requirements contract. (Weber himself remarked on this problem.)[71] Indeed, it is by no means clear that *legal* certainty is what a dynamic capitalist wants, except as a defense against attack. For expansion, he wants the rules changed in his favor, as, for example, the rule that you cannot take other people's land away except for a public purpose and except upon payment of just compensation.[72] Furthermore, while Liberal legal thought certainly was sometimes ideologically serviceable to powerful entrepreneurs, it was not designed as a weapon for a particular predatory class, despite the reputation that Progressive historians gave it and from which it is only just beginning to emerge. Nor was it even consistently used by the courts in favor of that class. Men like Cooley,

Dillon, Field, and Miller, who helped put the structure together, were old Jacksonians and intensely suspicious of corporate privilege. Their desire to limit legislative power stemmed as much from terror of a corrupt legislative-corporate alliance as from the specter of radicalism; they wanted to eliminate *all* patronage of particularism.[73] Besides, Liberal legal thought did not condemn the exercise of state power as long as it remained within its proper sphere, and the extensive regulation of public service corporations, occupations, and morals in the late nineteenth century, reviewed and approved by orthodox Liberal courts, showed how broad the sphere could be.[74]

Still, the thesis that the legal thought of this time was developed to legitimate and justify the newly emergent forms of domination can be made valid if it is broadened to mean much more than providing a cover for some particularly powerful interests. The program of defining rights is an attempt to deal with the problem of the perceived illegitimacy of forms of domination by making them seem to *disappear*, i.e., by making all coercion seem to be the result of either consent or natural necessity (e.g., of human biology or economic laws). Late nineteenth-century legal thought held out the theoretical possibility of seeing everything in the social order as either naturally determined or as the spontaneous creation of individual wills that were incapable of oppression because, as far as admittedly imperfect institutions could achieve this, they were bounded in their zones of free autonomous action by neutral rules of the game. The beauty of Liberal legal science as professional ideology was that, unlike Whig-Federalist science, it was not at odds with prevailing political ideology but dovetailed perfectly with it. The professional elite, instead of telling people how they should behave, would use their learning to specify the conditions under which people, or legislatures, were free to behave just as they pleased. Each person was handed at birth the same standard package of rights, defining the standard autonomous area of free movement, with the courts and their science standing by to identify and sanction nonconsensual invasions of zones. Thus the bar leadership's longstanding program of scientific rights definition finally found a secure institutional and political base, as well as a way of resolving the old Whig-Jacksonian quarrel, in the Liberal professionalism of the late nineteenth century. On this model, the progressive discovery of the underlying principles of the social order would provide the means for its neutral, disinterested management in everyone's interest so that conflict (between, for example, capital and labor) would seem pointless and illicit domination would become impossible.[75]

Of course, this whole mind-set began to collapse in the 1890s, when challenges were mounted against all three of the basic aims of Liberal legal science. Thus (1) the aim of the formal equality of juristic persons came to seem less attractive when such "persons" as U.S. Steel claimed to be endowed with the standard package of rights; (2) the aim of seeing all action within spheres of autonomy as resulting from free will came up against both sharper perceptions of visible coercion in the workplace and revised theories of social causation; and (3) the aim of formal realizability through the deductive process of neutral adjudication appeared increasingly silly and unjust in the attempt to practice it. The very abstraction and generality that the Liberals had sought to impart to legal form now seemed its chief defect. In such a form, the law was incapable of dealing with the realities of concrete social and economic problems. It concealed "real" interests under meaningless categories, and, as if this were not enough, it could not even approach the Liberal ideal of predictable application. Some Progressive critics (who came to include the "Legal Realists" of the 1920s and 1930s) delighted not only in showing the class bias of Liberal legalism as practiced but also in exploding its aspirations to technical coherence. The famous principles were exposed as empty formulae that could lead to totally contradictory results through logical manipulation. The act of judging, far from being nondiscretionary, involved at each step the necessity of social choice; the abstraction of Liberalism was a mask that illegitimately obscured the social bases of such decisions.[76] (The first-year law school curriculum to this very day consists of an enthusiastic Oedipal slaying of our grandfathers—the authors of "formalism" in private law and "Lochnerism" in constitutional law.)

By the "rule of law," advocates of Liberal legal science meant the subjection of all social actors to a regime of general rules that were to specify in advance the limits of autonomous conduct, within which boundaries the state was to abstain totally from regulating conduct. The Progressives, concluding that such line-drawing was impossible, also gave up on the ideal of state abstention. They saw conflict between social groups as inevitable but still manageable. When interests of social actors conflicted, each might have legitimate claims to recognition. In such a case, the legitimate claims had to be *balanced*. Questions of how far each actor could go were questions not of absolute right (having the right or not having it) but of *degree* and so bound to vary with varying circumstances.

Consider, for example, Liberal and Progressive treatment of the enforcement of contracts. In Liberal ideology a contract is either clearly enforceable or clearly not. Either the parties have wandered into a zone of state-sanctioned prohibitions on contracting behavior (such as those against making deals for illegal purposes or procuring them by duress or fraud), or they have not. If they have not, the content of the deal is nobody's business but their own. The Progressive lawmaker, by contrast, reasons along the following lines. The making of any contract potentially implicates many different kinds of social "policies" or "purposes" of which the policy promoting free bargaining is but one. Other pertinent policies include the promotion of informed and uncoerced choice in the bargaining process or the prevention of undue exploitation or the taking of advantage. Still other appropriate policies might be the protection of third parties from undesirable external effects of the bargain, such as restrictions on competition (a category that is especially liable to indefinite expansion, embracing anything from pollution, labor unrest, or increased ghetto unemployment to maldistribution of income). These policies underlie the contracting system as a whole. Indeed, they are the reasons for contracting being allowed in the first place, and the function of legal institutions is to see that they are carried out. In this Progressive conception, law is just like administration, economics, public finance, or scientific management of industrial production. It is but another policy science devoted to seeking "efficiency," the best possible resolution of the conflict of social policies.

But what, in this scheme, could conceivably have satisfied the ideal of the "rule of law"? It might have seemed completely arbitrary but for its adherents' convictions (1) that in every case, conflicting interests could be balanced in such a way as to approximate the ideally efficient adjustment of the underlying policies; and (2) that there was a rational technique available for identifying policies and the correct means of adjusting them. No less enthusiastically scientific than the generations that had gone before, the Progressive lawyers believed themselves capable of developing a method of expressing the immanent rationality of the social order. But unlike the Liberals, they believed that rationality was to be looked for in particularity (the "facts") rather than generality—that each social situation was unique, requiring regulation tailored to its uniqueness. Hence they tended on the whole to be more interested in legislative and administrative approaches to social problems than in adjudicative ones. Where the Liberals had sought to classify all conduct under abstractly defined individual roles (seller, buyer, landlord, tenant, creditor, stockholder, offeror, offeree) and obligations (contract and tort), the Progressives looked for categories corresponding to their ideas of concrete social groups in particular social relations (consumers, tenant farmers, odd-lot investors, or electrical workers, who were engaged respectively in buying cars, mortgaging farms, listening to stock promoters, bargaining with management) and sought to develop specialized agencies and bodies of rules to deal with each.

The key, I think, to understanding the Progressive legal mind-set is this idea of rationality in particularity: buried in each social conflict or dispute was an efficient solution in terms of some universally valid harmony of the underlying social policies. To find it, of course, you needed to consult experts. In general, the parties immediately concerned—individuals, labor unions, the construction trades, however they might be defined—were initially presumed to be the best experts on their own situations and thus most capable of working out efficient solutions to their problems by negotiation and compromise. But their judgment might be clouded by opportunism, guile, or short-sightedness, and in any case the immediate parties might take insufficient account of the policies favoring outside interests (affected third parties or the "public"). The legal system thus provided an elaborate system of review mechanisms that, while giving due deference to expert discretion at every level, sought to control the parochialism of that discretion through general standards of reasonableness or fairness, authorizing another tier of experts to undertake independent inquiry into the social efficiency of the solution.

Thus the rate-making commission let the utility (the presumptive best expert on its own profit structure) initiate the request and justification for a raise of rates, but the commission would subject that request to a hearing of other affected parties and independent review. The commission's decision on rates, in turn, might be reviewed in the courts, which would defer to the commission's fact-finding expertise but would try to provide an independent check on its reasonableness. To take another example, while Liberal constitutionalism sought to mark off definite boundaries between proper and improper exercises of legislative power, the Progressives recast judicial review as a process of initial deference to the expert legislative judgment on the prevailing political consensus (presumptively the most reliable index of a socially efficient solution), followed by independent review to control gross abuses of that discretion in the interests of a more detached perspective on the constitution's policies. As a final example, consider the case of contract adjudication with which I started. The Progressive judge, in the search for efficiency, gives primary deference to the norms and expectations of the parties themselves. What did they hope to achieve in this bargain? What solution would fairly satisfy their expectations? To obtain help in this, the judge looks at the detailed particulars of their circumstances, aided by experts from their trade. What are the customary expectations of the experts who do this for a living? Only if the immanent norms of the parties or trade seem unduly parochial will he look for outside sources of normative guidance—in, say, statutory expressions in other contexts of standards of fair dealing. If need be, however, the Progressive judge *will* look for them, stir them into his soup of policies, and serve up a solution.

To pause a moment for review, we have identified three distinct versions of the ideology of legal science: (1) the antebellum Whig-Federalist version, according to which the lawyer was qualified to prescribe obligations for his fellow citizens because of his superior knowledge of what ordinary people have long held to be customary and correct behavior (recorded in the common law) and the superior virtue that his learning and experience conferred; (2) the Liberal version, in which the lawyer was to clarify and make definite the boundaries within which state and individual action must remain to assure maximum autonomy for all, to keep individuals and the state from going outside their spheres, but to remove all restrictions on free action within them; and (3) the Progressive version, which viewed the lawyer as one contributor to expert management, whose goal was to promote the efficient attainment of an immanent social equilibrium (the "public interest") between the actual and potential conflicts of corporate interest groups.

Each of these conceptions of legal science produced not only a distinctive dogmatic literature (cases and commentary) but a distinct style of public service activity as well. For the Whig-Federalist, of course, the ideal way to appear in public was in full Ciceronian dress as an orator-statesman of the republic: arguing great constitutional causes, speaking on liberty and union in the Senate, and also (given the importance attached to eloquence and oratory in the civic humanist tradition) performing before juries. For the Progressive, the characteristic public role was that of neutral administrative expert, a specialist in a particular field. This expert was more properly to be found in appointive rather than elective office, perhaps as a member of a public service commission. If involved in politics, the Progressive lawyer was to be elected on a Fusion or Reform ticket, or else was to serve on a specialized bipartisan committee or league to rationalize some corrupt or sloppy practice—school administration, police training, street railway franchise awards.

Liberal lawyers, the focus of the present essay, tended to form the backbone of both Mugwump and regular legislative reform efforts of the 1880s—civil service reform, lobby reform, secret ballots, corrupt practices acts, the streamlining of court procedure, the removing of crooked judges, and the devising of procedures to select capable ones.[77] Academic and corporate lawyers, for all the name-calling and infighting that went on between them, often collaborated on these projects, in which the goal was to ensure objective and honest administration of the standing rules of the social game—in short, to patrol the boundaries. If "virtue" was the ideal quality aimed at by Whig science, and "expertise" or "efficiency" by the Progressives, perhaps "integrity" will do as a label for the goal of the Liberal scheme, a conception of the lawyer's role that fell somewhere between the other two. For the partisans of the Liberal scheme, education, especially legal education, would make men honest and objective by training their intelligences to realize when action by the government or their clients would transgress its proper sphere and therefore, in the long run, become futile and self-defeating. As George Fredrickson says of these reforms, "If the power elite . . . was really outside the government, it was still necessary to have an inside elite which would, paradoxically enough, act in a positive way to keep government from expanding beyond its 'natural sphere' as defined by the economics and sociology of the day."[78] Or as Geoffrey Blodgett says, more succinctly, these reforms were "the solution of Yankee lawyers for the abuse of Yankee law."[79]

Not so incidentally, this Liberal ideology helps to explain why the law schools took so little interest in statute law. (It only helps, since this situation continued well after the schools' own faculties—Holmes, Thayer, Pound, Corbin—had demolished the idea that common law is neutral and only statute is political. The rest of the explanation may very well lie in the reluctance of the law schools to become involved in controversial issues while training graduates for a conservative profession.[80]) In the Liberal view, legislation was just common law all over again, enacted in statute in order to provide a more efficient procedural mechanism for vindicating common-law rights—the Sherman Act, for instance, being considered a mere restatement of the common law on unlawful restraints of trade, albeit in such a way as to make it nationally effective.[81] Otherwise, legislation was the expression of the will of the state, which within its sphere was as unamenable to *legal* analysis as a bolt of lightning. All a court could do was to carry out the legislative mandate or decline to do so if it had exceeded its limits. The rules determining the *limits* of legislation were given by the law of the constitution, which in Liberal legal thought simply incorporated all the neutral principles of the common law. In the due process clause of the Fourteenth Amendment, for example, "property" derived its meaning from common law science.

For the Liberal, the major public service activity of the organized bar was exactly the same as the schoolmen's: the refinement of private-law science in order to make it more certain through law reform—yielding commentaries or limited codifications that clarified technical rules, restated them in more "principled" (general and abstract) form, and purged them of their putative archaisms and anomalies.[82] Like their Whig predecessors, Liberal lawyers were fond of emphasizing both the majesty of the common-law tradition and the confusion and obscurity into which it had fallen after generations of unscientific practice.

The Liberal reform efforts were plainly soaked in redemptive significance for the corporate lawyers who engaged in them. The duty to perfect legal science and its administration was what made possible the endless reiteration of the *thèse nobiliaire* amid much complaint that the bar was becoming commercialized. The *thèse nobiliaire* embodied the claim of the leading lawyers to act as mediators between capital and labor, that is, between plutocracy and socialism, despite the fact that they seemed actually to be working for and bound by ethics of loyalty to one side only. If the system as a whole was functioning, there should be nothing wrong with unrestricted advocacy of some client's will.[83] Up to a point, the lawyer could aggressively pursue his client's interest. But he could not go, and should try to discourage his client from going, beyond that point. Simultaneously, this Liberal lawyer was supposed to work to keep the boundaries in repair from the damage done by his own battering. Although some extremely conscientious attorneys tried to play the game in precisely this schizoid way,[84] most must have found it a difficult tightrope to walk if they thought about walking it at all. Such association and graduation speeches as "The Lawyer's Duty to Society and the State," a favorite theme between 1870 and 1910, are filled with the rhetoric of decline from the Ciceronian ideal, and, like their antebellum predecessors, these speeches stress the lawyer's obligation to rise in character and learning above all particularism.[85]

Some of these speeches, like Brandeis's famous "Opportunity in the Law," are openly critical of Liberal legalism in practice, portraying it as a lapse into irresponsible privatism and pointing the way to a revival of the old civic ideal in a conception of the public interest.[86] Yet it was not so much proto-Progressives like Brandeis as it was the ordinary Liberal lawyers themselves who destroyed Liberal legal science. Their clients did not really want to stay within the boundaries marked off for them. In the perfectly legitimate process of pursuing their interest, the lawyers pushed and pulled at the formal principles from which the boundaries were derived until their emptiness became manifest—an example of which I will later provide. But only for such unusual men as Dorman Eaton, Simeon Baldwin, or Charles Evans Hughes, who all left comfortable practices to give them full attention, did bar meetings, reform politics, and legal science amount to anything more than occasional diversions for corporate lawyers.

Fortunately for the historian, lines of specialization between the practitioner and the academic had not yet hardened in this period; corporate lawyers contributed regularly to the law reviews and to the political science and economics journals. Usually these articles were on current topics, but sometimes they included the sort of antiquarian exploration then fashionable of the Roman or Teutonic origins of some current doctrine. Such erudition—though perhaps impressive to a court, if they ever got to one—was almost surely not the principal source of the authority and independence of Liberal lawyers vis-à-vis clients. Rather, that authority and independence resided in the Liberal lawyers' contacts or technical ability, or in the client's demand for their judgment on powerful outsiders' assessments of their actions ("If you do this, the investors [or the commission] won't like it"). Yet the same basic Liberal consciousness that pervades the formal writing on law in this period can be found, I believe, at the heart of the practice of the legal elite.

Let me illustrate my point that Liberal legal science could find its way into legal practice with two examples: the first from a fairly well-known activity of the corporate bar, the drafting of state incorporation laws and corporate charters; the second, from the more obscure realm of reorganization practice.

Private corporation law is the better-known example and may be quickly summarized. In the first American corporations, no distinction was drawn between public and private. All corporations were "bodies-politic," chartered by the legislature to carry out some specific public purpose. Early in this century, however, there emerged the notion of a "private corporation," meaning property owned by individuals rather than the state but still granted special privileges in return for services to the public. In the 1830s, Jacksonian agitation for equal rights against monopolies had led to the generalization of corporate privileges in the form of incorporation statutes. But these statutes continued to specify, with some precision, limits on corporate purposes, life, and capitalization, and to prescribe financial and governance structures and rights of investors.[87] If corporations were on their way to becoming Liberal "persons," with the same rights and duties as those ascribed to all other individuals, they were still treated, in accordance with antebellum legal principle, as persons of special status with special obligations. Following the Civil War, the movement in private corporate law was to remove or redefine as state-willed the incidents of status that distinguished special legal persons from individuals with normal rights.[88] As the abstract objectified Liberal scheme became increasingly prominent, private corporations increasingly became defined as rights-bearing individuals, enjoying complete freedom of action within their spheres.

Some of the specific ways in which this shift was effected deserve mention here. Private corporations came to be included as persons within the Fourteenth Amendment's protection against state action that improperly interfered with liberty or property.[89] The doctrine of ultra vires—the claim that a corporate action was invalid because it went beyond some restriction in the corporate charter, usually asserted not against but *by* a corporation as a defense to claims against it for acts of its agents—was rapidly eroded in the courts.[90] Most important, following the lead of the almost legendary James' Dill, Liberal corporate lawyers undertook an effective campaign to "liberalize" corporation statutes in such a way that corporations could do anything that individuals might do. As part of this campaign, which culminated in New Jersey statutes of 1896 and 1898, corporations were freed from restrictions on their powers and capitalization and were granted an almost unlimited authority to arrange their internal affairs by contract.[91] The final step taken by the corporate lawyers who drafted these statutes was to knock down the simple democratic governance structures that had been provided in the general acts and in the common-law rules on the rights of security holders and to erect in their stead an intracorporate structure that centralized effective control in management, authorizing it to reshuffle the interests of investors through issuance, redemption, and retirement of various classes of securities.[92] In short, in its external relations, the private corporation assumed for most purposes the legal personality of the Liberal individual. Internally, it became an aggregate of contracting individuals who, as a consequence of their participation in the enterprise, were considered to have willed their consent to its hierarchical structures of management and control.

My other illustration of the Liberal scheme in practice comes from corporate reorganization, the largest and most time-consuming practice of eminent New York counsel after 1880 and the one that involved the most money. The same few firms did almost all of this work, which consisted in handling the legal aspects of reorganizing the capital structures of failing enterprises (in the earlier years, mostly railroads), the main aim being to reduce their debt and provide them with fresh operating capital.[93] Most of the railroad mileage in the country went through reorganization at some point after the Civil War.[94] The legal form under which reorganization took place, there being no federal bankruptcy act at all between 1878 and 1898, was the equity receivership. Early practice was exceedingly chaotic and became a creditors' race to get friendly receivers appointed in every state where the failing corporation did business. The procedure was centralized and rationalized in the 1880s by reorganization lawyers with the cooperation of the federal courts. The result was the emergence of the "consent" receivership, whereby corporate insiders could preempt any group of security-holders by acting before default to file a bill in equity against its creditors and to ask the federal court to appoint a receiver for the entire corporate property.[95] The courts, in the words of an experienced lawyer, threw "their protecting arms about the property without much pausing to consider the technical obstacles to their intervention."[96]

Reorganization practice grew up under this judicial protection. While the receivers (usually the old management, as there was much corruption here)[97] ran the business, investment bankers and their lawyers organized committees to represent the various classes of security-holders. The lawyer's first task was to draft documents giving the committee power to act for, say, the bondholders; the "powers conferred in this regard cannot well be too broad.... [The agreement should] place the committee practically in the position of owners of the bonds."[98] This goal could be accomplished by getting enough bondholders to deposit their bonds with the committee so that it had control over the trustee of the bonds-securing mortgage. How many bondholders was "enough" was determined by another contract, the trust indenture. The next step in this process of collapsing thousands of individuals into a committee was yet another contract, a deposit agreement by which a bondholder could pass his bonds into the control of the committee by depositing them with a trust company, in exchange for transferable certificates. (To get deposits, the bankers baited the certificates with fast-maturing coupons.)

The courts were often made uneasy by these arrangements, and so construed broad grants of power strictly against the committees. In response, the bar evolved contract documents of unbelievable specificity and length, sprayed with narrowly stated grants of discretion, elaborate provisions giving notice and chances to pull out, and exculpatory clauses. The courts worried about conflicts of interest since committee members were often known to deal in the securities they were protecting and to "act as reorganization managers, and also [to] form and manage the syndicates to provide the cash requirements."[99] The solution was clear authorization of all these transactions. The evolution of these instruments may be taken as an indication of the transition from a Whig-Federalist model of social hierarchy, in which the bankers were to act as trustees for the bondholders, to a Liberal model of formal equality, in which central managerial authority was derived from the exercise of contractual will, as objectively manifested in the deposit agreements. As long as the signs of consent were sufficiently explicit, a single reorganization manager was entitled to exercise his own will as the representative of a thousand others and thus to redistribute property rights free-handedly among investors.

In the next stage, all the committees got together to negotiate a reorganization plan, which usually stipulated that the junior bondholders would consent to reduce their current obligations considerably, the senior bondholders would reduce theirs somewhat, and the stockholders would contribute new capital, all in return for new shares in the rejuvenated enterprise. The lawyers, who came to play important parts in these negotiations, then drew up a plan and agreement of reorganization. The reorganization agreement was drawn to empower a new committee, the Reorganization Committee, to act as owner of the deposited securities. With that power, the Reorganization Committee typically bought the old corporation at a foreclosure sale and then transferred it to the new corporation in exchange for the new securities. Eventually the Committee set up voting trusts in the new corporation for a period long enough to empower it to carry out the plan. Of course, this only bound those who had deposited under the Committee, and it was necessary to pay off the rest of the bondholders at the foreclosure sale.

The real trouble at this stage came from those who held various kinds of rights against the old corporation but had not been included in the reorganization. These were usually representatives of general (unsecured) creditors who sued to hold up the adoption of the plan or to invalidate the sale on the grounds that they had not been fairly treated. Of course, one of the central aims of the Reorganization Committee's contrived foreclosures was precisely that of cutting off the floating debt. But through the 1870s and 1880s creditors were able to assert a plausible claim to priority over the bondholders for several reasons: (1) some states gave priority to certain preferred creditors (for materials and labor) by statute; (2) the courts developed the ingenious practice of issuing receiver's certificates that held priority over mortgages as a means of borrowing money to improve the company property and keep it going; and (3) the courts allowed receivers to prefer creditors who were currently furnishing labor and supplies.[100] The general justifications for preferences of this kind were obvious; a railroad would not be worth reorganizing if it were not kept going or were allowed to rust away during receivership. On the other hand, as a leading treatise put it (speaking of issuing receiver's certificates), "an unlimited exercise of power by the court in this direction would amount to improving the mortgagor out of his property."[101]

One of the significant achievements of the reorganization bar in the 1880s was to bring these practices under the control of rules. In general, the device used was consent: if the mortgagees agreed, other creditors could be given a superior lien. Otherwise, the granting of special status to particular creditors was to happen only in strictly defined and limited circumstances, usually also rationalized by contract theory such as the doctrine preferring current debts, on the theory that the bondholders' contracts gave them the right to rely only upon net earnings.[102] A judge who flouted the rules and made the appointment of a receiver conditional on the payment of *all* secured debt was slapped down by the United States Supreme Court (through Justice Brewer) in 1890: "Can anything be conceived which more thoroughly destroys the sacredness of contract obligations? . . . No one is bound to sell a railroad company or to work for it, and whoever has dealings with a company whose property is mortgaged must be assumed to have dealt with it on the faith of its personal responsibility and not in expectation of subsequently displacing the priority of its mortgage liens."[103] Only those "few unsecured claims" previously declared to have an equitable priority could be paid before the mortgagees.

With this case, and the practice that had developed, reorganization law seemed to have moved on to a firmly scientific foundation. Aside from enforcing some equitable claims on current debts, which was necessary to preserve the property, the court provided the rigid framework within which the lawyers could build their consent structure. If properly drafted, this consent structure was immune to attack and could not be set aside except for procedural defect or fraud.

Then came the *Monon* case (1899).[104] This was a general creditor's suit, alleging the invalidity of a plan whereby the stockholders and bondholders would both have interests in the new corporation. Here was a nice dilemma for legal science. The bondholders were, of course, entitled to buy the property at the foreclosure sale and shut *everyone* out. If they could do that, surely they could give whatever interests they wanted to anyone, including stockholders, but it was equally clear that stockholders' rights were legally inferior to any creditor's. This seemed to suggest that stockholders could *not* be brought into the reorganization unless the creditors were first paid off. Confronted with this dilemma, the Supreme Court (again speaking through Justice Brewer) generalized all the old preferred-creditors cases into a new theory:

> We have held in a series of cases that the peculiar character
> and conditions of railroad property not only justify but compel a
> court . . . to give to certain limited unsecured claims a priority
> over the debts secured by the mortgage. . . . It may be, and has
> often been said, that this rule implies somewhat of a departure

from the apparent priority of right secured by a contract obligation duly made and duly recorded, and yet this Court, recognizing that a railroad is not simply private property, but also an instrument of public service, has ruled that the character of its business and the public obligations which it assumes justify a limited displacement of contract and recorded liens.[105]

In fact, this case came to nothing after being returned to the lower court. "Yet even to this day," the reorganization lawyer Adrian Joline told Harvard Business School students in 1910, "reorganizers stand more or less in terror of the Monon case, and it looms as a perpetual spectre in their path."[106] Two years later, in *Northern Pacific Co. v. Boyd*,[107] the Supreme Court gave reality to the specter, holding that a reorganization plan that included stockholders as well as bondholders must make provision for the unsecured creditors. It was perfectly just for stockholders to combine with bondholders to buy the property, but they must first pay off other creditors, not necessarily in cash, but by a fair offer on equitable terms of bonds or stock.[108]

This famous case inaugurated a new order, as everyone knew it would at the time. For a season it created some havoc on Wall Street. Stockholders had to be included in reorganizations, since they were expected to put up the cash. (Justice Brewer once remarked that about all a railroad company stockholder had a right to do was to pay the corporate debts.[109]) Yet their inclusion made the whole beautiful contract structure of reorganization plans vulnerable to the strike suits of general creditors. Eventually everyone adjusted, but to completely changed conditions; the new task for reorganization committees was to draft the "fair, equitable, and feasible" plan for accommodating outsider interests, which the court must approve before confirming the foreclosure sale.[110]

To be sure, it could be argued that the new order ultimately had very little instrumental impact upon the practices of the legal-financial community. In time, lawyers for bondholders' committees proved sufficiently adept at ensuring that judicial scrutiny of the fairness of reorganization plans was cursory and ineffectual.[111] Yet ways of thinking about the legal regulation of social relations had undergone a fundamental shift.

1. The various committees participating in reorganizations gradually came to be seen, and to be legally analyzed, no longer as aggregations of individuals pooling their wills through contract, but rather as the managers of interest groups (a new theory of representation);

2. Correspondingly, the basic task of law shifted from that of defining

the boundaries of zones within which legal persons would be free to exercise their wills without interference of any kind to that of achieving equilibrium, through a balancing process, among a multitude of conflicting interests; and

3. Liberal legal science—the technique of rights definition by the elaboration of principles, their harmonious arrangement, and the deduction of subrules from them by a strictly legal logic—simply disintegrated. The principles themselves, in this case the rights of creditors who bought at foreclosure sales to do as they wished with their property and the priority of general creditors' rights to stockholders', were perceived to be in contradiction. The perception cracked open the system and drove lawyers to look for solutions outside it, either in a new role for the courts or outside the courts altogether. To encapsulate the changes in a phrase, the program of legal science as rights definition was replaced by a program of scientific social engineering.

Naturally these changes, which mark off what has been called the Liberal from the Progressive mentality, did not happen all at once. Through the first decades of this century, one can observe a fascinating shuttling back and forth between the old and the new. Brewer himself was now on one side, now on the other. The two views of science confronted one another squarely in the litigation over reorganization of the promoter-looted Chicago street railway systems in 1907.[112] After years of litigation, the city held out a chance to rescue the systems by offering the receivers a franchise for a consolidated system. But the only practical way to put together the various roads would have been to authorize their receivers to borrow new money secured by a first lien on their properties, and to empower a city committee of engineers to decide how much should be spent for improvements. Peter Grosscup, the federal circuit judge supervising the receiverships, knocked heads together and secured agreement from almost all of the interests involved; but a few securityholders in the old railroads continued to object. Grosscup finally overrode these objections, saying frankly there was no precedent for what he was doing but that the city's offer was the best the roads were ever likely to get, and in the interests of all, he ordered the receivers to accept it.[113] On appeal, Justice Brewer (sitting as circuit justice) set aside the order in a monument to Liberal ideology:

> The rehabilitating mortgage is not in terms limited in amount. . . . Now, what does that mean? It means that those improvements . . . are not made according to the judgment of the present corporate owner of the property . . . but a body outside

them.... Now, I have no doubt ... that the committee selected by the city of Chicago will deal fairly and honestly, and, perhaps, they being experts in their lines of business, with far better judgment than the trustees of these mortgages, or the officers of the corporations. But, at the same time, no man is compelled to turn over his property to the control and management of another.... These voluntary reorganizations ... do involve, sometimes, moral pressure upon certain interests to conclude something in the hope that they will get a larger benefit from the reorganization, but the action is voluntary. They are the acts of the parties themselves. They are making new contracts. They are entering into new relationship [sic] with one another. The individual is making the contract, and not the court for him.[114]

Yet with the continuing erosion of Liberal legal science, Brewer's approach came to seem no more an application of principle, no less an application of policy, than Grosscup's. Pressure built up to find a new theory of adjudication or else to restrict the judicial role so as to distribute the weight formerly placed upon rights definition somewhere else—toward administrative expertise, countervailing power, the expert judgment of businessmen and bankers. A federal judge who handled a lot of reorganizations proposed "a new scheme of law which would in some way confer upon an impartial and disinterested tribunal the entire supervision of corporate reorganization."[115] More specifically, some judges proposed a generalization of equitable powers already in force to a broad judicial power of supervision over the terms of reorganization plans; others proposed reenactment of the bankruptcy statutes, the solution adopted in 1933.[116] A young corporation lawyer, A. A. Berle, Jr., developed the most sophisticated theoretical articulation of the new modes of thought. He insisted that the whole contract theory of intracorporate organization should be discarded as a fiction. The reality was a network of relationships of hierarchic control, with insiders managing for the purported benefit of outsiders. While consent could not legitimate this regime, efficient management could, given a due regard for maximizing the interests of the various classes of participants. A new legal science had to develop that would recognize hierarchy as inevitable, potentially beneficial but dangerous, and invest it with fiduciary duties wherever it was found.[117]

So, then, what does all of this prove? I hope that a preliminary case has now been made for explaining changes in reorganization law in ideological rather than instrumental terms, for seeing them as reflections of, and contributions to, a fundamental change in ways of thinking about law. The main instrumental modes of explaining legal change, as set forth at the beginning of this essay, do not seem nearly so persuasive for the following reasons.

1. The story of reorganization law does not seem to be one of new social problems calling for responsive new developments in legal technology. In the social problems they presented—how to reconcile the conflicting claims of different participants in the old enterprise and what interest to give them in the new—the reorganizations of the 1920s were not really very different from those of the 1880s. Nor can it convincingly be argued that there was a lag, a failure of legal technology that was only repaired later on. The lawyers of the 1920s contributed no significant legal-technological inventions that were unknown to the generation of Liberalism. Liberals had available to them the category of "corporations affected by a public interest." They could have assigned corporations undergoing reorganization to that category and thus brought them under the supervision of public service commissions. In declining to do so, they argued that, although the rates and highways of railroads were public in their nature, their relations with stockholders and creditors concerned property just as private as any individual's—a classically Liberal division of zones.[118] Similarly, Congress could have provided for displacement of minority by majority interests by bringing reorganization under the federal bankruptcy power (the present system).[119] Bankruptcy had long been recognized as a situation that permitted the constriction of some creditors' vested property rights for the greater good of all. When the Congress did not act in this way, corporate lawyers were constrained to act within the rules of the ideological game and to justify all manipulation of outsider by insider interests as authorized by the outsiders' consent. And finally, of course, the courts could already have taken the expanded view of their equity powers which they eventually came to take in *Monon* and *Boyd*.[120] As the history of their practice shows, federal judges presiding over reorganizations were not at all timid about stretching their authority, nor was the bar in the least lacking in technological ingenuity. But the fact remains that in the 1880s those judges would not have dreamed of characterizing themselves as exercising a general discretion to review reorganization plans as "fair, equitable, and reasonable." By the 1920s, this discretion was taken for granted. The only question was whether they were really competent, or had been given adequate procedural tools, to use it efficiently.

2. It is similarly difficult to account for what happened in reorganization law by the theory of interest-group politics. As far as one can tell, no aroused army of general creditors or junior mortgagees influenced

the courts to their decisions in *Monon* and *Boyd.* In fact the courts justified those decisions by what would later become standard pluralist argumentation, to the effect that these interests deserved special protection because they were relatively weak and unorganized. Besides, when one looks at the players, one sees that they are often the same people (e.g., Justice Brewer); and though it is frequently true that the same man may hold in his head two contradictory ideologies, it is less likely that he will be found representing two opposing interest groups. Not so incidentally, the lawyers who may be credited with first serving up the argument that ultimately triumphed in *Boyd* were Wheeler Peckham and Francis Lynde Stetson, quintessentially blue-chip Wall Streeters, who would have been filled with horror at the thought that they were leading a battle against bankers' control of reorganization.[121] Like Justice Holmes, the intellectual pioneer of Liberal legal science in the 1870s and its most penetrating critic in the 1890s—or like Thomas M. Cooley, the Liberal judge and treatise writer who as I.C.C. chairman became a major prophet of Progressive regulatory ideology—these corporate lawyers helped to demolish their own creation. Without doubting for a moment that the pressure of the immediate self-interest of interest groups supplies the motive force or driving power behind a great deal of legal change, it is nonetheless possible to argue that long-run structural change takes on characteristics that are quite independent of the interests of such groups. Thus, while reference to interest-group politics supplies a plausible ad hoc explanation for any given short-run legal decision—often indeed the *most* plausible—such explanations do not satisfactorily take account of the conventional understandings that appear to underlie many such decisions and to be shared by participants with conflicting stakes in their outcomes. Such understandings, discourses, or ideologies, as they have been called here, can never of course determine particular outcomes, but they are the tools that must be used to construct the framework for decision. They encourage the perception of some alternatives as reasonable and realistic and of others as visionary or offensive, and still others they suppress before they can even be imagined. The project of trying to link legal changes in particular fields of law to large-scale ideological change derives much of its appeal from the fact that one seems to be able to see similar changes in the background conventions of discourse that take place concurrently across a variety of legal fields that are occupied by entirely different lineups of interests. The patterns of change that I have pointed to in reorganization law were, as I have argued (and in forthcoming work hope to demonstrate at length), paralleled by changes in torts, contracts, constitutional adjudication, administrative law, general jurisprudential thought, and, for all I know, many other fields as well.

When talking to lawyers about this project, I frequently come across a deeply ingrained suspicion of the notion that they should be depicted as a species of intellectuals producing ideology. Very few of them are self-consciously anything of the kind. Naturally they think of themselves as practical persons occupied with practical affairs, and doubtless this attitude helps to explain the tenacity of legal-technological and interest-group explanations of what they do. Yet when a lawyer helps a client arrange a transaction so as to take maximum advantage of the current legal framework, he or she becomes one of the army of agents who confirm that framework by reinforcement and extend it by interpretation into many niches of social life. The framework is an ideological one, i.e., a set of assertions, arguments, and implicit assumptions about power and right. A legal document such as a partnership agreement, a trust indenture, or a reorganization plan is a kind of political constitution. It embodies the following assumptions: (a) about representation, saying when the few may exercise power to bind or coerce the many; (b) about the scope and limits of decision-making discretion and the manner of its delegation; and (c) about individual entitlement and collective responsibility, propriety in various situations of refusing to share one's gains with others or insisting that others share one's losses. My hypothesis in this essay has been that these assumptions were embodied in a general background structure of ideological discourse that was elaborated in this period and then transformed and that one can detect the patterns of this discourse in elite lawyers' contributions to practices as diverse as advising bankrupt railroads and instructing law students in abstract and academic doctrines of private law. The hypothesis, of course, needs to be worked through a much larger number of examples.

Notes

Chapter 1

1. Talcott Parsons, "Professions," in *International Encyclopedia of the Social Sciences*, ed. David L. Sills (New York, 1968), 12:545.

2. Ibid., pp. 536–46. Parsons went so far as to say (p. 546) that "the professional complex has . . . even begun to dominate the contemporary scene in such a way as to render obsolescent the primacy of the old issues of political authoritarianism and capitalistic exploitation."

3. Abraham Flexner, "Is Social Work a Profession?" *School and Society* 1 (1915): 901–11. For an even earlier example of the *genre*, see W. H. Walker, "What Constitutes a Chemical Engineer?" *The Chemical Engineer* 2 (1905): 1–3. My thanks to my colleague John Servos for the latter reference.

4. Randall Collins, *The Credential Society: An Historical Sociology of Education and Stratification* (New York, 1979).

5. Parsons, "Professions," p. 536.

6. For an especially explicit example, see Vern L. Bullough, *The Development of Medicine as a Profession: The Contribution of the Medieval University to Modern Medicine* (Basel, 1966).

7. On the sociology and historiography of the professions before 1970, see Laurence Veysey, "Who's a Professional? Who Cares?" *Reviews in American History* 3 (1975) 419–23.

8. Jethro K. Lieberman, *The Tyranny of the Experts: How Professionals Are Closing the Open Society* (New York, 1970). For recent examples of the "revolt of the client," see Bernard Barber, "Control and Responsibility in the Powerful Professions," *Political Science Quarterly* 93 (Winter 1978–79): 599–615.

9. See, e.g., Robert Dingwall, "Accomplishing Profession," *Sociological Review*, n.s. 24 (1976): 331–49.

10. See, e.g., Burton J. Bledstein, *The Culture of Professionalism: The Middle Class and the Development of Higher Education in America* (New York, 1976); Magali Sarfatti Larson, *The Rise of Professionalism: A Sociological Analysis* (Berkeley, 1977); Mary O. Furner, *Advocacy & Objectivity: A Crisis in the Professionalization of American Social Science* (Lexington, 1975); Terence J. Johnson, *Professions and Power* (London, 1972); Jeffrey L. Berlant, *Profession and Monopoly: A Study of Medicine in the United States and Great Britain* (Berkeley, 1975); E. Richard Brown, *Rockefeller Medicine Men: Medicine and Capitalism in America* (Berkeley, 1979); David Noble, *America by Design: Science, Technology, and the Rise of Corporate Capitalism* (New York, 1977).

11. The virtues of a flexible and modulated Parsonian approach can be seen in the valuable recent work of Thomas L. Haskell. See his *The Emergence of Professional Social Science: The American Social Science Association and the Nineteenth-Century Crisis of Authority* (Urbana, 1977); and "Power to the Experts," *New York Review of Books*, 13 Oct. 1977, pp. 28–33.

12. Veysey in "Who's a Professional?" stresses this point in his review of the book by

Furner (note 10 above). It could equally well be made with respect to most of the other works in note 10 above, including notably Bledstein, *The Culture of Professionalism*.

13. This tendency is apparent in most of the works cited in note 10 above, including notably Larson, *Rise of Professionalism*.

14. Larson, *Rise of Professionalism*, p. xvii.

15. Ibid., p. xviii.

16. Cf. Wilfrid R. Prest, "The Social Identity of Early Modern English Barristers and Their Clients," paper delivered to the research seminar of the Davis Center for Historical Studies, Princeton University, 11 Apr. 1980; and Anthony J. LaVopa, "The Language of Profession: Germany in the Eighteenth Century," paper delivered to the research seminar of the Davis Center for Historical Studies, Princeton University, 25 Apr. 1980.

17. Cf. Haskell, "Power to the Experts," which begins and ends by quoting this phrase from the late American social critic Paul Goodman.

18. For examples of recent scholarship that tend to stress the monopolistic and self-seeking strategies of the American medical profession, see Berlant, *Profession and Monopoly*; James G. Burrow, *Organized Medicine in the Progressive Era: The Move toward Monopoly* (Baltimore, 1977); Larson, *Rise of Professionalism*, chap. 3; and E. Richard Brown, *Rockefeller Medicine Men*. For a striking statement of laissez-faire ideology by an American physician, see Robert Sade, "Health Care as a Right: A Refutation," *New England Journal of Medicine* 285 (Dec. 1971): 1288–92. Sade argues that medical care, like bread, should be thought of as a commodity that can be sold to the highest bidder. He totally fails to recognize (or at least to mention) that the federal government subsidizes medical education, facilities, and research, while also granting physicians monopoly power, including notably a monopoly over diagnosis and prescription. Cf. Gene Outka, "Social Justice and Equal Access to Health Care," *Journal of Religious Ethics* 2 (1974): 11–32. For evidence that many American physicians nonetheless share Sade's ideology, see *The Wall Street Journal*, 27 Mar. 1972.

19. Larson in *Rise of Professionalism* uses this phrase to cover the variety of strategies by which professionalizing groups seek to carve out and control a market for their services.

Chapter 2

1. "Editor's Easy Chair," *Harper's Monthly Magazine* 8 (Feb. 1854): 415; "Lectures and Lecturers," *Putnam's Monthly* 9 (Mar. 1857): 317; *New York Tribune*, 9 Sept. 1859.

2. This figure is based on an estimate that 2,000 lectures, with an average attendance of 250 people, took place each week during the season. See Robert J. Greef, "Public Lectures in New York, 1851–1878: A Cultural Index of the Times" (Ph.D. diss., University of Chicago, 1941), pp. 4–7.

3. Park Benjamin to Alfred Street, 26 Oct. 1849, Park Benjamin Papers, Butler Library, Columbia University, New York.

4. "The Lecture Season," *New York Tribune*, 20 Sept. 1854.

5. "Lectures and Lecturing," *Harper's Monthly Magazine* 14 (Dec. 1856): 124.

6. For the conceptual literature upon which much of the study of professions in the past and present has been based, see Wilbert E. Moore, *The Professions: Roles and Rules* (New York, 1970); Howard M. Vollmer and Donald L. Mills, eds., *Professionalization* (Englewood Cliffs, N.J., 1966); Kenneth Lynn, ed., *The Professions in America* (Boston, 1967); Talcott Parsons, "The Professions and Social Structure," in *Essays in Sociological Theory* (New York, 1964); Parsons, "Professions," in David L. Sills, ed., *International Encyclopedia of the Social Sciences* (New York, 1968), 12:536–47. Sev-

eral recent studies have pointed toward a broadening of these perspectives and contain a number of suggestive insights. See, especially, Thomas Haskell, *The Emergence of Professional Social Science* (Urbana, 1977); Burton Bledstein, *The Culture of Professionalism* (New York, 1976); and Magali Sarfatti Larson, *The Rise of Professionalism* (Berkeley, 1977). For a useful short critique of the contemporary models, see Laurence Veysey, "Who's a Professional? Who Cares?" *Reviews in American History* 3 (1975): 419–23.

7. Veysey, "Who's a Professional?" pp. 419–23.

8. For a full and highly suggestive discussion of the ideas of professionalism in nineteenth-century America see Bledstein, *The Culture of Professionalism*.

9. David F. Allmendinger, Jr., *Paupers and Scholars: The Transformation of Student Life in Nineteenth-Century New England* (New York, 1975), pp. 7–42. See also, Joseph Kett, *Rites of Passage: Adolescence in America, 1790 to the Present* (New York, 1977), pp. 11–61.

10. For discussions of overcrowding in the professions and the difficulty of getting established in them, see Daniel Calhoun, *Professional Lives in America* (Cambridge, 1965), pp. 88–197; Donald Scott, *From Office to Profession: The New England Ministry, 1750–1850* (Philadelphia, 1978); Lawrence Friedman, *A History of American Law* (New York, 1973), pp. 264–92; and Charles Gawalt, *The Promise of Power: The Emergence of the Legal Profession in Massachusetts* (Westport, Conn., 1979), pp. 39–81.

11. The problem of access is suggested in Allmendinger, *Paupers and Scholars*. See also Solon J. Buck, ed., "Selections from the Journal of Lucien C. Boynton, 1835–1853," *Proceedings of the American Antiquarian Society*, n.s. 43 (Oct. 1933): 329–80; and Mark Hopkins, *Early Lectures of Mark Hopkins and Others from His Brothers and their Mother* (New York, 1929).

12. Buck, "Selections from the Journal of Lucien C. Boynton," pp. 329–80.

13. The American Antiquarian Society, Worcester, Mass., has a superb collection of broadsides from a wide variety of nineteenth-century lecturers. For Graham, see Stephen Nissenbaum, "Careful Love: Sylvester Graham and Victorian Sexual Theory" (Ph.D. diss., University of Wisconsin, 1968); and, for the Fowlers, see John Davies, *Phrenology: Science and Fad* (New York, 1962).

14. George Fredrickson, *The Inner Civil War* (New York, 1964), contains a superb discussion of the vocational crises of such young persons. See also Gordon Milne, *George William Curtis and the Genteel Tradition* (Bloomington, 1956); Tilden G. Edelstein, *Strange Enthusiasm: A Life of Thomas Wentworth Higginson* (New Haven, 1968); and Ralph L. Rusk, *The Life of Ralph Waldo Emerson* (New York, 1949).

15. Merle M. Hoover, *Park Benjamin: Poet and Editor* (New York, 1948); Richard Croom Beatty, *Bayard Taylor: Laureate of the Gilded Age* (Norman, 1936); Eleanor M. Tilton, *Amiable Aristocrat: A Biography of Oliver Wendell Holmes* (New York, 1947).

16. Margaret Rossiter, "Benjamin Silliman and the Lowell Institute: The Popularization of Science in Nineteenth Century America," *New England Quarterly* 44 (Dec. 1971): 602–26.

17. Wilson Smith, *Professors and Public Ethics: Studies of Northern Moral Philosophy before the Civil War* (Ithaca, 1956).

18. Scott, *Office to Profession*, pp. 112–33, 148–56. Greef, "Public Lectures in New York," pp. 4–27.

19. Frank Sanborn in *Exhibition and Commencement Performances* (1845–55) 15, no. 44, Harvard Archives, quoted in Haskell, *The Emergence of Professional Social Science*, p. 59.

20. See John Higham, *From Boundlessness to Consolidation: The Transformation of American Culture, 1848–1860* (Ann Arbor, 1969).

21. This fabric of reporting and publicity is analyzed more fully in Donald M. Scott, "Print and the Public Lecture System, 1840–1860," in *Print and Early American Society*, eds. William L. Joyce, David D. Hall, et al. (Worcester, The American Antiquarian Society, 1983), pp. 278–98.

22. Barbara Hinds, "The Lyceum Movement in Maine" (M.A. thesis, University of Maine, 1949), pp. 77–78. The typicality of this course is clear from the records of the Worcester Lyceum, Petersboro, Mass.; Lyceum, Marlborough, Mass.; Lyceum in the American Antiquarian Society, Northampton, Mass.; Young Men's Association, Forbes Library, Northampton, Mass.; and the Albany Young Men's Association, Albany Public Library. See also, Joseph Schick, *The Early Theatre in Eastern Iowa* (Chicago, 1939); Hubert Hoeltje, "Notes on the History of Lecturing in Iowa," *Iowa Journal of History and Politics* 25 (Jan. 1927): 62–131; Mary Louise Hamilton, "The Lyceum in New Orleans" (M.A. thesis, Louisiana State University, 1948); and Jeffry Newman, "The Detroit Young Men's Society," *Michigan History* 43 (June 1959): 197–211.

23. *Hampshire Gazette*, 17 Feb. 1852.

24. "Circular" for 12 Sept. 1856, Elias Nason Papers, American Antiquarian Society.

25. See, for example, the correspondence between secretaries of societies and between lecturers and societies in Park Benjamin Papers, Butler Library, Columbia University; the Elias Nason Papers, American Antiquarian Society; George William Curtis Papers, Rockefeller Library, Brown University; The Papers of the Worcester Lyceum, American Antiquarian Society; Papers of the Northampton Young Men's Institute, Forbes Library; and Papers of the Albany Young Men's Association, Albany Public Library.

26. Edward Everett Hale, *James Russell Lowell and His Friends* (Boston, 1899), p. 107.

27. Public discourse was believed to need protection less from honest error than from partisanship and charlatanism, situations in which a speaker distorted knowledge for partisan ends or dishonest purposes. On the problem of the confidence man see Neil Harris, *Humbug: The Art of P. T. Barnum* (Boston, 1973), pp. 207–31.

28. Hale, *James Russell Lowell*, p. 110. See Bledstein, *Culture of Professionalism*, pp. 80–129, for a much fuller discussion of these assumptions.

29. Park Benjamin to president or secretary of the New Bedford Lyceum, 18 Oct. 1850, Park Benjamin Papers, Butler Library, Columbia University.

30. Daniel Calhoun's *Professional Lives in America* (Cambridge, 1965) has a superb discussion of these assumptions. See also Scott, *Office to Profession*; and Gawalt, *The Promise of Power*.

31. This incident is described fully in David Mead, *Yankee Eloquence in the Middle West: The Ohio Lyceum, 1850–1870* (East Lansing, 1951), pp. 133–41. In "Rights of Intellect," *New York Tribune*, Nov. 1855, the matter was also discussed at length.

32. For a superb discussion of this aspect of a professional's efficacy, see Gerald L. Geison, "Science and Efficacy in the Historiography of the Professions: Informal Reflections on the Case of Medicine," paper delivered to the Davis Center for Historical Studies, Princeton University, 9 May 1980.

33. See Scott, *Office to Profession*, for a fuller discussion of the clergy's role as public guardian. Perry Miller, *The Life of the Mind in America: From the Revolution to the Civil War* (New York, 1965), discusses the law as a framework defining the American nation.

34. For the idea of an explosion of information and knowledge, see Neil Harris, *Land of Contrasts* (New York, 1970), pp. 1–30.

35. Parsons Cooke, *Moral Machinery Simplified* (Andover, Mass., 1839), p. 4. Has-

kell, *The Emergence of Professional Social Science,* has a superb discussion of the crisis of cultural authority occasioned by this confusion.

36. *Hampshire Gazette,* 17 Feb. 1852.

37. *Hampshire Gazette,* 22 Jan. 1856.

38. See Donald M. Scott, "The Popular Lecture and the Creation of a Public in Mid-Nineteenth Century America," *Journal of American History* 66 (Mar. 1980): 802–5.

39. See "Lectures and Lecturing"; "Lectures and Lecturers"; J. G. Holland, "The Popular Lecture," *Atlantic Monthly* 15 (Mar. 1865): 367; and Thomas Wentworth Higginson, "The American Lecture System," *MacMillan's Magazine* 18 (May 1868): 49.

40. "Dr. Boyton's Lectures," *Hampshire Gazette,* 19 Feb. 1856; Dr. Antisell, "Volcanos and Volcanic Forces," *New York Daily Tribune,* 21 Jan. 1853; H. F. Maury, "The Sea and the Circulation of its Waters," ibid., 13 Jan. 1853. On the "wonders" of science, see George H. Daniels, *American Science in the Age of Jackson* (New York, 1968), pp. 40–41.

41. Bayard Taylor, "The Philosophy of Travel," *Hampshire Gazette,* 25 Dec. 1855.

42. See, for example, Wendell Phillips, "The Lost Art of Egypt," in *Modern Eloquence,* Ashley Thorndike, ed. (New York, 1932), 8: 831–45; Edwin Percy Whipple, "Wit and Humor," in *Modern Eloquence,* pp. 1189–210.

43. Holland, "The Popular Lecture," p. 367.

44. "Places of Public Amusement," *Putnam's Monthly* 3 (Feb. 1854): 148–49.

45. "Editor's Easy Chair," *Harper's Monthly Magazine* 24 (Jan. 1862): 266.

46. Higginson, "American Lecture System," p. 49.

47. See Carl Bode, *The American Lyceum* (New York, 1956), for the emergence of the lecture bureaus.

48. There is a rich literature bearing upon the emergence of the modern academic professions. See especially, Haskell, *The Emergence of Professional Social Science;* Paul Buck, ed., *The Social Sciences at Harvard* (Cambridge, 1965); Mary Furner, *Advocacy and Objectivity* (Lexington, 1975); Laurence Veysey, *The Emergence of the American University* (Chicago, 1965); Charles Rosenberg, *No Other Gods* (Baltimore, 1976); Alexandra Oleson and John Voss, eds., *The Organization of Knowledge in Modern America, 1869–1920* (Baltimore, 1979).

Chapter 3

1. James M. Schmotter, "The Irony of Clerical Professionalism: New England's Congregational Ministers and the Great Awakening," *American Quarterly* 31 (Summer, 1979): 148–68; Harry S. Stout, "The Great Awakening in New England Reconsidered: The New England Clergy as a Case Study," *Journal of Social History* 8 (1974–75): 21–47; J. William T. Youngs, *God's Messengers: Religious Leadership in Colonial New England, 1700–1750* (Baltimore, 1976). See also Donald M. Scott, *From Office to Profession: The New England Ministry, 1750–1850* (Philadelphia, 1978).

2. They included the Presbyterian, Congregational, Dutch Reformed, and eventually the Anglican churches.

3. Jon Butler, *Power, Authority, and the Origins of American Denominational Order: The English Churches in the Delaware Valley, 1630–1730,* American Philosophical Society *Transactions,* 68, pt. 2 (Philadelphia, 1978), pp. 52–64; Guy S. Klett, *Presbyterians in Colonial Pennsylvania* (Philadelphia, 1937), chaps. 2 and 9.

4. Klett, *Presbyterians in Colonial Pennsylvania,* chaps. 4–6; Alfred Nevin, *Churches of the Valley* (Philadelphia, 1852), p. 82.

5. *The Paxton Papers,* ed. John R. Dunbar (The Hague, 1957), p. 249.

6. The elders from each congregation were members of the presbytery; what part they played in the proceedings is difficult to determine.

7. Manuscript Minutes of Donegal Presbytery, vols. 1 and 2, Presbyterian Historical Society, Philadelphia (hereafter PHS); Klett, *Presbyterians in Colonial Pennsylvania*, chaps. 6–9.

8. Donegal Presbytery Minutes, 19 July 1733, 1: 10, PHS.

9. Ibid., 16 Oct. 1734, 3 Apr. and 12 June 1735, 27 May 1736, 1: 49, 53, 65, 101–2, 125, 135.

10. Ibid., 1: 45–48.

11. Ibid., Sept. and Nov. 1735, 14 Apr. 1736, 1: 70–75, 87–88, 92, 104–7, 115. Orr sailed for England that same year and was ordained a priest of the Anglican church by the bishop of London. Early in 1737 he returned to Charleston, South Carolina, where he became assistant rector at thriving St. Philips Church; Frederick Dalcho, *An Historical Account of the Protestant Episcopal Church in South-Carolina* (Charleston, 1820), pp. 127–28, 355–56.

12. Leonard J. Trinterud, *The Forming of an American Tradition* (Philadelphia, 1949), pp. 73–74.

13. *Records of the Presbyterian Church in the United States of America, 1706–1788*, ed. William M. Engles (Philadelphia, 1904), pp. 92–93. The 1729 act, which included a number of loopholes for those with scruples against subscription, was gradually tightened between 1730 and 1736; Bryan F. LeBeau, "The Subscription Controversy and Jonathan Dickinson," *Journal of Presbyterian History* 54 (1976): 317–35 (hereafter *JPH*).

14. *Records of the Presbyterian Church*, pp. 139–40. Trinterud, *Forming of an American Tradition*, pp. 74–75.

15. Douglas Sloan, *The Scottish Enlightenment and the American College Ideal* (New York, 1971), p. 22. A number of universities, especially Leyden, had an influence on Scottish thought in these years (pp. 14–23).

16. *Records of the Presbyterian Church*, p. 51; Thomas C. Pears, Jr., and Guy S. Klett, "Documentary History of William Tennent, and The Log College," *JPH* 28 (1950): 37–64, 105, 128, 167–204.

17. Besides personally directing his sons' education, Tennent entertained "some hopes" in 1725 of being made rector of Yale College; Pears and Klett, "History of William Tennent," p. 57, quote James Logan on this point. There is no evidence that Yale ever approached Tennent with an offer.

18. Trinterud, *Forming of an American Tradition*, chap. 3; Pears and Klett, "History of William Tennent," pp. 121–23.

19. *Records of the Presbyterian Church*, pp. 141, 148, 187.

20. Gilbert Tennent, *Remarks Upon a Protestation Presented to the Synod of Philadelphia* (Philadelphia, 1741), p. 4; *An Examination and Refutation of Mr. Gilbert Tennent's Remarks . . . By Some of the Members of the Synod* (Philadelphia, 1742), pp. 12–13; *Records of the Presbyterian Church*, p. 188; Lawrence A. Cremin, *American Education: The Colonial Experience, 1607–1783* (New York, 1970), pp. 324–25.

21. Pears and Klett, "History of Tennent," pp. 195, 120–21.

22. That William Tennent was not bound by convention is suggested in the legend of the recruitment of one Log College student. Charles Beatty was fourteen when he emigrated with his widowed mother from Northern Ireland; when of age he became a traveling peddler. One day Beatty was passing through Neshaminy, and "stopping at the Log College, he amused himself by surprising Mr. Tennent and his pupils with a proffer, in Latin, of his merchandise. Mr. Tennent replied in Latin, and the conversation went on in the same language, with such evidence of scholarship, religious

knowledge and fervent piety, that Mr. Tennent urged him to sell what he had, and prepare for the ministry. This he consented to do." See Alfred Nevin, ed., *Encyclopedia of the Presbyterian Church* (Philadelphia, 1884), p. 61. Beatty was ordained in 1742 and had a successful career; Guy S. Klett, ed., *Journals of Charles Beatty, 1762–1769* (University Park, Pa., 1962).

23. Historians disagree on the number of matriculants. For biographical information see Archibald Alexander, ed., *Biographical Sketches of the Founder and Principal Alumni of the Log College* (Philadelphia, 1851); George H. Ingram's three articles, "The Story of the Log College," *Journal of Presbyterian History* 12 (1927): 487–511; "Biographies of the Alumni of the Log College," ibid. 13 (1928–29): 358–59; ibid. 14 (1930): 1–27; Richard Webster, *A History of the Presbyterian Church in America . . . until 1760 with Biographical Sketches of its Early Ministers* (Philadelphia, 1857).

24. For a list of the academies started by the revivalists, with at least six that were founded by Log College men, see Sloan, *Scottish Enlightenment*, pp. 281–84. Finley's curriculum included Latin and Greek classics, logic, arithmetic, geography, geometry, ontology, and natural philosophy. Ingram, "Story of Log College," p. 506; Klett, *Presbyterians in Colonial Pennsylvania*, p. 207.

25. This does not mean that the College of New Jersey was an outgrowth of the Log College, however, since other institutions were equally active in supplying its leadership. Jonathan Dickinson and Aaron Burr, first and second presidents of the college, were Yale men and leaders of the academy movement in New Jersey. Thomas Jefferson Wertenbaker, *Princeton, 1746–1896* (Princeton, 1946), pp. 23–24, 27.

26. Trinterud, *Forming of an American Tradition*, pp. 74, 82, 143.

27. *Whitefield's Journals*, ed. William Wale (London, 1905), p. 351.

28. Gilbert Tennent, *The Danger of an Unconverted Ministry, Considered in a Sermon on Mark VI.34* (Philadelphia, 1740), in Alan Heimert and Perry Miller, eds., *The Great Awakening: Documents Illustrating the Crisis and Its Consequences* (New York, 1967), pp. 73–75.

Here Tennent sounds like the pietistic sectaries of Pennsylvania who criticized the church clergy for insisting on fixed salaries, insinuating that they looked upon the ministry as an office rather than a calling; see William J. Hinke, ed., *Life and Letters of the Rev. John Philip Boehm . . . 1683–1749* (Philadelphia, 1916), p. 162. An illuminating discussion of how the salary issue affected New England Congregationalism is in Stephen Botein, "Income and Ideology: Harvard-Trained Clergymen in Eighteenth-Century New England," *Eighteenth-Century Studies* 13 (Summer 1980): 396–413.

29. Tennent, *Danger of an Unconverted Ministry*, in Heimert and Miller, eds., *Great Awakening*, pp. 76–78, 86.

30. Ibid., pp. 84–90, 95–97.

31. Benjamin Franklin first published the sermon in Philadelphia in 1740, with a reprint appearing that same year; a second Philadelphia edition was published in 1741. The first Boston edition appeared in 1742 and was reprinted later that year. Christopher Sauer published a German edition in 1740. Charles Evans, *American Bibliography: A Chronological Dictionary of All Books, Pamphlets and Periodical Publications Printed in the United States . . . 1639–1800* (Chicago, 1903–59), vol. 2.

32. The synod repealed the rule that ministers were never to preach outside of their own presbyteries on the ground that the original language was insufficiently flexible, though what exceptions would be allowed was not specified. The synod further confirmed that presbyteries were the main licensing bodies, but it continued to assert that no minister could join the synod until his educational credentials had been approved by that organization. *Records of the Presbyterian Church*, pp. 151–52.

33. *Records of the Presbyterian Church*, pp. 155–58; Samuel Finley, *Christ Tri-*

umphing, and Satan Raging (1741), in Heimert and Miller, eds., *Great Awakening*, pp. 162–63, and Tennent, *Remarks Upon a Protestation*, p. 24.

34. But see note 39.

35. The Old Side ministers of the Philadelphia Synod included Francis Alison (1705–79), Adam Boyd (1692–1768), Robert Cathcart (?–1754), Samuel Caven (1701–50), John Craig (1710–74), Robert Cross (1689–1766), John Elder (1706–92), Robert Jamison (16??–1744), James Martin (16??–1743), Richard Zankey (1700?–1790), John Thomson (1690–1753), Samuel Thomson (1694?–1787).

36. Trinterud, *Forming of an American Tradition*, pp. 72–73. Samuel Caven may have been as old as thirty-six when he arrived in the colonies.

Of the twelve, Alison and Elder were educated at Edinburgh; Boyd, Cross, Martin, John Thomson, and possibly John Craig were educated at Glasgow. The others cannot definitely be traced through university registers, but as none attended Harvard or Yale, all were presumably educated abroad. Charles A. Briggs, *American Presbyterianism, Its Origin and Early History* (Edinburgh, 1885); Nevin, ed., *Encyclopedia*; Webster, *History of the Presbyterian Church*; William B. Sprague, *Annals of the American Pulpit* (New York, 1857–69), vols. 3 and 4.

37. New Side ministers of the New York Synod included Charles Beatty (1715–72), John Blair (1720–71), Samuel Blair (1712–51), Aaron Burr (1716–57), Eliab Byram (1718–54), Jonathan Dickinson (1688–1747), Samuel Finley (1715–66), Azariah Horton (1715–77), Simon Horton (1711–86), Timothy Jones (1717–94), Joseph Lamb (1690?–1749), James McCrea (1711–69), Charles McKnight (1720–78), Ebenezer Pemberton (1705–77), John Pierson (1689–1770), William Robinson (1700?–1746), Robert Sturgeon (?–1750), Charles Tennent (1711–71), Gilbert Tennent (1703–64), William Tennent, Jr. (1705–71), Richard Treat (1708–78), David Youngs (1719–52).

38. Besides the biographical sources cited above, information was drawn from Franklin Bowditch Dexter, *Biographical Sketches of the Graduates of Yale College, with Annals of the College History, October 1701–May 1745* (New York, 1885–1912), and Clifford K. Shipton, *Biographical Sketches of Those Who Attended Harvard College [Sibley's Harvard Graduates]* (Boston, 1873–).

39. Still, a more flexible approach to church government and presbyterial authority might have been forthcoming from the Philadelphia Synod had the Ulster side of its "Scotch-Irish" character outweighed the Scottish side before the split of 1741. The Irish practice of allowing each presbytery to set its own rules regarding creeds, ordination, and such had been followed in early eighteenth-century Pennsylvania. But as the struggle for power against the New Sides intensified in the early 1740s, the more orthodox members of the Old Side staked out and defended increasingly conservative positions. These were not always approved by the Irish members and probably would have been softened had not the competition and emotionalism of the times forced the Old Sides to close ranks. Elizabeth I. Nybakken, "New Light on the Old Side: Irish Influences on Colonial Presbyterianism," *Journal of American History* 68 (1982): 813–32; Klett, *Presbyterians in Colonial Pennsylvania*, chap. 8.

40. Klett, *Presbyterians in Colonial Pennsylvania*, p. 232.

41. Some conservative clergymen had urged in 1738 that the synod "fill our infant church with men eminent for parts and learning," thereby advancing its "honour ... both at home and among our neighbors, who conceive a low opinion of us for want of such favourable opportunities." *Records of the Presbyterian Church*, p. 139.

42. Tennent, *Danger of an Unconverted Ministry*, in Heimert and Miller, eds., *Great Awakening*, p. 78; Tennent, *Remarks Upon a Protestation*, p. 22.

43. Richard Warch, *School of Prophets: Yale College, 1701–1740* (New Haven, Conn., 1973), pp. 169–85.

44. Both groups came largely from middle-class circumstances; their fathers were ministers, magistrates, military officers, tradesmen, and merchants (see bibliographical sources above).

45. *A short reply to Mr. Whitefield's letter* . . . (Philadelphia, 1741) in Heimert and Miller, eds., *Great Awakening*, p. 144; Finley, *Christ Triumphing*, in ibid., pp. 157, 163, 161.

46. Ibid., p. 166. According to Tennent, "Opposition is an encouraging Sign. Let all the Followers of the Lamb stand up and act for GOD against all Opposers: Who is upon GOD's Side? who?" *Danger of an Unconverted Ministry*, in Heimert and Miller, eds., *Great Awakening*, p. 86.

47. *Records of the Presbyterian Church*, p. 156; Donegal Presbytery Minutes, 1:258, 253, PHS. I have relied heavily on the Donegal Minutes because they are the most detailed of any presbytery, but patterns similar to those discussed here can be found in "The Records of the Presbytery of New Castle upon Delaware," *JPH* 14 (1930): 289–308, 377–84, and *JPH* 15 (1932–33): 73–120, 159–68, 174–207, and in the Presbytery of Philadelphia Minutes in *Records of the Presbyterian Church*.

The battery of charges against ministers recorded in the Donegal Minutes has led one Presbyterian scholar to conclude that the Old Sides were "morally and personally . . . the worst of the synod's clergy" (Trinterud, *Forming of an American Tradition*, p. 165). This may have been true in an isolated case or two, but much of the "evidence" of wrongdoing was either proved false or is deeply suspect owing to its connection with Presbyterian factionalism.

48. Donegal Presbytery Minutes, 1: 206–10. Craighead later became a Cameronian Covenanter; he removed to Virginia in 1749, where he served a number of congregations until his death in 1766. Webster, *History of the Presbyterian Church*, pp. 434–37.

49. Donegal Presbytery Minutes, vol. 1, entries for April and May and p. 231. John Thomson, *The Government of the Church of Christ*, and Samuel Finley, *Christ Triumphing*, both in Heimert and Miller, eds., *Great Awakening*, pp. 110–26, 152–67.

50. Donegal Presbytery Minutes, 1: 273.

51. The adjustments in professional behavior and values made by Presbyterian clergymen in the post-Awakening years in order "to negotiate and maintain their special position," provides an early example of a phenomenon marked by Magali Sarfatti Larson in *The Rise of Professionalism: A Sociological Analysis* (Berkeley, 1977), quotation on p. xii.

52. Daniel Calhoun argues that small provincial communities often saw their minister as a champion of local interests; *The Intelligence of a People* (Princeton, 1973), p. 40. This idea is expanded upon by J. William T. Youngs in *God's Messengers*, who suggests that a major source of the minister's legitimacy in the post-Awakening years was his communal leadership (pp. 136ff).

53. Steel to the governor, Cumberland, 21 April 1756, *Pennsylvania Archives*, Ser. I, 2:623.

54. The Reverend Hugh Neill to the secretary, Oxford, 18 Oct. 1764, in William S. Perry, ed., *Historical Collections Relating to the American Colonial Church* (Hartford, Conn., 1878), 2:365; Klett, *Presbyterians in Colonial Pennsylvania*, chap. 13; Dietmar Rothermund, *The Layman's Progress: Religious and Political Experience in Colonial Pennsylvania, 1740–1770* (Philadelphia, 1961).

55. That rivalries continued behind the façade of unity was perhaps inevitable; Trinterud, *Forming of an American Tradition*; Nybakken, "New Light on the Old Side."

56. *Records of the Presbyterian Church*.

57. *Boston Weekly News-Letter*, 1 July 1742.

58. Tennent's letter to Jonathan Dickinson, dated 12 Feb. 1742, appeared in the *Boston Evening Post*, 26 July 1742, and was later republished in the Philadelphia papers. See also Gilbert Tennent, *The Necessity of Holding Fast the Truth* (Boston, 1743); and Milton J. Coalter, Jr., "The Radical Pietism of Count Nicholas Zinzendorf as a Conservative Influence on the Awakener, Gilbert Tennent," *Church History* 49 (1980): 35–46.

59. Samuel Finley, *Satan Strip'd of His Angelick Robe* (Philadelphia, 1743); Trinterud, *Forming of an American Tradition*, p. 133. Three moderate clergymen—Dickinson, Pemberton, and Pierson—initially held a middle position from which they tried to mediate between the two factions, but by 1746 the Philadelphia Synod claimed that the three had become "warm advocates" of the New Sides. *Records of the Presbyterian Church*, pp. 186–89.

60. Even the appointment of John Witherspoon as president of the college in 1768 did not resolve the problem; see Nybakken, "New Light on the Old Side," pp. 828–31.

61. *Records of the Presbyterian Church*, pp. 245, 205–6, 286–88.

62. Ibid., pp. 248–49, 254; Trinterud, *Forming of an American Tradition*, pp. 131, 205–6.

63. *Records of the Presbyterian Church*, pp. 274–75.

64. Samuel Finley, *The Approved Minister of God* (Philadelphia, 1749), pp. 5–6.

65. Edwin S. Gaustad, *Historical Atlas of Religion in America* (New York, rev. ed., 1976), p. 52. The Presbyterians surpassed the Congregationalists in 1825 to become the third largest denomination, but they lagged well behind the Methodists and the Baptists.

66. The Reverend Jacob Green to the Reverend Joseph Bellamy, Hanover, 22 Nov. 1775, Bellamy Papers (transcripts), I, Presbyterian Historical Society. Green himself was a Harvard graduate; see *Sibley's Harvard Graduates*, 11:405–14.

67. Finley, *Approved Minister*, pp. 5, 20.

Chapter 4

1. The major interpretive overview of the subject is Jerold S. Auerbach, *Unequal Justice: Lawyers and Social Change in Modern America* (New York, 1976), which barely mentions the judiciary. The term "professionalization," as used here, refers particularly to the 1900–1950 period.

2. A few exceptions will be noted below. The two genres that have dominated the secondary literature are studies of constitutional thought and judicial biography. Beginning with Jack W. Peltason, *Federal Courts in the Political Process* (New York, 1955), political scientists have explored the interaction of politics and professionalism in judicial recruitment and related areas, but there has been little such work done by historians.

3. See, for instance, Everett C. Hughes, "Professions," in *The Professions in America*, ed. Kenneth S. Lynn (Boston, 1965), pp. 2–3, on the importance of this "claim." In general the recent literature on American professionalism has stressed educational institutions, perhaps partly because it has been produced by professional academics; see Burton J. Bledstein, *The Culture of Professionalism: The Middle Class and the Development of Higher Education in America* (New York, 1976), for indications that this literature reflects concerns within the occupational environment of its authors.

4. Albert P. Blaustein and Charles O. Porter, *The American Lawyer: A Summary of the Survey of the Legal Profession* (Chicago, 1954), p. 8 and chap. 6; Robert Stevens,

"Two Cheers for 1870: The American Law School," *Perspectives in American History* 5 (1971): 493–511.

5. Blaustein and Porter, *American Lawyer*, chap. 5; Henry S. Drinker, *Legal Ethics* (New York, 1953), p. 310; Joel B. Grossman, *Lawyers and Judges: The ABA and the Politics of Judicial Selection* (New York, 1965), chap. 3.

6. Drinker, *Legal Ethics*, p. 309.

7. See, for example, Bernard Barber, "Some Problems in the Sociology of the Professions," in *Professions in America*, p. 18. The premise of what follows is that the "claim" of lawyers to be oriented toward the public good has been as important a part of their professional ideology as their "claim" to "esoteric knowledge." Successful assertion of both "claims" has produced such results as higher status and greater "market control." The usefulness of a quasi-literary approach to professional language is suggested by the general argument of Clifford Geertz, *The Interpretation of Cultures* (New York, 1973), pp. 193–233.

8. These and other strikingly apt terms of analysis may be drawn from Antonio Gramsci, *Selections from the Prison Notebooks*, eds. Quintin Hoare and Geoffrey N. Smith (New York, 1971), pp. 5–14. Obviously, modern American lawyers qualify for inclusion among Gramsci's "organic" intellectuals ("organisers" of a "new legal system" for the "capitalist entrepreneur"); at the same time, it may be argued that they have cultivated the appearance of Gramsci's "ecclesiastics." From what follows, however, it should be evident that the motivations of particular individuals at different times have been various and complex.

9. See Vernon K. Dibble, "Occupations and Ideologies," *American Journal of Sociology* 68 (1962–63): 229–31; Magali Sarfatti Larson, *The Rise of Professionalism: A Sociological Analysis* (Berkeley, 1977), pp. 166–69. The symbolic significance of judgeship has been noted most succinctly by David Riesman, *Individualism Reconsidered and Other Essays* (Glencoe, Ill., 1954), pp. 441–42.

10. Henry A. Boardman, *The Federal Judiciary: A Thanksgiving Discourse* (Philadelphia, 1862), pp. 6, 51–52, 28, 35–36, 10, 26–27, 47. Dr. Boardman's attitudes are further revealed in an earlier discourse, *The Importance of Religion to the Legal Profession . . .* (Philadelphia, 1849).

11. Daniel Duman, "The English Bar in the Georgian Era," in *Lawyers in Early Modern Europe and America*, ed. Wilfrid Prest (London, 1981), pp. 98–99; Robert Robson, *The Attorney in Eighteenth-Century England* (Cambridge, 1959), pp. 18–19; Brian Abel-Smith and Robert Stevens, *Lawyers and the Courts: A Sociological Study of the English Legal System, 1750–1965* (Cambridge, Mass., 1967), p. 38, and see also pp. 34–35, 44–45.

12. See, generally, John M. Murrin, "The Legal Transformation: The Bench and Bar of Eighteenth-Century Massachusetts," in *Colonial America: Essays in Politics and Social Development*, ed. Stanley N. Katz (Boston, 1971), pp. 415–49; Milton M. Klein, "The Rise of the New York Bar: The Legal Career of William Livingston," in *Essays in the History of Early American Law*, ed. David H. Flaherty (Chapel Hill, 1969), pp. 392–417; A. G. Roeber, *Faithful Magistrates and Republican Lawyers: Creators of Virginia Legal Culture, 1680–1810* (Chapel Hill, 1981); Joseph H. Smith, "Administrative Control of the Courts of the American Plantations," in *Essays in the History of Early American Law*, pp. 281–335. In the first few decades of the eighteenth century, at least in Massachusetts, the situation was reversed; provincial judges acted to upgrade the caliber of the bar.

13. Richard E. Ellis, *The Jeffersonian Crisis: Courts and Politics in the Young Republic* (New York, 1971), part 1; Kermit L. Hall, *The Politics of Justice: Lower Federal Judicial Selection and the Second Party System, 1829–61* (Lincoln, Neb., 1979).

14. Ellis, *Jeffersonian Crisis*, part 2; Alexis de Tocqueville, *Democracy in America*, ed. Phillips Bradley (New York, 1945), 1:279; Francis R. Aumann, *The Changing American Legal System: Some Selected Phases* (Columbus, Ohio, 1940), pp. 184–89. On the other hand, Tocqueville's comments on judicial influence over juries are worth noting, *Democracy*, 1:280–87; and see William E. Nelson, *Americanization of the Common Law: The Impact of Legal Change on Massachusetts Society, 1760–1830* (Cambridge, Mass., 1975), chap. 9.

15. Maxwell Bloomfield, *American Lawyers in a Changing Society, 1776–1876* (Cambridge, Mass., 1976), pp. 139–42; Aumann, *Changing American Legal System*, pp. 141–49. The judicial record here bears on the issue mentioned in note 68 below.

16. Gary B. Nash, "The Philadelphia Bench and Bar, 1800–61," *Comparative Studies in Society and History* 7 (1964–65): 219. The significance of formally "unspecialized" practice in America is stressed by Daniel J. Boorstin, *The Americans: The Colonial Experience* (New York, 1958), chap. 32.

17. Perry Miller, ed., *The Legal Mind in America: From Independence to the Civil War* (Garden City, N.Y., 1962), pp. 252–53. This is the best collection of professional oratory from the antebellum period; more of same may be found in Charles M. Haar, ed., *The Golden Age of American Law* (New York, 1965).

18. *Legal Mind in America*, p. 87 (1823 lecture by David Hoffman).

19. Ellis, *Jeffersonian Crisis*, chap. 8; and see, generally, Robson, *Attorney in Eighteenth-Century England*, for evidence of how inferior practitioners in the formally ranked English system readily became scapegoats for the sins of the profession.

20. *Eakin v. Raub* (Pennsylvania Reports, 1825); and see Charles Grove Haines, *The American Doctrine of Judicial Supremacy* (Berkeley, 1932), chaps. 10–11; Aumann, *Changing American Legal System*, pp. 189–94.

21. *Legal Mind in America*, p. 71 (1821 address to the Suffolk Bar).

22. So said Story, for example, ibid., p. 180 (1829 Harvard inaugural lecture); so said everyone. This metaphorical tradition was well established in the sermon literature of the Revolution; see, generally, Alice M. Baldwin, *The New England Clergy and the American Revolution* (Durham, N.C., 1928).

23. Murrin, "Legal Transformation," pp. 427, 430–31, 433–34. The religious background of law in nineteenth-century New England is noted by Gerard W. Gawalt, *The Promise of Power: The Emergence of the Legal Profession in Massachusetts, 1760–1840* (Westport, Conn., 1979), p. 118, and see Daniel J. Boorstin, *The Americans: The National Experience* (New York, 1965), pp. 35–42.

24. Ellis, *Jeffersonian Crisis*, p. 193; John D. Cushing, "The Judiciary and Public Opinion in Revolutionary Massachusetts," in *Law and Authority in Colonial America*, ed. George Athan Billias (Barre, Mass., 1965), pp. 168–86.

25. Aumann, *Changing American Legal System*, pp. 167–71; Ellis, *Jeffersonian Crisis*, pp. 216–18. See, too, Stephen Botein, "Income and Ideology: Harvard-Trained Clergymen in the Eighteenth Century," *Eighteenth-Century Studies* 13 (1979–80): 396–413; Daniel H. Calhoun, *Professional Lives in America: Structure and Aspiration, 1750–1850* (Cambridge, Mass., 1965), chap. 4.

26. Frederic Hathaway Chase, *Lemuel Shaw: Chief Justice of the Supreme Judicial Court of Massachusetts, 1830–1860* (Boston, 1918), p. 10.

27. The business orientation of Shaw and other nineteenth-century jurists is evident from general consultation of Leonard W. Levy, *The Law of the Commonwealth and Chief Justice Shaw* (Cambridge, Mass., 1957); Lawrence M. Friedman, *A History of American Law* (New York, 1973); Morton J. Horwitz, *The Transformation of American Law, 1780–1860* (Cambridge, Mass., 1977).

28. *Legal Mind in America*, p. 180 (1829 Harvard inaugural lecture).
29. John Shaw, *Holding Forth the Word of Life* . . . (Boston, 1761), pp. 25–26.
30. Joseph G. Baldwin, "The Career of Judge Field . . . ," in *Personal Reminiscences of Early Days in California, with Other Sketches*, ed. Stephen J. Field (n.p., 1893), pp. 139–40; Carl Brent Swisher, *Stephen J. Field: Craftsman of the Law* (Washington, 1930), pp. 95–98.
31. Perry Miller, *The Life of the Mind in America: From the Revolution to the Civil War* (New York, 1965), pp. 109, 104–6; this would be the definitive study of antebellum professional ideology in law if Miller had not obscured his analysis by using such literary categories as nature and artifice, heart and head.
32. George Martin, *Causes and Conflicts: The Centennial History of the Association of the Bar of the City of New York, 1870–1970* (Boston, 1970), p. 58; and see, generally, Benjamin R. Twiss, *Lawyers and the Constitution: How Laissez Faire Came to the Supreme Court* (Princeton, N.J., 1942).
33. James Willard Hurst, *The Growth of American Law: The Law Makers* (Boston, 1950), pp. 297–98.
34. Recent literature on the modern American legal profession recognizes this development quite clearly but tends to neglect many of the topics that occupied leaders of the organized bar; the state of the judiciary and related problems were the stuff of bar association meetings in the first half of the twentieth century. In what follows, the underlying "conservatism" of the organized bar is taken for granted; what needs emphasis is how bar leaders tried to demonstrate orientation to the "community interest" through "reformist" activity. For recent work suggesting the value of such an approach, see John Austin Matzko, "The Best Men of the Bar: The Founding of the American Bar Association," *Essays in History* 21 (1977): 7–28; Wayne K. Hobson, "Professionals, Progressives and Bureaucratization: A Reassessment," *The Historian* 39 (1976–77): 639–58. Arnold M. Paul, *Conservative Crisis and the Rule of Law: Attitudes of Bar and Bench, 1887–1895* (Ithaca, 1960), identifies a period of political reaction beginning in 1892, but much of the atmosphere described in his study had lifted by the early Progressive years.
35. *Chicago Legal News* 44 (1912): 274. A good detailed account of professional response to this issue is available in Barbara C. Steidle, "Conservative Progressives: A Study of the Attitudes and Role of Bar and Bench, 1905–1912" (Ph.D. dissertation, Rutgers University, 1969), chap. 8.
36. On the importance of the new "national scheme" in professional organization as old "island communities" in America disappeared, see Robert H. Wiebe, *The Search for Order, 1877–1920* (New York, 1967), chap. 5.
37. See Auerbach, *Unequal Justice*, chaps. 1–4, where the overriding concern with ethnicity sometimes diverts attention from the significance of the widening gap between corporate and solo practice.
38. *Case and Comment* 18 (1911): 296–97; George E. Mowry, *The California Progressives* (Berkeley, 1951), pp. 140–42; *Current Literature* 51 (1911): 240–45.
39. American Bar Association *Reports* 34 (1911): 544–76, 51, 61. (Hereafter ABA *Reports*).
40. See, generally, M. Louise Rutherford, *The Influence of the American Bar Association on Public Opinion and Legislation* (Philadelphia, 1937), pp. 142–53.
41. Rome Brown, "The Judicial Recall—A Fallacy Repugnant to Constitutional Government," *Annals of the American Academy of Political and Social Science* 43 (1912): 275; ABA *Reports* 35 (1912): 575; ABA *Reports* 36 (1913): 61–65, 581–83.
42. ABA *Reports* 37 (1914): 380–81, 37–40.

43. ABA *Reports* 38 (1915): 34. In the end, California but not Colorado and Nevada eliminated recall of judges; North Dakota later adopted it.

44. James Grafton Rogers, *American Bar Leaders: Biographies of the Presidents of the American Bar Association, 1878–1928* (Chicago, 1932), p. 124.

45. Hurst, *Growth of American Law*, pp. 122–23; *Case and Comment* 18 (1911): 296–97; Rome Brown, "The Judiciary as the Servant of the People," pp. 14–16, in *Addresses, Discussions, Etc.* (Minneapolis, 1917). (The last item is a two-volume collection of Brown's and related writings, privately produced without continuous pagination; the copy in Widener Library, Harvard University, includes miscellaneous press clippings and the like.) Speaking before the Tennessee State Bar Association in June 1913, Brown was hard pressed to cite examples of judicial recall in practice.

46. *Case and Comment* 18 (1911): 312–13; *Ohio Law Bulletin* 56 (1911): 320. For guidance through the entire body of such opinion, see ABA *Reports* 35 (1912): 585–89; ABA *Reports* 36 (1913): 593–604.

47. See, generally, the various reports of the Committee to Oppose the Judicial Recall in the annual ABA *Reports* from 1912 (vol. 35) through 1919 (vol. 42). Several congressmen helped circulate committee literature as government documents, and a few private citizens contributed to the cause.

48. According to the *Nation* 94 (1912): 227, there was very "little sign" that judicial recall was "regarded with approval by any considerable part of the American people." Theodore Roosevelt proposed a system allowing for recall of judicial *decisions* but was usually careful to distinguish the idea from recall of judges; see Stephen Stagner, "The Recall of Judicial Decisions and the Due Process Debate," *American Journal of Legal History* 24 (1980): 257–72.

49. *Case and Comment* 22 (1916): 256–57; other biographical information is included in Brown, *Addresses*, as described in note 45 above. On Brown's reputation in his home state, see *The Papers of Walter Clark*, eds. Aubrey Lee Brooks and Hugh Talmage Lefler (Chapel Hill, 1950), 2:246–51, 259. The unflattering report here had been provoked by an incident in North Carolina that is described below.

50. Brown, "The Socialist Menace to Constitutional Government" (Louisiana State Bar Association, 1917), p. 19, in *Addresses*; *New Republic* 2 (1915): 215–16. Opposing Brown, in the Oregon minimum-wage case before the Supreme Court, was Louis Brandeis.

51. Brown, "Judiciary as the Servant of the People," pp. 12–13; Rome Brown, "Recall of Judges" (Minnesota State Bar Association, 1911), pp. 6–9, in *Addresses*; Rome Brown, "The Recall of Constitutional Safeguards," p. 11, in *Addresses*; ABA *Reports* 36 (1913): 581.

52. See, generally, Aubrey Brooks, *Walter Clark, Fighting Judge* (Chapel Hill, 1944), especially pp. 204, 250. Clark's most startling statement on the American judicial system had come in January 1914, in a speech at New York's Cooper Union. William Howard Taft would say of Clark, jestingly, that he could not be trusted with the constitution overnight.

53. Brown, "Muckraking the Constitution," pp. 6, 14, 16, in *Addresses*; Brooks, *Walter Clark*, pp. 192–93; Brown, "The Dilemma of the Judicial Recall Advocate" (Missouri State Bar Association, 1914), pp. 18–22, in *Addresses*; and see note 49 above. In fact, Clark had never endorsed judicial recall, but Brown assumed otherwise.

54. Edson R. Sunderland, *History of the American Bar Association and Its Work* (n.p., 1953), p. 97; Hurst, *Growth of American Law*, pp. 287–89, notes that other bar associations in the country were trying to expand at this time. Taft's tribute, made in June 1921, is cited in biographical reprint material attached to Brown, *Addresses*, as described in note 45 above.

55. Hurst, *Growth of American Law*, pp. 360–62, makes clear that the organized bar of this period relied on amateur enthusiasm to make an impact in the public arena. Wiebe, *Search for Order*, pp. 111–17, points out that national organization in law was "looser" than that in medicine; in 1920, for example, the American Medical Association accounted for 60 percent of the nation's doctors.

56. ABA *Reports* 36 (1913): 61; ABA *Reports* 37 (1914): 38. The assumption here is that Brown's committee did affect discourse simply by arranging for speakers—usually Brown himself—to address meetings. Apart from its mailings of anti-recall literature, the only other committee activity to reach the lay public was its assistance to student debaters; see ABA *Reports* 36 (1913): 580–81.

57. Brown, "Judicial Recall," p. 275; Stagner, "Recall of Judicial Decisions," pp. 265–66; *Ohio Law Bulletin* 57 (1912): 200. Roosevelt's proposal for recall of decisions did attract limited support within the profession.

58. ABA *Reports* 42 (1919): 344–45; Hurst, *Growth of American Law*, p. 289.

59. ABA *Reports* 42 (1919): 65–70.

60. Hurst, *Growth of American Law*, pp. 342–52; William B. Hornblower, the New Yorker on Brown's committee, was even more of a business lawyer than his chairman. On "reformers" in law, there is illustrative material in Richard Hofstadter, *The Age of Reform* (New York, 1955), pp. 156–64.

61. ABA *Reports* 33 (1910): 425, 430; Wilson gave the ABA's annual address that year. ABA *Reports* 35 (1912): 285, 287. Gregory practiced what he preached; see Rogers, *American Bar Leaders*, pp. 165–69.

62. ABA *Reports* 35 (1912): 415; ABA *Reports* 36 (1913): 934–35 (speech to the Association of American Law Schools). Taft added that "circumstances" had driven lawyers into an apparently unprogressive position.

63. *Minneapolis Tribune*, 21 Feb. 1913 (clipping in Brown, *Addresses*, as described in note 45 above). *Lawyer and Banker* 4 (1911): 278, compared judicial recall to "assassination."

64. ABA *Reports* 34 (1911): 231–32, 236–44; Rogers, *American Bar Leaders*, pp. 161–64.

65. Ibid., pp. 170–75, and see Kellogg's annual address in ABA *Reports* 35 (1912): 341–70; Brown, "Recall of Constitutional Safeguards," p. 17.

66. William Howard Taft, *Popular Government: Its Essence, Its Permanence and Its Perils* (New Haven, Conn., 1913), pp. 182–83; *Ohio Law Bulletin* 57 (1912): 329.

67. See ABA *Reports* 29 (1906): 395–417, for Pound's controversial speech, "The Causes of Popular Dissatisfaction with the Administration of Justice"; Hurst, *Growth of American Law*, p. 362. For all the furor that he provoked, Pound had little to say that was inconsistent with the views of a Taft or Kellogg; the controversy may have resulted mainly from the novelty of his youthful academic style.

68. ABA *Reports* 36 (1913): 420, 427; and see Hurst, *Growth of American Law*, pp. 138–46. Taft's premises here were—and remain—empirically unverified. In its very origins, however, the bar association movement was committed to depoliticization of the bench. For an early statement of orthodoxy, drawing on crime statistics to make its point, see D. B. Eaton, *Should Judges Be Elected? Or the Experiment of an Elective Judiciary in New-York* (New York, 1873), especially pp. 74–85.

69. ABA *Reports* 35 (1912): 422–28 (speech of Frederick N. Judson). It was not only that judges had to be more interventionist in the courtroom (instead of acting merely as "umpires"); they also had to be free to formulate their own rules without heavy-handed legislative interference.

70. See, for example, Roscoe Pound, "Courts and Legislation," *American Political Science Review* 7 (1913): 363–68. Similar political ambiguity among academic law-

yers during the next decade is noted in Steven F. Lawson, "Progressives and the Supreme Court: A Case for Judicial Reform in the 1920s," *The Historian* 42 (1979–80): 427-28.

71. ABA *Reports* 42 (1919): 336-37; and see ABA *Reports* 29 (1906): 408-9, where Pound noted that judicial inefficiency made businessmen reluctant to use the courts.

72. *Case and Comment* 18 (1911): 296-97.

73. ABA *Reports* 35 (1912): 394.

74. Ibid., p. 411.

75. ABA *Reports* 34 (1911): 53.

76. Ibid., p. 232; Brown, "Judicial Recall," p. 274.

77. Henry Pringle, *The Life and Times of William Howard Taft: A Biography* (New York, 1939), 1:531; Alpheus Thomas Mason, *Brandeis: A Free Man's Life* (New York, 1946), pp. 489-90; Daniel S. McHargue, "President Taft's Appointments to the Supreme Court," *Journal of Politics* 12 (1950): 478-510. The controversy over Brandeis's nomination revealed the limits of cautious reformism in the organized bar. Seven former ABA presidents spoke out against him. The motives of some opponents were obviously unstated; one criticism of his ethics was that he was too "judicial" a lawyer.

78. See Joseph Alsop and Turner Catledge, *The 168 Days* (Garden City, N.Y., 1938). The best short account is by William E. Leuchtenburg, *Franklin D. Roosevelt and the New Deal, 1932-1940* (New York, 1963), pp. 231-38; his definitive full-length treatment has yet to appear as this essay goes to press.

79. ABA *Journal* 23 (1937): 236, 233.

80. Ibid., pp. 354, 316-17.

81. Sunderland, *History of the American Bar Association*, pp. 221-23, 173-82.

82. ABA *Journal* 23 (1937): 271, 335.

83. Ibid., pp. 318, 323, 335; and see Auerbach, *Unequal Justice*, pp. 195-96.

84. ABA *Journal* 23 (1937): 355, 364.

85. See Auerbach, *Unequal Justice*, pp. 193-95.

86. Hurst, *Growth of American Law*, pp. 289-90.

87. Auerbach, *Unequal Justice*, pp. 198-200; *National Lawyers Guild Quarterly* 1 (1937-38): 83, 1.

88. G. Edward White, "From Sociological Jurisprudence to Realism: Jurisprudence and Social Change in Early Twentieth-Century America," *Virginia Law Review* 58 (1972): 999-1028; Charles Evans Hughes, *The Supreme Court of the United States: Its Foundation, Methods and Achievements* (New York, 1928), pp. 45-46; David J. Danelski and Joseph S. Tulchin, eds., *The Autobiographical Notes of Charles Evans Hughes* (Cambridge, Mass., 1973), p. xxviii.

89. Harlan B. Phillips, ed., *Felix Frankfurter Reminisces* (New York, 1960), pp. 244-46. Supposedly, Frankfurter told FDR that the Supreme Court appointment would just "have to take care of itself," if ever the opportunity arose; presumably, FDR feared a replay of the Brandeis affair.

90. ABA *Journal* 23 (1937): 315.

91. Ibid., pp. 339, 384-85.

92. Ibid., p. 342.

93. Frank Cantwell, "Public Opinion and the Legislative Process," *American Political Science Review* 40 (1946): 924-35. Events in late March were unfavorable to FDR's cause—for example, the intervention of Chief Justice Hughes in the controversy and the seeming change-of-heart by Justice Roberts in the Court's decision upholding Washington's minimum-wage law. The timing of the ABA poll was such that only nonmembers could have been influenced by these developments.

94. ABA *Journal* 23 (1937): 278, 384–85; *America at the Polls: A Handbook of American Presidential Election Statistics, 1920–1964* (Pittsburgh, 1965), pp. 9–10. Particularly striking was the response of nonmembers from Mississippi, who divided on the question almost evenly.

95. In 1949, as the ABA prepared for major expansion in the next decade, its constitution was amended to omit the words of 1936 promising coordination of professional activity "on a representative basis"; Sunderland, *History of the American Bar Association*, pp. 173–74.

96. William O. Douglas, *Go East, Young Man: The Early Years* (New York, 1974), pp. 465–69; Merlo J. Pusey, *Charles Evans Hughes* (New York, 1951), vol. 1, chap. 31.

97. Albert J. Reiss et al., *Occupations and Social Status* (New York, 1961), pp. 218–23. The generational differences reported there apparently show up in the general findings a decade and a half later of Robert W. Hodge et al., "Occupational Prestige in the United States, 1925–1963," *American Journal of Sociology* 70 (1964–65): 290. Shortly afterward, it might be noted, the people of one state, Pennsylvania, narrowly expressed a preference to continue the partisan system of choosing judges; see Lynne Warfield Kaltreider and George D. Wolf, "Let the People Decide: Judicial Selection in the 1967 Pennsylvania Constitutional Convention," *Western Pennsylvania Historical Magazine* 63 (1980): 16.

Chapter 5

1. This essay is a preliminary report on work-in-progress on the ideology of the metropolitan elite of the American legal profession between 1870 and 1920. I am grateful to participants in the seminar of the Shelby Cullom Davis Center for Historical Studies at Princeton University, the Ford Foundation Program for Basic Research in Law at Harvard Law School, and the Law and Development Seminar of the SUNY/Buffalo Law School, who heard and criticized earlier versions; to Victor Brudney, Alfred Chandler, Charles Donahue, Willard Hurst, Al Katz, Jack Schlegel, and Detlev Vagts, for specific suggestions and insights; to David Hollinger, Morton Horwitz, Stanley Katz, Andrew Kaufman, and Duncan Kennedy for critical readings of draft manuscript; to Marilyn Spracker, Jan Stornelli, Nikki Kowalski, and James Schroeder, for research assistance; and to Gerald Geison for his expert editing. None of them is to blame for my errors and distortions.

Research on this project has been supported by a Fellowship of the American Council of Learned Societies (funded by the National Endowment for the Humanities), the Graduate School of the University of Wisconsin-Madison, and the American Bar Foundation.

2. The premier practitioner of this approach to the history of American law is my colleague James Willard Hurst. He also expounds, however, a quite different approach to legal history as the study of changes in the consciousness of people occupying specialized institutional roles ("lawmakers"), an approach very similar to the "ideological" view proposed here.

The legal-technical approach is still vital; for a recent example, see Tony Allan Freyer, *Forums of Order: The Federal Courts and Business in American History* (Greenwich, Conn., 1979), which describes how judicial lawmaking of federal, general common law in the diversity jurisdiction helped create the institutional framework for nineteenth-century economic growth.

3. A classic in this vein, mixed somewhat with the legal-technological, is Lawrence Friedman and Jack Ladinsky, "Social Change and the Law of Industrial Accidents,"

Columbia Law Review 67 (1967): 50–82, among whose virtues is explicit discussions of theory and methodology. This mode has of course a vulgar-Marxist version as well as a liberal-pluralist one, in which law is not the instrument of just any social group engaged in politics but specifically that of the capitalist ruling class.

4. For the sources of this tradition, see my "J. Willard Hurst and the Common Law Tradition in American Legal Historiography," *Law and Society Review* 10 (1975): 9–55.

5. For the present, I would confine the scope of this claim to the metropolitan elite, since the class origins, social status, practice jobs, and political roles of this elite were perhaps even more distinctive then than now, and they were not at all representative of those of the legal profession as a whole.

6. The approach is basically that of treating legal history as, among other things, a branch of the history of political thought, broadly conceived. I have found inspiring theoretical support for the enterprise in J. G. A. Pocock, *Politics, Language, and Time: Essays on Political Thought and History* (New York, 1971); Quentin Skinner, "Meaning and Understanding in the History of Ideas," *History and Theory* 8 (1969): 3–53; Clifford Geertz, *The Interpretation of Cultures: Selected Essays* (New York, 1973); and Antonio Gramsci, *Selections from the Prison Notebooks*, ed. and tr. by Quintin Hoare and Geoffrey N. Şmith (New York, 1971). The practice of the enterprise is brilliantly exemplified in other works of the same writers. Legal-intellectual history, encouraged by these examples and others, is in a process of revival: see the works cited in notes 60 and 75 below. My only complaint about this increasingly abundant literature on ideological aspects of law is that so far most of it has remained fixed on the most formal and academic expressions of legal thought—appellate cases and learned commentary on them. An exception, as well as an exemplary model for the whole enterprise, is Douglas Hay's essay, "Property, Authority and the Criminal Law" in Hay et al., *Albion's Fatal Tree: Crime and Society in Eighteenth-Century England* (New York, 1975), pp. 17–63.

7. *Annual Reports of the President and Treasurer of Harvard College, 1870–71* (Cambridge, Mass., 1872) (hereafter *Annual Reports*), cited in Charles Warren, *History of the Harvard Law School* (New York, 1908), 2:381.

8. T. W. Dwight, *Education in Law Schools in the City of New York Compared With That Obtained in Law Offices, A Lecture . . .* (New York, 1876), pp. 4–9; C. C. Langdell, "Dean's Report," in *Annual Reports, 1876–77* (1878), pp. 89–91; *Annual Reports, 1878–79* (1880).

9. *Annual Reports, 1886–87* (1888), p. 92.

10. For this shift generally, see James Willard Hurst, *The Growth of American Law: The Lawmakers* (Boston, 1950), pp. 301–5 (hereafter Hurst, *Lawmakers*).

11. The most famous battles of this kind were immortalized in the Adams brothers' stories of the Vanderbilt-Gould-Fisk fight for control of the Erie Railroad and the Gould-Fisk conspiracy to corner the market in gold in the late 1860s. Charles Francis Adams, Jr., and Henry Adams, *Chapters of Erie* (New York, 1886). Professor Andrew Kaufman's biography-in-progress of Benjamin Cardozo sheds interesting new light on the practical legal ethics of the time through its account of the role played in the legal maneuvers of the gold conspirators by Thomas Shearman, cofounder of the firm of Shearman and Sterling. For other unusually detailed accounts of such litigation in this period, see Robert T. Swaine, *The Cravath Firm and Its Predecessors, 1819–1948* (New York, 1946–48), 1:327–37 (injunction warfare between express companies and railroads, nominally contesting the express companies' exclusive right to express business, actually to settle the price they should pay for those rights); and Chester M.

Destler, *Roger Sherman and the Independent Oil Men* (Ithaca, 1967), chaps. 5–9 (struggle of the independent producers with the Rockefeller syndicate for control of the Pennsylvania Oil Regions).

Harry Scheiber has forcefully and persuasively argued the thesis that nineteenth-century entrepreneurs perceived the diverse, scattered, and unruly nature of decentralized decisionmaking as a positive advantage: "If powerful corporate interests took full advantage of federalism's enclave effects to gain subsidies from state governments or to exercise virtually total control over policy in certain states they also had in hand a ready instrument to counteract the *unfavorable* effects of decentralized power when their situation dictated such a strategy." Harry Scheiber, "Federalism and the American Economic Order, 1789–1910," *Law and Society Review* 10 (1975): 117.

12. Swaine, *Cravath Firm*, 1:657.

13. This course has an interesting little history of its own. It was promoted by an active and meddlesome alumnus, Louis D. Brandeis. Langdell saw it as a concession to localism and paid no attention to it. Brandeis saw in the course an opportunity, never apparently realized, to teach the "individuality" of Massachusetts law, its expression of the "local customs, traditions, and the peculiar habits of mind of its people." Brandeis to Langdell, 10 Apr. 1893; Brandeis to Eliot, 25 Apr. 1893, *Letters of Louis D. Brandeis*, ed. Melvin I. Urofsky and David W. Levy (Albany, N.Y., 1971), pp. 113–14. This sort of historicism, which eventually was to help undo legal science, was of course quite foreign to Langdell's way of thinking.

14. Theodore W. Dwight, Lectures on Municipal Law (1875). Columbiana MS 191 (Butler Library, Columbia University). The famous "Dwight Method," rivalling Harvard's "Case Method" at one time in prestige, appears from these lectures to have been warmed-over and predigested Blackstone and Kent, in both organization and substance. But Dwight was said to have been a man of extraordinary personal presence. On the diploma privilege, see Alfred Z. Reed, *Training for the Public Profession of the Law* (New York, 1921), pp. 259–70.

15. Harvard curricular information from *Annual Reports*, passim.

16. Jeremiah Smith, *A Selection of Cases on Private Corporations*, 2 vols. (Cambridge, Mass., 1897).

17. Eliot to James Barr Ames, 24 July 1900, and Ames to Eliot, 1 Aug. 1900, C. W. Eliot Papers, Harvard University Archives (hereafter Eliot Papers).

18. On the animosity, see Julius Goebel et al., *A History of the School of Law, Columbia University* (New York, 1955), pp. 130–31; R. Gordon Hoxie et al., *A History of the Faculty of Political Science, Columbia University* (New York, 1955), pp. 45–63; on the demand by law students for political science courses, ibid., pp. 96–97.

19. See, e.g., William A. Keener to Seth Low, 23 May 1893 (advising against giving a course on international law in the Law School), Keener MSS, Butler Library, Columbia University.

20. Joseph H. Beale to William Rainey Harper, 2 Apr. 1902, cited in "Comment, Ernst Freund: Pioneer of American Administrative Law," *University of Chicago Law Review* 29 (1962): 767, n. 40.

21. Ames to Harper, 31 Mar. 1902, ibid., pp. 764–65, n. 11. The whole episode is related in detail (how Beale compromised and came to Chicago anyway; how Freund's teaching public law was not suppressed but strictly controlled and his "political science" subjects expelled; and how Freund himself humbled to routine library-administrative duties) in William L. Chase, "The Influence of the American Law School: University Legal Scholarship and the Rise of Modern Administrative Government, 1870–1978," (Ph.D. dissertation, Harvard University, 1978), pp. 157–208. See also

Frank L. Ellsworth, *Law on the Midway: The Founding of the University of Chicago Law School* (Chicago, 1977), pp. 68–77.

22. "Law is certainly a living interest at Harvard University. The Law School is the most successful department of the entire University and enjoys a reputation throughout the nation which is higher than that of any other Department." Eliot to A. V. Dicey, 2 May 1913, Eliot Papers.

23. Robert Stevens, "Two Cheers for 1870—The American Law School," *Perspectives in American History* 5 (1971): 403–548, particularly 430–41.

24. Swaine, *Cravath Firm*, 2:2–6. The system was apparently started by Walter Carter, Cravath's mentor at the bar. Otto E. Koegel, *Walter S. Carter, Collector of Young Masters or the Progenitor of Many Law Firms* (New York, 1953).

25. Anthony Chase, "The Birth of the Modern Law School," *American Journal of Legal History* 23 (1979): 329–48; Chase, "Origins of Modern Legal Education: The Harvard Case Method Conceived as Clinical Instruction in Law" (LL.M. thesis, Harvard University, 1979).

26. Jerold S. Auerbach, *Unequal Justice: Lawyers and Social Change in Modern America* (New York, 1976), pp. 74–101.

27. The papers of James Bradley Thayer (Box 20-1, Harvard Law School Archives) are a tribute to the aggressiveness of alumni, especially John Sargent, Victor Morawetz, J. C. Carter, and J. H. Choate, who assisted in broadening the financial base of the school beyond Boston to include New York in the late 1880s. For a capsule history of the association and its work, see Warren, *History of the Harvard Law School*, 2:428.

28. See, e.g., Auerbach, *Unequal Justice*, p. 184.

29. Andrew L. Barlow, "Coordination and Control: The Rise of Harvard University: 1825–1910" (Ph.D. dissertation, Harvard University, 1979), pp. 215, 244.

30. An incomplete portion of this project is the assembling of a synoptic collective biography of Wall Street lawyers which will attempt to give a statistical report on their participation in business and politics. For some useful earlier work on this subject, see William Miller, "American Lawyers in Business and Politics—Their Social Backgrounds and Early Training," *Yale Law Journal* 60 (1951): 66–76.

31. For an extensive discussion of the Bryce thesis and its merits, see David C. Hammack, "Elite Perceptions of Power in the Cities of the United States 1880–1900 . . . ," *Journal of Urban History* 4 (1978): 363–75.

32. By far the most valuable general survey of lawyers' roles in American political and economic life remains Hurst, *Lawmakers*, pp. 295–375.

33. This is based on an examination of the biographies of 1,150 men who entered the New York City bar between 1860 and 1910. A precise breakdown and description of the sample will be given upon completion of the collective biography project, see above n. 29.

34. See, e.g., George W. Edwards, *The Evolution of Finance Capitalism* (London, 1938); Lewis Corey, *The House of Morgan: A Social Biography of the Masters of Money* (New York, 1930).

35. Chandler's work on the structure of nineteenth- and twentieth-century enterprise, *Strategy and Structure: Chapters in the History of the Industrial Enterprise* (Cambridge, Mass., 1962) and *The Visible Hand: The Managerial Revolution in American Business* (Cambridge, Mass., 1977), has led to further studies both by himself and others comparing American to French, British, and German enterprise in the same period: *Recht und Entwicklung der Grossunternehmen im 19. und Frühen 20. Jahrhundert*, ed. Norbert Horn and Jürgen Kocka (Göttingen, 1979); and *Managerial Hierarchies: Comparative Perspectives on the Rise of the Modern Industrial Enterprise*, ed. Alfred D. Chandler, Jr., and Herman Daems (Cambridge, Mass., 1980).

36. The business history literature for this period is simply vast. These generalizations are distilled from the following research: I went through Chandler's *Visible Hand*, looking for passages that suggested directly or indirectly an involvement of law and lawyers; two of my research assistants then read through all of the secondary sources that Chandler cites for those passages, looking for references to law and lawyers; they marked these and I read them. Very few had *any* extended treatment of the role of law or lawyers; most of those few are cited elsewhere in the notes to this essay.

37. The most extreme example is perhaps William Nelson Cromwell's work on behalf of his client, the French New Panama Canal Co. He helped start the Panama revolution of 1903. See Charles D. Ameringer, "The Panama Canal Lobby of Philippe Bunau-Varilla and William Nelson Cromwell," *American Historical Review* 68 (1963): 346–63.

38. See, e.g., Chandler, *Visible Hand*, pp. 193–94, which also suggests national linkage through, first, entrepreneurs and, later, investment bankers on corporate boards.

39. Gerald T. White, *Formative Years in the Far West: A History of Standard Oil Co. and of California Predecessors Through 1919* (New York, 1962), p. 435.

40. For the exceptional fastidiousness of Boston investors, see Paul Goodman, "Ethics and Enterprise: The Values of a Boston Elite, 1800–1860," *American Quarterly* 18 (1966): 437–51; and Frederic Cople Jaher, "The Boston Brahmins in the Age of Industrial Enterprise," in Jaher, ed., *The Age of Industrialism in America: Essays in Social Structure and Cultural Values* (New York, 1968), pp. 188–262. Eminent outside counsel were sometimes solicited for endorsements of bond issues even when they could hardly be as expert as locals in matters of local law—cf. Samuel J. Tilden's opinion sought by the Illinois Central Railroad on an Illinois issue; he had to have "refreshed his knowledge" on the Illinois statute. IC RR Archives 2.5 (Newberry Library). The role of municipal bond counsel, who specialized in the scandal-ridden local grants of railroad aid, is illuminated in Oliver Wendell Holmes Devise, *History of the Supreme Court of the United States*, vol. 6: Charles Fairman, *Reconstruction and Reunion, 1864–1888* (New York, 1971), pt. 1, pp. 918–1116. Through the 1880s the opinion of counsel was not critical in securing investor confidence because the U.S. Supreme Court virtually *always* disallowed defenses against the validity of bonds in the hands of holders; so all the risk was taken by the issuers. In the 1890s, however, investors did not wish to risk prolonged and expensive enforcement efforts even if the law could help them force a favorable settlement. The appearance of responsible bond counsel filled this need for an independent intermediary appraiser.

41. Thomas R. Navin and Marian V. Sears, "The Rise of a Market for Industrial Securities, 1887–1902," *Business History Review* 29 (1955): 105–38. John Dos Passos, lawyer for the Sugar Trust and inventor of a number of the new forms of securities, was an active promoter of securities issues in this period.

42. See, e.g., James Willard Hurst, *The Legitimacy of the Business Corporation in the Law of the United States, 1780–1970* (Charlottesville, Va., 1970); David F. Noble, *America by Design: Science, Technology, and the Rise of Corporate Capitalism* (New York, 1977), chap. 6 (patent monopoly); Spencer L. Kimball, *Insurance and Public Policy: A Study in the Legal Implementation of Social and Economic Public Policy* (Madison, 1960) (devices to create adequate insurance funds and maintain their integrity); Arthur H. Dean, *William Nelson Cromwell, 1854–1948: An American Pioneer in Corporation, Comparative, and International Law* (New York, 1957), pp. 189–211 (open-end mortgage); Chandler, *Visible Hand*, pp. 122–44 (railroad associations), pp. 315–36 (trusts, holding companies, vertical integration). For some unusually in-

teresting historical work in the legal-technological mode on other countries, see Richard Danzig, "Hadley v. Baxendale: A Study in the Industrialization of the Law," *Journal of Legal Studies* 4 (1975): 249–84 (legal limits on contract damages); and D. S. Landes, "The Structure of Enterprise in the Nineteenth Century: The Cases of Britain and Germany," *Rapports du XI Congrès Internationale des Sciences Historiques* 5 (Uppsala, 1960): 107–28 (corporate form).

43. See Chandler, *Visible Hand*, pp. 315–39, 375–76; Alfred D. Chandler, Jr., and Stephen Salsbury, *Pierre S. DuPont and the Making of the Modern Corporation* (New York, 1971), pp. 110–20; Alfred S. Eichner, *The Emergence of Oligopoly: Sugar Refining as a Case Study* (Baltimore, 1969); Leslie Hannah, "Mergers, Cartels, and Concentrations: Legal Factors in the U.S. and European Experience," in *Recht und Entwicklung*, ed. Horn and Kocka, pp. 306–16; Jürgen Kocka, "The Rise of the Modern Industrial Enterprise in Germany," in *Managerial Hierarchies*, ed. Chandler and Daems, p. 106.

44. Chandler, *Visible Hand*, pp. 375; see also ibid., p. 334.

45. See Alfred D. Chandler, Jr., "The Origins of Progressive Leadership," in *The Letters of Theodore Roosevelt*, Vol. 8: *The Days of Armageddon, 1914–1919*, ed. Elting E. Morison et al., (Cambridge, 1954), pp. 1462–65; Samuel P. Hays, "The Politics of Reform in Municipal Government in the Progressive Era," *Pacific Northwest Quarterly* 55 (1964): 157–69; Geoffrey Blodgett, *The Gentle Reformers: Massachusetts Democrats in the Cleveland Era* (Cambridge, Mass., 1966); David C. Hammack, *Power and Society in Greater New York* (New York, 1982).

46. Hammack, *Power and Society in Greater New York*, chap. 8; see also Hammack's "Problems in the Historical Study of Power in the Cities and Towns of the United States, 1800–1960," *American Historical Review* 83 (1978): 328–30. Hammack's index of influence is participation in major decisions. Of course there is another way of looking at power and influence—i.e., as control over the mental universe in which decisions are framed that govern people's views of what counts as a "problem" to be decided, what kinds of options are thinkable and what kinds are (literally) unimaginable, what counts as a respectable argument and what does not, and what counts as a responsible or efficient solution. This is the "ideological" perspective I am arguing for in this essay. It is developed in the specific context of "power" by Steven Lukes, *Power: A Radical View* (London, 1974), which also sharply criticizes instrumental theories of power.

47. James Bryce, *The American Commonwealth* (rev. ed. New York, 1913), 2:307. See also Hurst, *Lawmakers*, pp. 356–59 (lawyers as symbol-makers).

48. The story has yet to be told. For the European background, see Donald R. Kelley, "Gaius Noster: Substructures of Western Social Thought," *American Historical Review* 84 (1979): 619–48. For English use of legal science, see Barbara J. Shapiro, "Law and Science in Seventeenth Century England," *Stanford Law Review* 21 (1969): 727–66; and especially the major work in progress of Daniel Coquillette on the gradual incorporation of civilian ideas into English law. See Part 1, "The English Civilian Writers, 1501–1637," *Boston University Law Review* 61 (1981): 1–89.

49. There is still no really adequate treatment of antebellum legal theory, which would set it in relation to its English and European sources and contemporary views of science and political economy; perhaps no field has suffered more from the once prevailing view that Americans, especially busy ones, do not have ideas. Our only general treatment is Perry Miller, *The Life of the Mind in America: From the Revolution to the Civil War* (New York, 1965), pp. 99–265, which suffers from its exclusive reliance on ceremonial speeches and introductions to law books to the exclusion of

the content of the books themselves; the great historian clearly never felt really at home in this field. Other helpful secondary works include the following. On Blackstone and Mansfield, whose influence was enormous, see Charles Gray, "Blackstone's History of English Law" (unpublished MS 1979); Duncan Kennedy, "The Structure of Blackstone's Commentaries," *Buffalo Law Review* 28 (1979): 209–382, C. H. S. Fifoot, *Lord Mansfield* (Oxford, 1936). On the significance of Bacon for American conceptions of science, see especially T. D. Bozeman, *Protestants in an Age of Science: The Baconian Ideal and Antebellum American Religious Thought* (Chapel Hill, 1977). On the Whig ideology, Morton J. Horwitz, *The Transformation of American Law, 1780–1860* (Cambridge, Mass., 1977) is indispensable; see also Stephen Botein, "Cicero as a Role-Model for Early American Lawyers: A Case Study in Classical Influence," *Classical Journal* 73 (1978): 313–21; Daniel Walker Howe, *The Political Culture of the American Whigs* (Chicago, 1979); and Jean V. Matthews's excellent biography, *Rufus Choate: The Law and Civic Virtue* (Philadelphia, 1980). For the tradition of civic humanist ideas carried forward by the Whigs, see especially J. G. A. Pocock, *The Machiavellian Moment: Florentine Political Thought and the Atlantic Republican Tradition* (Princeton, 1975), and Gordon S. Wood, *The Creation of the American Republic, 1776–1787* (Chapel Hill, 1969). On Jeffersonian legal ideas, see Richard Ellis, *The Jeffersonian Crisis: Courts and Politics in the Young Republic* (New York, 1971), and Linda K. Kerber, *Federalists in Dissent: Imagery and Ideology in Jeffersonian America* (Ithaca, 1970); on Jacksonian, the best work available is still Marvin Meyers, *The Jacksonian Persuasion: Politics and Belief* (Stanford, 1957), but Charles McCurdy's work in progress on Jacksonian lawyers promises to be definitive.

The works of the lawyers themselves are the best guides to their ideas. For leading representative expressions of the Whig line, see Joseph Story, "The Value and Importance of Legal Studies" [1829], in *The Miscellaneous Writings of Joseph Story*, ed. William W. Story (New York, 1852), pp. 503–48, and Rufus Choate, *Addresses and Orations of Rufus Choate* (Boston, 1891), pp. 133–66; of the Jacksonian, Robert Rantoul, "Oration at Scituate" [1836], in *Memoirs, Speeches, and Writings of Robert Rantoul, Jr.*, ed. Luther Hamilton (Boston, 1854), pp. 251, 277–90.

50. On neutralization, see Ellis, *Jeffersonian Crisis*, passim; and Gerard W. Gawalt, *The Promise of Power: The Emergence of the Legal Profession in Massachusetts, 1760–1840* (Westport, Conn., 1979), pp. 81–118.

51. Dennis R. Nolan, "Sir William Blackstone and the New American Republic: A Study of Intellectual Impact," *New York University Law Review* 51 (1976): 731–68.

52. James Wilson, "Lectures on Law," in *The Works of James Wilson*, ed. Robert G. McCloskey (2d ed., Cambridge, Mass., 1967), p. 505.

53. H. W. Warner, *A Discourse on Legal Science* ... (New York, 1832), pp. 10–11.

54. See Maxwell H. Bloomfield, *American Lawyers in a Changing Society, 1776–1876* (Cambridge, Mass., 1976), pp. 144–62.

55. On the revival, see Gawalt, *The Promise of Power*, pp. 139–58.

56. For these experiments, see Reed, *Training For the Public Profession of the Law*, pp. 121–25.

57. Ibid., pp. 142–49.

58. See, e.g., the dicta of two of the leading exponents of the case-method: "Law, considered as a science, consists of certain principles and doctrines.... It seemed to me ... to be possible to take such a branch of the law as Contracts, for example, and without exceeding comparatively moderate limits, to select, classify, and arrange all the cases which had contributed in any important degree to the growth, development, or establishment of any of its essential doctrines." Christopher Columbus Langdell, *A*

Selection of Cases on the Law of Contracts (Boston, 1871), pp. vi–vii. "The student must look upon law as a science consisting of a body of principles to be found in the adjudged cases, the cases being to him what the specimen is to the geologist." William A. Keener, *A Selection of Cases on the Law of Quasi-Contracts* (New York, 1888–89), preface.

The apparent contradiction that we may see between the historicism of the case method and the analytic pretensions of legal science did not exist for them. They saw legal doctrine as having been *evolving towards* ever-increasing rationality and internal consistency. In theory, therefore, historical and analytic-deductive methods for deriving correct doctrine should in most instances (the exceptions were the occasions when cases had historically taken a misguided wrong turning) lead to exactly the same results.

59. Frederick Pollock, *Essays in Jurisprudence and Ethics* (London, 1882), pp. 237, 147–53. In fact one of the remarkable aspects of the common consciousness developed by English and American lawyers at this time is that at the level of general jurisprudence (whether the law was mostly command or mostly custom) they agreed on almost nothing; but when they came to write about substantive legal problems, the underlying structure of their work was the same.

60. For examples of this phenomenally casual method, look at C. C. Langdell, *A Brief Survey of Equity Jurisdiction* (Cambridge, Mass., 1905); James Barr Ames, *Lectures on Legal History and Miscellaneous Legal Essays* (Cambridge, Mass., 1913).

61. The account that follows is my own version of an emerging synthesis in recent scholarship on late nineteenth-century legal thought. This scholarship has largely built on special studies of private law subjects, especially contract and tort, of constitutional law, and of the jurisprudential writing of the period, particularly that of Holmes. See especially P. S. Atiyah, *The Rise and Fall of Freedom of Contract* (Oxford, 1979); Lawrence M. Friedman, *Contract Law in America: A Social and Economic Case Study* (Madison, 1965), pp. 82–139; Peter Gabel, "Intention and Structure in Contractual Conditions: Outline of a Method for Critical Legal Theory," *Minnesota Law Review* 61 (1977): 601–43; Grant Gilmore, *The Death of Contract* (Columbus, 1974); Morton J. Horwitz, "Work in Progress on Late Nineteenth-Century Legal Thought" (unpublished MS, 1979); Duncan Kennedy, "Form and Substance in Private Law Adjudication," *Harvard Law Review* 89 (1976): 1685–778; Ian MacNeil, "Contracts: Adjustment of Long-Term Economic Relations Under Classical, Neo-Classical, and Relational Contract Law," *Northwestern University Law Review* 72 (1978): 854–905; Charles McCurdy, "Justice Field and the Jurisprudence of Government-Business Relations: Some Parameters of Laissez-Faire Constitutionalism, 1864–1897," *Journal of American History* 61 (1975): 970–1005; Mark Tushnet, *Considerations of Humanity and Interest: An American Law of Slavery, 1810–1860* (Princeton, 1981); Roberto Mangabeira Unger, *Law in Modern Society* (New York, 1976); G. Edward White, *Tort Law in America: An Intellectual History* (New York, 1979).

62. I owe this point on the double meaning of "principles" to Atiyah, *Freedom of Contract*, pp. 345–52.

63. F. A. Hayek, *The Constitution of Liberty* (Chicago, 1960), pp. 153–54.

64. Ibid., p. 153.

65. William E. Nelson, "The Impact of the Antislavery Movement upon Styles of Judicial Reasoning in Nineteenth Century America," *Harvard Law Review* 87 (1974): 513–66.

66. See, e.g., Harold M. Hyman, *A More Perfect Union: The Impact of the Civil War and Reconstruction on the Constitution* (New York, 1973), pp. 367–90.

67. Atiyah, *Freedom of Contract,* concerning England; John P. Dawson, *The Oracles of the Law* (Ann Arbor, 1968), 392 ff., 450ff., and Franz Wieacker, *Privatrechtsgeschichte der Neuzeit: Unter Besonderer Berücksichtigung der Deutschen Entwicklung* (Göttingen, 1967), pt. 5, concerning Germany.

68. I do not know of any study of the thought of this group; their biographies are in F. H. Lawson, *The Oxford Law School, 1850–1965* (Oxford, 1968), pp. 61–92.

69. See Hyman, *A More Perfect Union,* and Stanley I. Kutler, *Judicial Power and Reconstruction Politics* (Chicago, 1968), for this thesis.

70. Horwitz, *Transformation of American Law,* takes the general position that legal formalism developed as a shield against the redistribution of the profits of entrepreneurs who had bent the law in their favor in the previous generation. Lawrence Friedman suggests a "functionalist" variant—that *judicial* formalism was a stopgap means of standardizing high-volume transactions before the development of administrative formalism. "On Legalistic Reasoning—A Footnote to Weber," *Wisconsin Law Review* 1966: 148–71, particularly 167.

71. Max Weber, *On Law and Economy in Society,* Max Rheinstein ed. (Cambridge, Mass., 1954), p. 308.

72. See Horwitz, *Transformation of American Law;* and Harry N. Scheiber, "Property Law, Expropriation, and Resource Allocation by Government: The United States, 1789–1910," *Journal of Economic History* 33 (1973): 232–51, for accounts of how nineteenth-century law did just that.

73. See, e.g., McCurdy, "Justice Field"; Alan M. Jones, "Thomas M. Cooley and Laissez-Faire Constitutionalism: A Reconsideration," *Journal of American History* 53 (1967): 751–71; Charles Fairman, *Mr. Justice Miller and the Supreme Court, 1862–1890* (Cambridge, Mass., 1939).

74. For an extensive catalogue of regulatory legislation in the late nineteenth century, see Morton Keller, *Affairs of State: Public Life in Late Nineteenth Century America* (Cambridge, Mass., 1977), pp. 409–38, 473–521; Lawrence M. Friedman, "Freedom of Contract and Occupational Licensing, 1890–1910," *California Law Review* 53 (1965): 487–534. Work in progress by Janet Lindgren which surveys all New York legislation reviewed in the courts between 1880–1920 has found that (a) the great majority of regulatory statutes survived constitutional challenge; and (b) in virtually every case in which a statute was found unconstitutional, the legislature subsequently reenacted its substance in another form. Her findings suggest that the judges wanted primarily to make sure that legislation satisfied the criteria of Liberal legal ideology—especially that of *generality*—and that this explanation better fits the evidence than the traditional accusation that they were simply laissez-faire mossbacks. Janet S. Lindgren, "Judicial Review Reviewed," *Wisconsin Law Review* (1983, forthcoming).

75. On the connections among liberalism, scientism, and professionalism, see David Montgomery, *Beyond Equality: Labor and the Radical Republicans, 1862–1872* (New York, 1967), especially pp. 379–86; Thomas L. Haskell, *The Emergence of Professional Social Science: The American Social Science Association and the Nineteenth-Century Crisis of Authority* (Urbana, Ill., 1977); Magali Sarfatti Larson, *The Rise of Professionalism: A Sociological Analysis* (Berkeley, 1977), chap. 9.

76. The sketch—and it pretends to be nothing more than that—of Progressive legal ideology which follows represents my effort to synthesize a model from my reading in the area. Prior work that has been especially important in putting together these ideas includes, in addition to the works cited in notes 60 and 63 above: on Progressive ideology at the level of formal thought, Morton White, *Social Thought in America:*

The Revolt against Formalism (Boston, 1957), and David A. Hollinger, *Morris R. Cohen and the Scientific Ideal* (Cambridge, Mass., 1975); on legal thought, Edward A. Purcell, Jr., *The Crisis of Democratic Theory: Scientific Naturalism and the Problem of Value* (Lexington, Ky., 1973), G. Edward White, "From Sociological Jurisprudence to Realism: Jurisprudence and Social Change in Early Twentieth-Century America," *Virginia Law Review* 58 (1972): 999–1028, John Henry Schlegel, "American Legal Realism and Empirical Social Science: From the Yale Experience," *Buffalo Law Review* 28 (1980): 459–586, and William Twining, *Karl Llewellyn and the Realist Movement* (London, 1973); on economic thought (institutional economics), Ben B. Seligman, *Main Currents in Modern Economics: Economic Thought since 1870* (New York, 1962), pt. 1: "The Revolt against Formalism," pp. 3–253; on business ideology, Samuel Haber, *Efficiency and Uplift: Scientific Management in the Progressive Era, 1890–1920* (Chicago, 1964); Samuel P. Hays, *Conservation and the Gospel of Efficiency: The Progressive Conservation Movement, 1890–1920* (Cambridge, Mass., 1959); James Weinstein, *The Corporate Ideal in the Liberal State, 1900–1918* (Boston, 1968); on administrative ideology, Thomas K. McCraw, "Regulation in America: A Review Article," *Business History Review* 49 (1975): 159–83; and Barry Dean Karl, *Executive Reorganization and Reform in the New Deal: The Genesis of Administrative Management, 1900–1939* (Cambridge, Mass., 1963); and on Progressive reform generally, Robert H. Wiebe, *The Search for Order, 1877–1920* (New York, 1967); Richard M. Abrams, *Conservatism in a Progressive Era: Massachusetts Politics, 1900–1912* (Cambridge, Mass., 1964); Samuel P. Hays, *The Response to Industrialism, 1885–1914* (Chicago, 1957); and David B. Tyack, *The One Best System: A History of American Urban Education* (Cambridge, Mass., 1974).

It is probably unnecessary, but may be useful, to emphasize that Progressive ideology (like its predecessors) was capable of taking very different forms in different minds while preserving its essential structural characteristics. The idea of efficiency as "rationality in particularity," for example, had both left-wing Romantic forms that identified particularity with individuality, variety, and growth—stressing the need for personal and local autonomy—and right-wing forms that drew from the ideal of particularity the program of finding standard, uniform, centrally managed procedures for each of the detailed tasks and decisions of everyday life. One would expect to find most corporate lawyers somewhere toward the right of this spectrum, and most academic lawyers somewhat further left (though never very far). Louis Brandeis, in his simultaneous embrace of Romantic individuality and scientific management, is a fascinating example of someone who covers the whole spectrum.

77. See generally Blodgett, *The Gentle Reformers*; Ari Hoogenboom, *Outlawing the Spoils: A History of the Civil Service Reform Movement, 1865–1883* (Urbana, Ill., 1961); Gerald W. McFarland, "Partisan of Nonpartisanship: Dorman B. Eaton and the Genteel Reform Tradition," *Journal of American History* 54 (1968): 806–22; John G. Sproat, *The Best Men: Liberal Reformers in the Gilded Age* (New York, 1968).

78. George M. Fredrickson, *The Inner Civil War: Northern Intellectuals and the Crisis of the Union* (New York, 1965), p. 207.

79. Blodgett, *The Gentle Reformers*, p. 118.

80. For similar pressures on teachers of economics, see Mary O. Furner, *Advocacy and Objectivity: A Crisis in the Professionalization of American Social Science, 1865–1905* (Lexington, Ky., 1975).

81. William Letwin, *Law and Economic Policy in America: The Evolution of the Sherman Antitrust Act* (New York, 1965), pp. 77–99.

82. See George W. Martin, *Causes and Conflicts: The Centennial History of the*

Association of the Bar of the City of New York, 1870–1970 (Boston, 1970); Hurst, Lawmakers, pp. 359–66.

83. William Simon, "The Ideology of Advocacy: Procedural Justice and Professional Ethics," Wisconsin Law Review (1978): 29–144, at 39–61, establishes the connections between Liberalism in law and adversary ethics.

84. A striking example is Elihu Root, who was an aggressive advocate for whatever corporate clients retained his services, but who was also a major architect of both Liberal and Progressive varieties of law reform activities to curb such clients. See Hurst, Lawmakers, pp. 368–75. The case of Richard Olney, counsel to the Boston and Maine and the Chicago, Burlington, and Quincy Railroads, is probably far more typical; cf. his advice to the Burlington on issuing free passes after the practice had been made a criminal offense by state law: "'Personally and unofficially'—as you put it—I should like to see the C., B. & Q. go on issuing passes if, as you say, that course would promote its pecuniary interest. On the other hand, I do not see any way to advising any such course, because the penalties of the law are severe and fall upon the personal offenders and not upon the corporation itself. How can the C., B. & Q. indemnify an officer or employee against the risks or consequences of a sentence to the penitentiary? . . . The subject is one attended with great practical difficulties and about which there ought to be some concert of action among the railroad companies." Olney to Charles E. Perkins, 20 Jan. 1892, CB&Q Archives 3-05:1 (Newberry Library, Chicago).

85. My main source is a collection of about 130 addresses on legal science and the lawyer's public duty, collected in 148 volumes of nineteenth-century legal pamphlets in the Cornell Law Library (apparently the personal collection of A. D. White). I am grateful to Elizabeth Mensch for finding these pamphlets, letting me see them, and giving me the benefit of her ideas.

A quite typical rhetorical production of this time—deploring the fall of the bar from its antebellum Whig-Federalist ideal of aristocratic virtue, civic-mindedness, learning, eloquence, and devotion to "principle" rather than "precedent," into its modern condition of commercialism, technical sharp practice, easy admission to the bar, deficiency in liberal culture, political selection of judges, and taking of contingent fees—is interesting because of its authorship by John R. Dos Passos, father of the novelist, who was a lawyer for the Sugar Trust, promoter of stock subscriptions, and aggressive apologist for corporate concentration. Dos Passos, The American Lawyer As He Was—As He Is—As He Can Be (New York, 1907). There are valuable insights on the rhetoric of decline and its meaning in Samuel Haber, "The Legal Profession among the Others at the End of the Nineteenth Century" (unpublished paper presented at the annual meeting, American Society for Legal History, Williamsburg, Va., October 1979).

86. Louis D. Brandeis, Business—A Profession (Boston, 1914), p. 313.

87. See Oscar Handlin and Mary Handlin, Commonwealth: A Study of the Role of Government in the American Economy, Massachusetts, 1774–1861 (Cambridge, Mass., 1969), chaps. 6–8; Louis Hartz, Economic Policy and Democratic Thought: Pennsylvania, 1776–1860 (Cambridge, Mass., 1948), pp. 109–30, 254–62; J. W. Hurst, Legitimacy of the Business Corporation, pp. 31–51; Edwin Merrick Dodd, American Business Corporations until 1860, with Special Reference to Massachusetts (Cambridge, Mass., 1954).

88. The phrase is Thomas Erskine Holland's, in The Elements of Jurisprudence (Oxford, 1880), p. 87.

89. See Hurst, Legitimacy of the Business Corporation, pp. 66–88.

90. See Keller, *Affairs of State*, pp. 432–33.

91. James B. Dill, *The Statutory and Case Law Applicable to Private Companies under the General Corporation Act of New Jersey* . . . (New York, 1899); E. Merrick Dodd, Jr., "Statutory Developments in Business Corporation Law, 1886–1936," *Harvard Law Review* 50 (1936): 27–59.

92. Adolph A. Berle, Jr., *Studies in the Law of Corporate Finance* (Chicago, 1928); Adolph A. Berle, Jr., and Gardiner C. Means, *The Modern Corporation and Private Property* (New York, 1932), book 2, pp. 127–287.

93. The Cravath firm was one of the few, and it has left us a detailed account of the practice. Swaine, *Cravath Firm*, passim.

94. The most useful accounts of the major reorganizations are Edward G. Campbell, *The Reorganization of the American Railroad System, 1893–1900: A Study of the Effects* . . . (New York, 1938), and Stuart Daggett, *Railroad Reorganization* (Boston, 1908); of the general *business* procedures for going through reorganization, Arthur S. Dewing, *The Financial Policy of Corporations* (New York, 1920), vol. 5; of the detailed *legal* procedures, James Byrne, "The Foreclosure of Railroad Mortgages in the United States Courts" and Paul D. Cravath, "The Reorganization of Corporations . . .," both in Francis Lynde Stetson et al., *Some Legal Phases of Corporate Financing, Reorganization, and Regulation* (New York, 1917), pp. 77–152, 153–234.

95. This odd procedure was pioneered in *Wabash, St. Louis & Pacific R.R. Co. v. Central Trust Co.*, 22 F. 138 (1884). For details, see Byrne, "Foreclosure of Railroad Mortgages," in *Some Legal Phases*, ed. Stetson, pp. 82–88.

96. Adrian H. Joline, *The Method of Conduct of the Reorganization of Corporations* (Cambridge, Mass., 1910), 24.

97. For a contemporary account of the practice by a judge who presided over many reorganizations, see William H. Taft, "Recent Criticisms of the Federal Judiciary," *American Bar Association Reports* 18 (1895): 262–65.

98. Cravath, "Reorganization of Corporations," in *Some Legal Phases*, ed. Stetson, p. 163.

99. Ibid., p. 171.

100. On all these practices, see M. M. Cohn, "Railroad Receiverships—Questions of Practice Concerning Them," *American Law Review* 19 (1885): 400–423; Albert Gallup, "Railway Mortgages and Receiver's Debts in the United States," *Law Quarterly Review* 4 (1888): 300–311; Byrne, "Foreclosure of Railroad Mortgages," in *Some Legal Phases*, ed. Stetson, pp. 117–24.

101. Charles F. Beach, Jr., *Commentaries on the Law of Receivers* (New York, 1887), §391, p. 393.

102. *Fosdick v. Schall*, 99 U.S. 235, 255 (1878).

103. *Kneeland v. American Loan & Trust Co.*, 136 U.S. 89, 97 (1890).

104. *Louisville Trust Co. v. Louisville, New Albany & Chicago Railway Co.*, 174 U.S. 674 (1899).

105. Ibid., 682.

106. Joline, *Reorganization of Corporations*, p. 48.

107. 228 U.S. 482 (1913).

108. Ibid., 508.

109. Quoted by Joline, *Reorganization of Corporations*, p. 46.

110. The new procedure was devised by Robert T. Swaine of the Cravath firm. Swaine, *Cravath Firm*, 2:168–69, 172–74. Its ingenuity lay in the fact that, once the court had confirmed the sale, the confirmation incorporated a decision that the plan *was* "fair, equitable, and feasible," thus immunizing it from subsequent attack.

111. Such at least was the conclusion of the exhaustive study of reorganization committees conducted by the Securities and Exchange Commission under the direction of William O. Douglas. U.S. Securities and Exchange Commission, *Report on the Study and Investigation of the Work, Activities, Personnel and Functions of Protective and Reorganization Committees* (Washington, 1940), pt. 8, 47–60.

112. The best account of the fantastic career of Charles Tyson Yerkes, Jr., the financier of these systems, is Theodore Dreiser's novel, *The Titan* (New York, 1914).

113. *Guaranty Trust of N.Y. v. Chicago Union Traction Co.*, 158 F. 913 (N.D. Ill. 1907).

114. *Merchants' Loan & Trust Co. v. Chicago Rys. Co.*, 158 F. 923, at 929–30 (C.A. 7th Cir. 1907).

115. Charles M. Hough, Jr., cited in James N. Rosenberg, *Corporate Reorganization and the Federal Court* (New York, 1924), p. 1.

116. See contributions by various lawyers to Rosenberg in ibid.

117. A. A. Berle, Jr., *Corporate Finance*.

118. There are some suggestions that the Supreme Court was preparing to classify at least *railroad* reorganizations as affected with a public interest in the 1870s: see C. J. Waite, in *Fosdick v. Schall*, 99 U.S. 235 (1878). But under the pressure of liberal classifications in the 1880s, the doctrine was generally accepted that railroads were private in their intracorporate relations. Victor Morawetz, *A Treatise on the Law of Private Corporations Other Than Charitable* (Boston, 1882), §445, p. 433, n. 1.

119. The Supreme Court made it clear that Congress possessed authority to do this, *Canada Southern Railway v. Gebhard*, 109 U.S. 527 (1883), though the states did not, *Gilfillan v. Union Canal Co.*, 109 U.S. 401 (1883).

120. The device available would have been for the court to label foreclosure sales that it believed injurious to junior security-holders and unsecured creditors as "constructively" (i.e., fictitiously) fraudulent against those interests, justifying the traditional exercise of equitable jurisdiction.

121. Swaine, *Cravath Firm*, 1:497, 508.

Index

Academic lawyers, 62, 66–69, 125 (n. 70); and legal theory, 72, 91, 94, 97, 100, 128 (n. 6), 136 (n. 76)
Academic professions, 3–4, 13, 27; history of, 14–16; displace public lecturing, 27–28
Academic specialization, 8, 27–28
Access to professions, 15–16
Administrative efficiency of judges, 62–64, 126 (n. 71)
Advocacy law, 73, 86, 99, 137 (n. 84)
Age of clergy, 39–40
Agents for lecturers, 23, 27
Alison, Francis, 37, 118 (nn. 35–36)
American Bar Association: and lawyer's public image, 9–10, 55–65, 68–69, 123 (n. 36), 124 (n. 47); response to FDR court packing, 10, 64–69, 126 (n. 93), 127 (nn. 94–97); code of ethics, 49–50, 58–59, 62–64; Committee to Oppose Judicial Recall, 55–64, 68, 124 (n. 47); organization of, 55–56, 65, 123 (n. 36); membership, 57–59, 65, 67–69, 124 (n. 54), 125 (n. 55), 127 (nn. 94–97); and legal education, 76–77
American Bar Association Journal, 65–66
American Judicature Society, 65
American Law Institute, 65
American Liberty League, 66
American Medical Association, 125 (n. 55)
Ames, James Barr, 74–75, 88
Anglican church, 30, 35, 40, 115 (n. 2), 116 (n. 11)
Anglo-American relations, 51, 91
Antebellum legal theory, 10–11, 83–88, 97, 100; judicial theory, 50–55, 63–64, 123 (n. 31)
Antislavery natural-law jurisprudence, 91
Antitrust litigation, 61, 79–81
Arizona statehood, 55–56, 63–64

Arminianism, 35
Arnold, Thurman, 66
Attendance at lectures, 12, 18–21, 112 (n. 2)
Attorney: defined, 73
Auerbach, Jerold, 76
Autonomy of professionals, 13–14

Bacon, Francis, 82, 87
Baldwin, Joseph G., 54
Baldwin, Simeon, 99
Baptist church, 45, 47, 120 (n. 65)
Barlow, Andrew, 77; thesis, 77–81
Beale, Joseph H., 75, 129 (n. 21)
Beatty, Charles, 116 (n. 22), 118 (n. 37)
Beecher, Henry Ward, 23
Benjamin, Park, 12
Bentham-Burke debate, 83
Berle, A. A., Jr., 107
Blackstone, William, 82, 85, 129 (n. 14)
Blair, John, 118 (n. 37)
Blair, Samuel, 37, 118 (n. 37)
Boardman, Henry A., 50–51
Bond counsel, 79, 131 (n. 40)
Bondholders, 102–5
Boston and Maine Railroads, 137 (n. 84)
Boston investors, 79, 131 (n. 40)
Boyd, Adam, 118 (nn. 35–36)
Boynton, Lucian, 15–16
Brace, Charles Loring, 24
Brandeis, Louis, 64, 66–68, 99, 126 (n. 77), 129 (n. 13)
Brewer, David Josiah, 104–7, 109
Brown, Rome Green, 56–63, 68, 124 (nn. 45, 49, 54), 125 (n. 56)
Bryan, William Jennings, 59
Bryce, James, 77, 81, 130 (n. 31)
Burr, Aaron, 117 (n. 25), 118 (n. 37)
Business: judicial role in, 54–55, 62, 122 (n. 27), 123 (n. 34), 126 (n. 71); and legal theory, 60–64, 77–82, 92–94, 99, 125 (n. 60), 130 (nn. 30, 32, 35), 131 (nn. 36–37, 40–42), 135 (nn. 70, 74),

Index

137 (nn. 84–85). *See also* Corporate law; Reorganization and receivership litigation
Business schools, 75
Byran, Eliab, 118 (n. 37)

Capitalism: and professionalization, 5–7; and legal theory, 11, 70–71, 80–81, 92
Cardozo, Benjamin, 128 (n. 11)
Carter, J. C., 74
Carter, Walter, 75, 130 (n. 24)
"Case method," 74–76, 87, 129 (n. 14), 133 (n. 58)
Cathcart, Robert, 118 (n. 35)
Caven, Samuel, 118 (n. 35)
Chandler, Alfred D., Jr., 78, 80
Chase, Anthony, 76
Chicago Bar Association, 55
Chicago, Burlington and Quincy Railroads, 137 (n. 84)
Chicago street railways, 106–7
Choate, Rufus, 74
Circulars sent by lecturers, 19–20
Clark, Walter, 58–59, 124 (n. 52)
Class politics: and professionalization, 5; and legal theory, 10–11, 71–72, 77–81, 89, 92–93, 95–97, 127 (n. 3), 128 (n. 5); and Presbyterian schism, 41, 119 (n. 44); and judicial selection, 51–54; and legal education, 76–77. *See also* Elites; Legal elites
Clergy: and capitalism, 6; decline in prestige, 18, 34, 42–48
College of New Jersey (later Princeton University), 37, 45
College presidents: as cultural spokesmen, 18
Columbia Law School, 74–75, 78, 129 (nn. 14, 18)
Common-law theory, 74, 89, 98
"Communities of the competent," 8, 13–14, 28
Community service and legal profession, 50, 52–54, 97, 121 (n. 7), 123 (n. 34)
Comparative legal theory, 84, 88–89
Conestoga Indians, 43
Conflicts of interest, 102
Congregational church, 29, 115 (n. 2), 117 (n. 28), 120 (n. 65)

Congress. *See* Legislation and corporate law
"Consent" receivership, 102, 104, 138 (n. 95)
Constitutional theory, 74, 87, 98, 120 (n. 2)
Contract law, 89–90, 95–96, 104, 107
Cooley, Thomas M., 109
Corporate charters, 11, 79, 100–101
Corporate law, 65, 70–74, 77–81, 91–92, 94, 97, 99–110, 131 (n. 37), 137 (n. 84)
Corporate trusts, 80–81
Corporate vs. solo legal practice, 55, 61, 123 (n. 37)
Counselor: distinguished from attorney, 73–74
Craig, John, 118 (nn. 35–36)
Craighead, Alexander, 41–43, 119 (nn. 47–48)
Cravath law firm, 75, 130 (n. 24), 138 (nn. 93, 110)
Cream of Wheat Company, 58
Creditors, 102–6, 108–10, 138 (n. 110)
Cromwell, William Nelson, 131 (n. 37)
Cross, Robert, 118 (nn. 35–36)
Culture: and professionalization, 8, 11, 49–50; and elites, 16–17; and public lecturers, 23–27
Curtis, George William, 16

"Danger of an Unconverted Ministry, The" (Tennent sermon), 37–39
Davenport, James, 44–45
Davis, John W., 65
Deposit agreement, 102
Dickinson, Jonathan, 117 (n. 25), 118 (n. 37), 120 (nn. 58–59)
Dill, James, 101
Dillon, John Forrest, 74
Doctrine of ultra vires, 101
Donegal Presbytery, 31–33, 42, 119 (nn. 47–48)
Dos Passos, John, Sr., 131 (n. 41), 137 (n. 85)
Douglas, William O., 68–69, 139 (n. 111)
Dutch Reformed church, 115 (n. 2)
Dwight, Theodore W., 72–75, 129 (nn. 14, 18)
"Dwight method," 74, 129 (n. 14)

Eaton, Dorman, 99
Education: and professions, 3–4; historical development, 15; clerical, 35–48, 116 (nn. 17, 22), 117 (n. 32). *See also* Academic professions; Legal education
Elder, John, 118 (nn. 35–36)
Elders of the Presbyterian church, 31–33, 46, 116 (n. 6)
Election of judges, 54–57
Eliot, Charles W., 72–73, 75–77, 129 (n. 21), 130 (n. 22)
Elites: and professionalization, 11, 80–81; and intellectual leadership, 16. *See also* Legal elites
Emerson, Ralph Waldo, 16
English law: and judicial selection, 51–52, 122 (n. 19); and American legal theory, 73–74, 83, 89, 91, 132 (nn. 48–49), 134 (n. 59)
Equity receivership, 101–2
Erie Railroad, 128 (n. 11)
Ethics: and public lecturers, 21–23, 114 (n. 27); and judicial selection, 49–50, 53–54, 58–59, 121 (nn. 7–8); and legal profession, 60–64, 72–73; 128 (n. 11)
European legal theory, 83, 89, 132 (nn. 48–49)
Evangelical movement, 9, 29, 34–48, 117 (n. 24)

Farrar, Edgar, 61
Fees, for lawyers, 23
Field, David Dudley, 55
Field, Stephen J., 54–55
Finley, Samuel, 37, 39, 41, 47–48, 118 (n. 37)
Fiske, James, 128 (n. 11)
"Formalism" in legal theory, 71, 89, 92, 94, 102–3, 135 (nn. 70, 76)
Fourteenth Amendment, 98, 101
Fowler brothers, 16
Franchise litigation, 79
Frankfurter, Felix, 59–60, 67, 77, 126 (n. 89)
Franklin, Benjamin, 117 (n. 31)
Freedom: Liberal conception of, 90
Freeman, Edward Augustus, 88
French and Indian War, 43
French New Panama Canal Co., 131 (n. 37)

Freund, Ernst, 75, 129 (n. 21)
Frontier settlements and clergy, 43–44, 119 (n. 52)
Fusion party, 97

German law, 91
Gompers, Samuel, 59
Gould, Jay, 128 (n. 11)
Governmental lawyers, 50, 66–67
Graham, Sylvester, 16
Gray, John Chipman, 74
Great Awakening, 8–9, 29–30, 34, 41–42, 45, 47
Great Northern Railway, 58
Green, Jacob, 47–48
Gregory, Stephen, 60, 125 (n. 61)
Grosscup, Peter, 106–7
Guthrie, W. D., 74

Hale, Matthew, 82
Hannah, Paul F., 66
Harper, William Rainey, 75, 129 (n. 21)
Harper's, 12, 21
Harvard College, 9; and clerical education, 35–40, 118 (n. 36)
Harvard Law School, 74–78, 91, 129 (nn. 13–14, 21), 130 (nn. 22, 27)
Harvard Medical School, 76
Hayek, Fredrich, 90
Hierarchy in judicial system, 51–52. *See also* Legal elites
Higginson, Thomas Wentworth, 16, 26
Historical legal theory, 84, 89, 134 (n. 58)
Historiography of professionalization, 3–14. *See also* Legal historiography
Hitchcock, Edward, 17
Hoffmann, David, 86–87
Holland, Josiah, 25
Holmes, Oliver Wendell, 16, 88, 91, 99, 109
Hornblower, William B., 125 (n. 60)
Horton, Azariah, 118 (n. 37)
Horton, Simon, 118 (n. 37)
Hughes, Charles Evans, 64, 66, 99, 126 (n. 93)
Hungarian Revolution (1848), 24
Hutchinson, Thomas, 51

Ideology: of professionalization, 7–8, 13, 113 (n. 8); of judgeship, 9–10, 49–50,

61–62; of legal theory, 9–11, 70–72, 77–81, 127 (n. 10), 132 (n. 46); of status, 71. See also Class politics
Illinois Central Railroad, 131 (n. 40)
Income from lecturing, 12. See also Salaries
Independent judgeships, 62–69, 125 (nn. 69–70)
Information explosion, 23–24
Institutionalization: of lecturing, 20–28; of learning, 27–28
Instrumental approach to law, 71–73, 76
Insurance law, 74
Intellectuals: and professionalization, 13–17; and judicial system, 50, 121 (n. 8)
Interest group politics, 71, 78, 105–9, 127 (n. 3)
International law, 129 (n. 19)
"Interpretive imperative," 25
Itinerant preaching, 37–39, 45, 117 (n. 32)

Jacksonian democracy, 64, 83, 86–87, 100
Jamison, Robert, 118 (n. 35)
Jeffersonian-Jacksonian legal theory, 83–84, 93
Jewish lawyers, 77
Joline, Adrian, 105
Jones, Timothy, 118 (n. 37)
Judges: and rights definition, 84, 87; and Liberal legal theory, 91, 108
Judicial biography, 120 (n. 2)
Judicial recall movement, 10, 55–64, 68, 123 (n. 35), 124 (nn. 45, 48), 125 (nn. 56, 63)
Judicial selection, 49–52, 62–64
Junior Bar Conference, 65–66
Jurist: defined, 72

Kane, E. K., 24
Keener, William A., 75
Kellogg, Frank B., 61, 125 (n. 67)
Kent, James, 85–86, 129 (n. 14)
King, Starr, 20

La Follette, Robert, 59
Labor and lawyers, 58, 92, 126 (n. 93)
Laissez-faire theory, 7, 71
Laity and clergy, 8–9, 31–33, 41–48, 116 (n. 6)

Lamb, Joseph, 118 (n. 37)
Langdell, Christopher C., 72–75, 77, 83, 89, 129 (n. 13)
Lawyer as statesman, 53–54
Learning as profession, 3–4, 13–16, 27–28, 113 (nn. 10, 14)
Lecture season, 19, 114 (nn. 22, 25)
Legal education, 49, 72, 74–77, 86–87, 99, 129 (nn. 13–14, 18–20). See also specific law schools
Legal elites: and judicial selection, 9–11, 51–54, 67–69; and legal theory, 70–73, 76–82, 84–85, 88–91, 110, 127 (n. 1), 128 (n. 5), 130 (n. 33), 131 (nn. 40–41)
Legal historiography, 10–11, 70–72, 82, 87–88, 127 (nn. 2–3), 128 (nn. 4–6)
Legal practitioners, 71–74, 76
Legal science, 82–97, 133 (n. 58)
Legal theory vs. practice, 10–11, 70–81, 94–110, 127 (n. 3), 136 (n. 76), 137 (n. 85). See also specific legal theories
Legislation: and judgeships, 62–64, 125 (n. 69), 135 (n. 74); and corporate law, 79, 93, 96, 98, 108–10, 135 (n. 74), 139 (n. 119)
"Liability behavior," 89–90
Liberal legal theory, 10–11, 88–101, 106–10, 134 (n. 61), 135 (n. 74), 137 (n. 84)
Life tenure for judges, 57, 62
Lippmann, Walter, 58
Local law, 73–74
Log College, 35–40, 116 (n. 22), 117 (nn. 23–25)
Lord, John, 16
Louisville Trust Co. v. *Louisville, New Albany & Chicago Railway Co.* See Monon case

McCrea, James, 118 (n. 37)
McKnight, Charles, 118 (n. 37)
Maine, Henry James Sumner, 88
Mansfield, William Murray, first earl of, 82, 85
"March of the Paxton Boys," 43
Martin, James, 118 (nn. 35–36)
Massachusetts legal system, 51, 74, 121 (n. 12), 129 (n. 13)
"Mechanical jurisprudence," 71, 89
Mediators: clergy as, 23; lawyers as, 23, 71–72, 82–83, 99
Medical profession, 7, 13, 112 (n. 18), 125

(n. 55)
Methodist church, 47, 120 (n. 65)
Middle Octerara Church, 41–42
Military life, 43–44
Minimum wage laws, 58, 126 (n. 93)
Minnesota State Bar Association, 56
Models of professionalization, 3–8, 13, 112 (n. 6), 113 (n. 8)
Monon case, 104–9
Monopolies, 61, 80–81
Monopolization by professional groups, 5, 7, 13, 112 (nn. 18–19)
Moral discipline in Presbyterian church, 31–33, 41–48
Moral guardians: clergy as, 18, 23; public lecturer as, 21–28; judges as, 49–54, 68–69; lawyers as, 84–85, 88
Moravian church, 45
Morgan, J. P., 78
Mugwump movement, 80, 96
Murphy, William J., 58

Nason, Elias, 20
National Lawyers Guild, 66
Networks: informal and lecturers, 15; and legal elite, 76–81
New Brunswick Presbytery, 34–35, 37
"New Nationalism," 61
New Sides Presbyterians, 8–9, 34, 39–40, 42–48, 118 (nn. 37–39), 120 (n. 59)
New York Code of Procedure, 74
New York Tribune, 12, 21
Northern Pacific v. *Boyd*, 105–9
Nottingham Presbyterian church, 33–34

Old Sides Presbyterians, 8–9, 34–35, 37, 39–40, 42–48, 118 (nn. 35–37)
Olney, Richard, 137 (n. 84)
Opinion polls: U.S. Supreme Court and, 67–69, 126 (n. 93), 127 (nn. 94–97)
Orr, William, 33–34, 116 (n. 11)
Overcrowding in professions, 15–16, 113 (nn. 10, 14)
Oxford Law School, 91

Panama Canal, 131 (n. 37)
Park, Benjamin, 16
Parsons, Talcott: theory of professions, 3, 5–7, 11, 111 (nn. 2, 11)
Peckham, Wheeler, 109
Pemberton, Ebenezer, 118 (n. 37), 120

(n. 59)
Philadelphia Presbytery, 36
Phillips, Wendell, 16
Pierson, John, 118 (n. 37), 120 (n. 59)
Political science, 75, 91, 129 (n. 18)
Politics: clergy's role, 43–44, 119 (n. 52); and judicial recruitment, 50–52, 55–64, 120 (n. 2), 123 (n. 34), 125 (nn. 68, 70); and legal ideology, 77–81, 91, 93, 97, 128 (n. 5), 130 (nn. 30, 32), 132 (n. 49). *See also* Class politics; Interest group politics; Judicial recall movement
Pollock, Frederick, 87–88, 134 (n. 59)
Populism, 29, 41, 44–48
Pound, Roscoe, 61, 98, 125 (n. 67), 126 (n. 71)
Power: of professionals, 7, 13–14, 112 (nn. 18–19); of clergy, 31–33, 38–48; of legal elites, 78–82
Presbyterian church: clerical authority, 8–9, 31–33, 41–48; schism in, 9, 34–48; early organization, 29–31, 116 (n. 6); reconciliation, 44–48; settlement of 1758, 46; membership, 47–48
Print media, 19–20, 24, 114 (n. 21)
Private-law theory, 76–77, 88, 98–99, 134 (n. 61)
Procedural reform, 62
Professionalization: Parson's theory, 3, 5–7, 11, 111 (n. 11); criteria for, 3–4, 13, 112 (nn. 6, 8); of clergy, 34–35, 39–48, 119 (n. 51); of judiciary, 48–54, 62–64, 120 (nn. 1–2)
Progressive legal theory, 10–11, 94–99, 106, 135 (n. 76), 137 (n. 84)
Progressive movement, 57, 61, 63–65, 67, 80–81, 108–10, 123 (n. 70)
Public image: of clergy, 8–9; of judges, 9–10, 49–65, 68–69, 123 (n. 36), 124 (n. 47); of lecturers, 18–26; of lawyers, 81–82
Public lecture system, 19–20
Public response: to judicial recall, 57–58, 60, 124 (nn. 47–48), 125 (n. 56); to court packing, 67–69, 126 (n. 73), 127 (nn. 94–97)
Public utilities, 74, 96
Puritans, 31–32
Putnam's Magazine, 12, 21

146   Index

Railroads: legal protection of, 55, 101–10, 128 (n. 11), 137 (n. 84)
Reason and legal theory, 84–85, 89
Reconstruction era, 91
Redpath Agency, 27
Reform movements, 80–81, 92–93, 96
Reform party, 97
Religious metaphor in law, 53–54, 122 (n. 23)
Reorganization and receivership litigation, 74, 79, 101–10, 138 (n. 110), 139 (nn. 111, 118–19)
Research universities, 27–28
Revivalist academies, 36–37, 117 (n. 24)
Revivalist movement. *See* Evangelical movement
Right of ordination, 35
Rights definition, 11, 83–84, 88–91, 93, 106–7
Roberts, Owen Josephus, 126 (n. 93)
Robinson, William, 40, 118 (n. 37)
Roman law, 83, 87, 91, 99
Roosevelt, Franklin Delano, 10, 64–68, 126 (nn. 89, 93)
Roosevelt, Theodore, 61, 124 (n. 48), 125 (n. 57)
Root, Elihu, 57, 137 (n. 84)
Ross, Elizabeth, 32–33
Ross, John, 32–33
Rowland, John, 35, 37
"Rule of law," 94–95

Salaries: for clergy, 22, 117 (n. 28); for public lecturers, 22–23; for judges, 53–54, 112 (n. 27). *See also* Fees for lawyers; Income from lecturing
Sanborn, Frank, 18
Sauer, Christopher, 117 (n. 31)
Scholarship: and professionalism, 27
Science, 17–18, 25; and legal theory, 83, 87, 132 (n. 49). *See also* Legal science
Scotch-Irish Presbyterians, 30–31, 39–40, 118 (n. 39)
Scottish common-sense philosophy, 92
Secularization, 43–48
Securities and Exchange Commission, 139 (n. 111)
Securities financing, 79–80, 131 (n. 40)
Sequenced curriculum in law, 76
Shaw, George Bernard, 7
Shaw, Lemuel, 53

Shearman, Thomas, 128 (n. 11)
Sherman Act, 80, 98
Silliman, Benjamin, 17
Smith, Jeremiah, 74
Smith, Sylvester C., Jr., 65–66
Social Darwinism, 92
Social prestige: of professionals, 3–7, 11; of clergy, 8–9, 31–33, 41–48; of judges, 9–10, 51–52, 68–69, 127 (n. 97); of public lecturers, 13, 17–18, 20–28
Social work, 3–4, 111 (n. 3)
Standard Oil of California, 79
State laws, 73–74, 139 (n. 119)
Statute law, 98
Steel, John, 43
Stetson, Francis Lynde, 109
Stinchfield, Frederick, 64
Stockholders, 104–6, 108–10
Story, Joseph, 52–54, 68, 85, 87
Strike litigation, 78–79
Stubbs, William, 88
Sturgeon, Robert, 118 (n. 37)
Sugar Trust, 131 (n. 41), 137 (n. 85)
Supreme Court, U.S.: court packing, 10, 64–69, 126 (nn. 89, 93); prestige of, 50–54, 69; Taft appointments, 63–64, 126 (n. 77); Liberal legal theory and, 91, 104, 139 (n. 118)
Survey of Legal Profession (ABA), 49–50
Swaine, Robert T., 138 (n. 110)
Symbolism of judgeship, 52–54, 62–64, 68–69, 85
Synod of New York, 39, 44–47, 118 (n. 37)
Synod of Philadelphia, 30, 34, 37–40, 44, 118 (nn. 36, 39), 120 (n. 59)

Taft, William Howard, 55–56, 61–64, 79, 124 (nn. 52, 54), 125 (nn. 62, 67–68)
Taylor, Bayard, 12
Technology: law as, 70, 72–73, 76, 80–81, 127 (nn. 2–3), 131 (n. 42)
Tennent, Charles, 35–36, 39–40, 118 (n. 37)
Tennent, Gilbert, 35–39, 44–45, 117 (n. 28), 118 (n. 37)
Tennent, William, 35–36, 116 (nn. 17, 22)
Tennent, William, Jr., 35–39, 118 (n. 37)
Tennessee State Bar Association, 124 (n. 45)
Thèse nobiliaire, 82–83, 99

Thayer, James Bradley, 88, 98
Thomson, John, 118 (nn. 35–36)
Thomson, Samuel, 118 (n. 35)
Tilden, Samuel J., 131 (n. 40)
Tocqueville, Alexis de, 52
Travel lectures, 25
Treat, Robert, 118 (n. 37)
Trust indenture, 102
Trustee principle, 84, 102

Ulster Irish, 29–31, 39–40, 118 (n. 39)
Ulster Scots, 30–31, 40, 118 (n. 39)
Unity among clergy, 33–34, 43–48. See also Presbyterian church, schism in
University of Chicago Law School, 75, 129 (n. 21)
University of Edinburgh, 40, 118 (n. 36)
University of Glasgow, 39–40, 118 (n. 36)
Upward mobility, 15–16, 19–22
"Useful knowledge," 8, 18–21, 24–26

Vanderbilt, Cornelius, 128 (n. 11)
Vocational crises, 16–18, 21–22, 53, 113 (n. 14)
Voluntary associations, 19–22, 55–56. See also American Bar Association

Walker, Timothy, 52
Wall Street lawyers, 76, 130 (n. 30). See also Corporate law
Weber, Max, 91–92
Westminster Confession (1729), 34–35, 116 (n. 13)
Whig-Federalist legal theory, 10–11, 82–88, 93, 97, 99, 102
Whitefield, George, 37
Wilkie, Thomas, 32–33
Will and legal contracts, 89, 94, 106
Wilson, Woodrow, 60, 68, 126 (n. 61)
Witherspoon, John, 120 (n. 60)

Yale College, 9, 35, 40, 116 (n. 17), 117 (n. 25), 118 (n. 36)
Yerkes, Charles Tyson, Jr., 139 (n. 112)
Youngs, David, 118 (n. 37)

Zankey, Richard, 118 (n. 35)
Zinzendorf, Nicholas, Count, 45, 120 (n. 58)

Notes on Contributors

Patricia U. Bonomi did her doctoral work at Columbia University and is currently professor of history at New York University. Her publications include *A Factious People: Politics and Society in Colonial New York* (1971) and essays on churchgoing in colonial America and eighteenth-century revivalism. She is now writing an interpretive history of the religious culture of colonial America.

Stephen Botein is associate professor of history at Michigan State University. He has published articles on the history of American printers and clergymen as well as lawyers. He is currently at work on a book about "expertise" in eighteenth-century America.

Gerald L. Geison is associate professor in the Program in History of Science at Princeton University. His publications include *Michael Foster and the Cambridge School of Physiology: The Scientific Enterprise in Late Victorian Society* (1978) and numerous articles for the *Dictionary of Scientific Biography*.

Robert W. Gordon is professor of law at Stanford University. He has published articles on the history of the legal profession, contract law, legal theory, and legal historiography. His current work concerns the relation of corporate and administrative law and practice to political and economic thought in the late nineteenth and early twentieth centuries, as well as problems of theory and method in legal historiography.

Donald M. Scott teaches history at Brown University. He is the author of *From Office to Profession: The New England Ministry, 1750–1850* and, with Bernard W. Wishy, co-author of *America's Families: A Documentary History*. He is currently at work on a book on the popular lecture and the formation of public culture in mid-nineteenth-century America.